D0031818

# Bitch Doctrine

BY THE SAME AUTHOR

*Unspeakable Things*

# BITCH DOCTRINE

*Essays for Dissenting Adults*

LAURIE PENNY

B L O O M S B U R Y
NEW YORK • LONDON • OXFORD • NEW DELHI • SYDNEY

Bloomsbury USA
An imprint of Bloomsbury Publishing Plc

1385 Broadway
New York
NY 10018
USA

50 Bedford Square
London
WC1B 3DP
UK

www.bloomsbury.com

BLOOMSBURY and the Diana logo are trademarks
of Bloomsbury Publishing Plc

First published in Great Britain 2017
First U.S. edition 2017



The text of this book has been excerpted and extended from articles and blogs written by the author for *New Statesman*, *Baffler*, *Buzzfeed*, *New York Times*, *Time* Magazine and *New Inquiry*



ISBN: HB: 978-1-63286-753-7
EPUB: 978-1-63286-754-4

**Library of Congress Cataloging-in-Publication Data is available.**

2 4 6 8 10 9 7 5 3 1

Typeset by NewGen Knowledge Works (P) Ltd., Chennai, India
Printed and bound in the U.S.A. by Berryville Graphics Inc., Berryville, Virginia

For my sisters, now and always

# CONTENTS

Individuals bearing witness do not change history; only movements that understand their social world can do that.

Ellen Willis

Sometimes you have to be a bitch to get things done.

Madonna

# BITCH LOGIC

In case you hadn't noticed, there's a war on. The field of battle is the human imagination. This is a book about the hard stuff, about the painful places where theory crashes into flesh and bone. It's a book about desire and control and contested bodies. It's a book about gender and power and violence, and about a world beyond them, which is scarier still.

As I write, it feels like the world is falling apart. A craven billionaire real-estate mogul and reality television shyster has just been elected to the presidency of the United States, swept to power by a wave of racist rage and violent populism. The British government is collapsing after the worst political crisis in living memory, the centre-left opposition is eating itself, bigots are getting brave in the streets and the stock markets are tumbling. Not for the first time in my years as a writer and a political thinker, I find myself wondering why I still care as much as I do about gender, about sexism, about power and identity. Aren't there bigger things to worry about? Why can't we put these girlish things aside until after the revolution, when it comes, if it comes?

I'll tell you why. Because if the women don't win, nobody wins. If queer people and marginalised people and freaks and outsiders cannot live free, freedom is not worth the paper it's printed on.

It is no longer an overstatement to suggest that toxic masculinity is killing the world. Feminists, of course, have been banging on about this in our shrill, hysterical way for years, but until the election of Donald J. Trump, the victories of the far right across Europe and the waves of violence against women and minorities that followed, nobody took us seriously. This book deals directly with that violence – with the alt-right and the radicalisation of young men into extremism across the world, with the apoplectic male resentment that is consuming our culture from within. The feeling that men, particularly white, working-class men, have been cheated of their birthright is the root and centre of this discord. They are right that they have been cheated, but dangerously wrong about who pulled the con.

Some people believe that at times like this, the correct approach is to abandon 'identity politics' and speak, instead, about class and only class. Even on the notional left, the usual suspects are at pains to point out that geopolitical disaster could have been avoided if we had all been less precious about gay rights and women's rights and Black Lives and concentrated on the issues that matter to real people. Real people meaning, of course, people who aren't female, or queer, or brown, or from another country. You know, the people who really matter.

In the wake of successive victories for a new, frightening Nationalist Capitalism, commentators from all sides of the self-satisfied chin-stroking debate school are blaming 'identity politics'. What they seem to mean by 'identity politics' is 'politics that matter to people who aren't white men in rural towns or young boys in bedrooms convinced that their inability to get laid is an injustice that must be answered in blood and suffering'.

This is an idea that has remarkable staying power across a fractious and divided left: the idea that issues of race, gender and sexuality are at best a distraction from class politics and at worst a bourgeois tendency that will be destroyed after the revolution. The logic is that by focusing on issues of social justice, the political class has abandoned 'real' working people to the vicissitudes of economic hardship.

This notion is horribly wrong, and the worst thing is that it's wrong in the right direction, in the manner of a passenger plane that maintains a perfect flight path right until it slams into the field next to the runway. The political class has indeed rolled over and let kamikaze capitalism wreck the lives of working people around the world. 'Identity politics', however, have little to do with that cowardice. That the two are now yoked together in the popular imagination is something everyone who believes in a better world must answer for.

All politics are identity politics, but some identities are more politicised than others. The notion that the politics of identity and belonging have been allowed to overwhelm seemingly intractable issues of class, power and poverty is, in fact, entirely correct – but this is not a problem for the traditional left. It is a problem for the traditional right, which has pursued a divide-and-conquer strategy for centuries, pitting white workers against black and brown workers, men against women, native-born citizens against foreigners in a hierarchy of victimhood that diverts energy and anger away from the vested interests bankrolling the entire scheme. When they promise to give you 'your country back', is that not identity politics? When they tell you that Muslims and migrants and uppity women are the real threat to your security, is that not identity politics? When they tell you that you will feel 'great again' if only you stand behind the strong men waving the flag of white nationalism and chauvinist violence, what is that, if not a politics of identity infinitely more dangerous than any we've seen since the 1930s?

It's a shell game. A con. It did not start with Donald Trump, but the real-estate mogul and social-media tantrum artist has taken the Ponzi scheme to its logical conclusion. The president and his fellow travellers and sugar daddies have committed political fraud against the entire Western world. They have compounded it by making us believe – as all good fraudsters do – that it was our fault for being so naive in the first place.

It is, to some extent, reassuring to believe that it's all our fault. If it's all our fault for being too politically correct, too committed to 'diversity', if it was liberals and leftists who messed up by listening to these whining hippies with their patchouli-scented ideals of fairness and tolerance and police not shooting young black men dead for no reason, we might not have to face the more frightening notion that what's happening is, in fact, beyond our control.

The truth is that social justice and economic justice are not mutually exclusive. Those who would sacrifice one for the other will end up with neither, which is of course what the unscrupulous narcissists manspreading at the gates of power are counting on. The mainstream political left has, for generations, been unable to answer the core economic issues that – shocking, I know, but hear me out – affect the lives of all human beings, of every race, gender and background. For decades, in the face of late capitalist hegemony, all that the established left could realistically achieve has been to tweak the system incrementally, making things a little fairer for individual groups, without challenging the structural inequalities that created the injustice in the first place. This must change, and soon. Not just because of 'fine moral principles'. Trying to fix economic policy without tackling structural inequality is not just morally misguided – it is intellectually bankrupt.

Race, gender and sexuality are not side-issues in the current crisis. They are the bedrock and expression of that crisis. Capitalism has always divided its labour supply along lines of race and gender, ensuring that in times of crisis, we don't start setting fire to the machine, but to one another. All politics are identity politics, and this is no time to back away from our commitment to women's rights, racial justice and sexual equality. This is when we double down. The fight against the corporate neo-fascism funnelling out of every television set is not a fight that can be won if liberals, leftists and social-justice campaigners turn on one another. It is a fight that we will win together, or not at all.

I called this book *Bitch Doctrine* because when I present what seem to me quite logical, reasonable arguments for social change, I find myself called a bitch, and worse. Bitches, however, to borrow a phrase from Tina Fey, get stuff done.

The title is a provocation, but so is the rest of the book. How could it be otherwise? Anything any woman ever writes about politics is considered provocative, an invitation to dismissal and disgust and abuse, in much the same way that a short skirt is considered an invitation to sexual violence. That's the point. I have learned through years of writing in public that if you are a woman and political, they will come for you whatever you say – so you may as well say what you really feel. If that makes me a bitch, I can live with that.

Bitch is a verb as well as a noun: to bitch, meaning to complain groundlessly about petty, unimportant things. When I tell people I'm a political writer, they often ask me when I'm going to chuck in 'the women thing' and concentrate on 'real politics' – but gender and power and love and sex and selfhood are not footnotes to political reality. They are the places where identity and economics meet. I have always placed women's politics and gender politics front and centre in my writing and analysis because I believe it is not just wrong to do otherwise, it is also intellectually bankrupt. I am told on a daily basis that the things I write about gender and identity, about love and work and the way that one, by degrees, becomes the other, are insignificant next to the struggles of women somewhere across the sea. I am usually told this by those who have no interest in those struggles except as a means to silence women closer to home.

I've been a journalist, a columnist and an essayist since I was nineteen. I tell stories about people, and I listen to the stories they tell about what it means to be human in this anxious age where all the old rules are cracked open and spilt on the shifting ground of socio-economic certainty. People often ask me if I'm a journalist or an activist. The answer is yes. The answer is both. To write and speak and think about the world is to act on it. Everyone who does so brings their own issues to the table, their own passions, their own prejudices, their foibles and broken hearts.

Any writer who claims objectivity is lying to you or to themselves, or both. I have never held with the notion of objective journalism: too often that's a modesty slip for the enduring suspicion that only a certain sort of well-to-do Western man can possibly have a viewpoint worth listening to. When I started out, my world was overfull of stern men imploring me to strive for objectivity – which meant, in practice, that I ought to tell the story as a rich older man might see it. To wash all the dirty politics out of what I wrote. I have never been equal to the work of that compromise, and I've walked out of jobs that wanted me to make it. That still feels far too much like arrogance, but the alternative was complicity, which was, and still is, worse.

Arrogance is an occupational hazard for any writer, especially those who manage to make writing their living, but only in women writers is it seen as a problem. Women writers aren't supposed to be too brave, too sure of ourselves. Instead, we are supposed to dissemble, to approach with one knee bent, supplicant, to thank the men who helped us on our way, to blush and prevaricate if anyone asks what we hope to achieve. We're taught, as women – especially as women – that before anything else, we must make ourselves likeable. We must make ourselves agreeable. We must shrink ourselves to fit the room, and shave down our ideas to fit the times. That sort of thing is death to creativity, death to good writing, death to clear thinking. Accepting that you're going to be called a bitch isn't about acquiescence. It's about choosing freedom. There are a great many worse things that can happen to you than someone not liking what you have to say.

I have great respect for those who are able to write and speak about gender in a more conciliatory fashion than I do. For those who are able to put on the dress and the heels and do the thankless work of pretending to men in power that feminism isn't coming to destroy every certainty they cling to. I've never been able to do it, so I thank those who can. I consider my work well done whenever I receive emails from teenage strangers telling me that something I wrote helped them feel a little less alone, even for a moment. There is a school of liberal thought that seeks only to persuade the undecided through sober and sanguine debate. This has never been my approach to culture war. I place as much importance on comforting the afflicted as I do on afflicting the comfortable, and doing the former with any success tends to achieve the latter.

In the ten years since I started writing about feminism online, tentatively posting about assault statistics in blogs read by fifteen people and their flatmates, there has been an explosion in thought, writing and action about gender politics, and those ideas have translated directly into lived experience. There is no longer any 'view from nowhere'. There is, as the writer Chimamanda Ngozi Adichie puts it, no single story to tell about the world – and there never has been. The best we can do is strive to be honest – to identify and interrogate our assumptions, and to stand firm where it matters. To be honest with our readers and ourselves.

So here's some honesty. All I've ever wanted to achieve with writing is to move the world in small ways with words. That's no more or less valuable than any other way of making change. I write simply because it's the best way I know to make change in the world while bringing in rent money. I'm beyond lucky to be able to do this for a living. I hope for nothing more for myself than to be able to do it until such time as writing about social change is unnecessary, at which point I will happily go away and write about shoes. Every so often I wonder why I didn't become a restaurant critic. They get free dinners. Being a feminist journalist, I get free death threats.

Being a woman and a writer these days means being told by armies of strangers every day that you don't deserve to speak or to live, that you're ugly and worthless and stupid. I considered growing a thick skin, then I remembered a thick skin is the last thing a writer needs. One of their hypotheses is that all these carping bitches really need is a good shag. I have empirically tested this hypothesis, and I still have a list of demands. Top of that list is a kinder world.

I'm not going to tell you that it gets better. I can't pretend that there's a point where they stop coming for you. What happens is that you get stronger. You grow up, and you find your allies in the most curious places. Life, including political and creative life, is as much the result of the choices you don't make as the ones you do. Every time I make a choice not to capitulate, it gets easier to make that choice again. Every time I make a choice to be a difficult bitch, I notice other difficult bitches standing beside me and wonder what sort of trouble we might make together.

It's easier for me to make those choices, of course, than it is for some people. I'm middle-class, white, well educated. I have less to lose by taking my own advice than others do. I have less to lose by seeking freedom than my mother did, and she had less to lose than her mother, although they both had far more to win. There is still a world to win.

I'm not writing as everygirl, because there is no such thing. The idea that any person could speak 'for women' is cartoonish in its misunderstanding of what feminism is, what women are. No man is ever asked to speak for his entire sex. The experiences of men are acknowledged to be broad, varied, complex, but women are always women first, no matter what else we are. This must change if we are to be taken seriously, not just as writers but as human beings.

When I write about gender and power and desire, I know that my experience and understanding are not, and never will be, complete. Not all women's struggles are the same. My audience is largely European and North American, but even here there's a diversity in pent-up experience that terrifies those with a vested interest in shutting up women and queers. I could read and research for a lifetime and still not know what it is to be a woman of colour, or a woman in a non-English-speaking country, or a working-class woman. I have done my best to listen, and to educate myself on experiences outside my own. I continue to be challenged. If it's true that nobody can speak for all women, that goes double for someone like me.

Women of colour, indigenous women, trans women, poor and working-class women are never asked to speak for 'all women' – even though they have more right to do so. The assumption is that a person's thinking gets more universal the more they look like the accepted face of social power in the West – white, straight, cis, well educated, well-to-do and, if possible, male. In fact, if anything, the opposite is true. The theory and writing of oppressed people already contains within it the assumptions of the oppressor class it has been forced by the nature of its oppression to acknowledge. Queer and LGBT people, for example, know more about straight people than straight people will ever know about us, because we grew up in a homonormative world, were taught its customs and punished for insulting them, if only by our existence. Black women know more about the total experience of womanhood than white women ever will in a white supremacist world.

So this book, like any other book written by a white, middle-class author, cannot be universal. That does not mean it lacks value. It means I will inevitably get things wrong, leave things out, mess up and have to make amends. I mean to do so in good faith, if I get the chance.

I draw on my own experiences here, but they are not representative. At best, they are symptomatic. When women write and speak the truth of their own lives, it is called 'confessional', with the implication of wrongdoing, of sharing secrets that ought not to be spoken aloud, at least not by nice girls. When men do the same, it is called literature, and they win prizes. The reason that society at large is dismissive of and disgusted by the avalanche of personal writing by women, girls and queer people is the same reason we're doing it: because these stories have not been told before in such numbers.

Writing and sharing those stories helps us feel less alone but, more than that, comparing experiences of oppression and hardship and hurt makes it possible to believe that the problem might not just be with us, as individuals. The problem might not be that we are not strong enough. The problem might be broader, more structural, something that those with privilege have to answer for personally and together. And that is a terrifying notion for anyone with a vested interest in the status quo. No wonder our words are dismissed as the confessional chatter of hysterics. If they weren't, they might have to be taken seriously.

These are frantic, fearful times. History and language are accelerating, and unexpected people are taking control of both in unexpected ways. If there was ever a time when a clear line existed between writing and living, that time is over. Today we think, work and agitate in text. We conduct our social lives in text. The public sphere is a whole lot more public, and a whole lot less predictable, than mid-century theorists ever anticipated. Dissatisfied by the stories told about what women are and what they do, new writers are emerging to reshape the narrative. The public sphere now includes a great many people whose voices, if they were ever noted at all, were included in footnotes. Women, girls, queer people, people of colour, people living in the margins of our collective cultural script, are suddenly rewriting it. That changes what it means to be a writer, just as it changes what it means to be a human being living and thinking and acting in the world.

That means the way we think about sex is changing. The way we think about gender identity is changing. The way we think about how to live and love and fight and fuck is changing so fast that you can, on a clear day, feel the breeze of it in your hair. We have gone, in the space of a decade, from the collective assumption that there was no such thing as 'date rape' to public discussion of 'rape culture', to holding public figures to account for their treatment of women, girls and children. We have gone from the understanding that the best women could hope for was to balance exhausting paid employment and childcare, to teenagers talking about wages for housework.

It has become commonplace to speak of 'waves' of feminism. I've never seen it that way. Feminism, for me, is not a set of waves, but a great grumbling tsunami, moving slow, sweeping across a blighted landscape of received assumptions, washing away old certainties. The big wave has hardly begun to hit, and already all of us are changed. This pace of change, of course, is rather frightening to some people, and the backlash is on.

Many of my energies in the past decade have gone into contesting that backlash. Across the world, parochialism, racism and vintage sexism are offered as answers to the climate of fear in which we find ourselves. We are told that we ought to be looking back to the certainties of a fantasy, fictional past that is perpetually just out of reach. I prefer to look to the future. Feminism, of course, has always been an exercise in science fiction.

Here it comes: I don't hate men as individuals. I'm obliged to start out by saying that, of course, for the benefit of the fragile among us who believe that talking about women's rights is akin to calling for some sort of androcaust. In my case, the not-hating-men thing also happens to be true. I have, however, increasingly little patience with men as a social phenomenon.

Over the years, I've been attacked with such relentless spleen that I have become more timid with my heart when I sit down to pour it out on the page. I have learned to fear my own capacity for empathy, where men are concerned. They can be so fragile. So often, they take any challenge to their received narratives, any questioning of their ideas about the world, as a profound identity threat, especially if the question or the challenge comes from a woman. Of course, of course, not all men. But enough of them.

Sometimes, men and boys ask me whether and how they can be feminists. I don't think anyone needs permission for that, let alone my permission. But merely identifying as a thing is just a start. You also have to take responsibility for your goddamn actions. Feminism is active. It's not something you are; it's something you do. It's what you fight for that matters. Feminism is not an identity but a movement, a way of living. And feminism isn't just about women – it's about liberating everyone from gender oppression, but since women are most oppressed by modern gender norms and laws, and since the movement has always been driven by women's politics, 'feminism' is an appropriate name – it's almost as if men can't bear to be part of a movement that suggests for a moment that women might lead.

Feminism isn't about fighting men all the time. But I'm not interested in making my politics safe and sweet and unthreatening for men, because ultimately, feminism does threaten the status quo, and the status quo is one where men have more social power than women. Feminism is about fairness, redistribution of wealth and power and influence; it's about changing the old order whereby men have had most of those things for most of human history. There's only so far you can dilute the message, make it nice and fluffy and safe, before you lose the point altogether. So, again, you may as well say what you mean. The stakes are too high to apologise before we've even begun. There's no point being nice in a burning world.

I've heard it said that for a progressive, equal society to come about, the one we have now has to collapse completely. I've heard this said almost overwhelmingly by men on the left who nurse guilty hard-ons over visions of dying in battle as martyrs. Civilisation, they say, needs to collapse completely before we can have the revolution we need. I have heard almost no women argue this, partly because women and queers have less reason to fantasise about civil unrest, and partly because in practice, what the slow collapse of society actually entails is women picking up the pieces, mending the broken bones and broken hearts and shouldering the extra work where the fabric of society rots and rends.

When I was a child, I was afraid of almost everything. I was afraid of nuclear war, of global warming. I was afraid of the ozone layer and the government and getting my SAT results. I spent much of my young life convinced that I would not make it to adulthood, that some planet-wide disaster would inevitably sweep away not just me and my family and my favourite teachers and everyone I loved, but the entire society we lived in, the whole species, everything solid in the world. That hasn't happened – not to me, not yet, and not to many of us. But we still live in a society convinced of its own imminent collapse. Fascists are mustering on the fringes of politics to dominate the mainstream. The Middle East is fighting to be rid of the rule of murderous clerics. The floodwaters are rising, and that's no longer a metaphor.

When I found feminism as a young person, it was a comfort in unexpected ways. Not just because it gave words to the injustices of sex and gender I saw around me every day, but because I had found something I could do. All right, I couldn't stop the world sliding into chaos, but maybe I could do my part, in some small way, to make that chaos fairer. To make it more liveable.

It is precisely at times of crisis that utopian thinking is most necessary. I am not going to stop writing and dreaming about a better world for women, for queer people and for everyone left out of mainstream discourse just because the planet is half alight. These things don't matter less at times like this. They matter more. What type of world would possibly be worth winning if women can't win too?

In all this chaos it can be hard to separate signal from noise. This book is an attempt to do so – to bring together some of the writing that has mattered most to me and form it into a coherent whole. These columns and essays were written between 2013 and 2016, usually under savage deadline pressure in the full glare of online scrutiny. Together, they're something more. The articles in this book are intended to start conversations, not finish them. In the words of the Coilhouse magazine collective: to inform, inspire and infect.

There is a sense of urgency to the writings collected here. Urgency is appropriate. We are trying to change the world for the better in the middle of stacking crises, and this is no time to go on the defensive, no time to capitulate, to accept a diluted definition of freedom. On the contrary. This is a good time to gather our weapons. If it's all going to end in ruins, let's have them be beautiful ruins. Let's have fairness there, and care, and mutual aid. Let's have men and women and everyone else meet each other as equals in the clearing dust. And let's start now, while we still have Wi-Fi and central heating.

And meanwhile, I'll keep on writing as if – to borrow Alasdair Gray's phrase – we lived in the early days of a better nation. I hope you'll read this book the same way, though if you turn the page, you'll find it starts on treacherous terrain. It starts with politics.

# 1

# Of Madness and Resistance: A US Election Diary 2016

## A GREAT GROPE FOR POWER

*Late October 2016*

There's no drug quite like the confidence of a mediocre white man, and even lifelong users like Donald Trump have to be careful when mainlining in public. Witness, if you will, the epic meltdown captivating headline writers across the globe as the Republican nominee for president of the goddamn United States of America disintegrates into a hot mess of misogynist sleaze, jawing fascist buzzwords as the global audience he always craved looks on in disbelief. Trump's supporters may be shamefaced, but the whole cringeworthy spectacle is hardly less humiliating for anyone who still half-believes in democracy and the rule of law.

The second presidential debate between Hillary Clinton and Donald Trump resembled an extended exchange between a piece of online political punditry and the comments section beneath it. On the eve of the debate – a mere forty-eight hours after the leak of the now infamous video which featured Trump bragging that his celebrity status enabled him to kiss, grope and try to have sex with women – he held a press conference to which he invited any female he could find who had ever made a sexual complaint against Bill Clinton, attempting to smear Hillary by association. The man who boasted about 'grabbing' women 'by the pussy' had no compunction about showcasing alleged assault victims to aid his own sleazy fumble for power.

Hillary didn't rise to it. She remained the picture of dignity throughout, which wasn't hard given what was standing opposite her. It was clear from the start of the debate that there was something badly wrong with Trump: that the yammering personification of the white male nationalist id was not just unprincipled but actively unwell. Over ninety excruciating minutes, he prowled about the stage, gurning and muttering to himself like a matinee murderer debating the devil on his shoulder. At one point he seemed so incensed that the cameras were not on him that he actually started humping his own chair. It was the sort of slow-moving car crash that sends reality TV ratings through the ceiling, specifically, in this case, a glass ceiling.

The entire election campaign of 2016 has resembled a wet dream that David Lynch might have had after falling asleep watching Fox News. Trump rapidly lost his grip not just on propriety but on human language, shouting made-up words and incoherent statements such as 'Syria is no longer Syria. Syria is Russia . . . I believe we need to get ISIS' and promising to 'bring economics to the people'. He threatened to prosecute his opponent as soon as he became president. He sounded, more than anything, like a conservative hatebot of your drunken racist uncle, algorithmically spunking out gobs of truthiness.

The rhetorical model did not recall Abraham Lincoln so much as it did Tay, Microsoft's short-lived artificial intelligence Twitter chatbot, who was taught by armies of alt-right trolls with time on their hands to say things like 'feminism is cancer' and 'I love Hitler'. I was reminded that back in the heyday of what was once called the blogosphere, editors went through a phase of believing that the comments section amounted to the voice of the people, rather than whoever was bored, angry and hateful enough to dedicate hours to recreational harassment, particularly of women, people of colour and anyone with the temerity to hold an opinion who was not white, male, straight and conservative. We learned, but not quickly enough. The comments section is now alive and chewing at the heart of Western democracy.

This is no accident. Trump's entire campaign is an exercise in industrial-scale trolling, which does not for a second mean that it is not dangerous. It means that he is playing to an entirely different set of win conditions whereby victory goes to whoever screams the loudest. Democracy, to this man and his followers, is just a new system to game, and if it doesn't deliver, they'll try something else. What they want most is not the presidency – not in any serious way. I'm sure that Trump wants to sit in a shiny chair in the Oval Office and have people tell him all day that he's the most powerful and impressive man in the world, and I'm just as sure that he doesn't want to be bothered with the actual business of government. No, what his followers want is to scream and throw things until someone tells them they're still special. Why? Because they can. Because it's cathartic. Because they feel they have little to lose. Because it's fun and it makes them feel big and powerful, and so little else does.

I'm sorry to say this, because it really doesn't help, but some of us did warn the public about these people years ago. Back then they were confining their recreational bigotry to women and people of colour who were told to shut up and stop being so sensitive. It gives me no pleasure to be proved right on this one. Right now, anyone who fails to see the connection between gender politics and geopolitics either has their hands over their eyes or is looking over their shoulder to a time when a bit of boyish sexual violence didn't disqualify you for elected office. But this is not just about feminism. This is, specifically, about consent. This is about people who feel entitled to dominate and control the bodies of one half of the population also feeling entitled to run the world, and the pathological pattern at play. What we're dealing with is a man who wants to grab the whole world by the pussy and is bewildered and furious when the pussy grabs back.

And he's not the only one of his kind. This has, lest we forget, been the pattern of patriarchal power-play for generations. For years, we've had to deal with household names, politicians, entertainers being revealed as serial sexual predators. We've had to come to terms with the truth that they were allowed to get away with it because that was just what it meant to be a successful man. You could grab whatever, whoever, you wanted. Women and girls were status objects there for the seizing, willing or not. That's changing, because there are a lot of people out there who want it to change, but there are also a lot of other people who found that model of social violence comforting, people who are angry at these so-called 'feminazis' and their hormone-crazed demands to be treated like human beings with agency, people whose sense of being cheated out of their male birthright is an outlet for a more dangerous sense of socioeconomic betrayal, and most of those people have been rooting for Trump since day one. The new assault allegations are unlikely to damage his standing in their eyes.

Most Republican commentators with any sense are already consigning their party to cold storage, putting it into an induced coma to preserve whatever might survive this humiliation. The lemming-like rush to the political precipice may be premature. Trump is not going to pull out. He decided he wanted the presidency and now he believes himself entitled to it. He's determined to fuck the world whether or not it's willing, and you'd better hope the US is on some sort of birth control. People who do not respect the consent of individuals also tend to lack respect for the consent of the governed. They conceive of democratic consent exactly as they conceive of sexual consent: nice if you can get it, but if you can't, you still deserve the spoils. This is the dictionary definition of chauvinism, and it is unlikely to be purged from the public mood come 9 November when this deeply unpleasant spectacle is finally over.

The kamikaze chauvinism of the alt-right did not emerge from nowhere. It's the inevitable end-point of decades of popular discontent channelled and chaperoned by vested interests, the same vested interests that have funded the Republicans and their ilk for generations. For all their maidenly blushes over Trump's crass misogyny, their tardy protestations over his attitude to the half of the population who are mothers, wives and daughters and, somewhat inconveniently, voters, conventional conservatives know that what Trump has done is simply to take contemporary right-wing rhetoric to its logical conclusion. He has torn away the modesty curtain of mainstream neoliberal debate and shown the jabbering psychopath behind it. That is profoundly embarrassing, and embarrassment is as likely to make people lash out as it is to make them roll over.

If your entire identity is built on a certain narrative, it is very hard to abandon that narrative even if it is destroying your chances of winning. Living with that sort of dissonance does strange things to the psyche. All sorts of wild, weird notions start creeping in. Words start coming out that make you sound cruel, crazed or both, although if you're running for office, you usually try to hold back from saying them when there are cameras in the vicinity.

Trump is unusual only in that he lacks a filter. He really does say what many people are thinking, and the problem is that just because many people are thinking something does not make it right, or safe, or true. What America and the global conservative consensus see in Trump is their own faces in the haunted mirror of the modern media engine; they are not the only ones staring in horror.

The problem with being an arrogant sack of hair with the raw energy of the American id sustaining your own swollen ego is that when someone punctures it, you deflate with a fart sound that echoes around the world. Trump deserves every bit of this humiliation, but the movement behind him is driven by the wounded pride of millions. It is ferocious, unpredictable and not at all funny. I'm not laughing. This got beyond a joke years ago. Whoever wins this race, the war for decency and democracy will continue, and right now all of us are losing.

## AND NOW WE GET SERIOUS

*9 November 2016*

The writing was on the wall, for those who knew how to read it. Specifically, it was on the wall of a black church in Mississippi, which was set on fire last week and spray painted with the words 'Vote Trump'. It was plastered across the rolling news when voters were shot down outside a polling booth in California last night. The democratic sentiment in the United States has been tortured and twisted into a dark, violent thing. That does not make it undemocratic. It also doesn't make it just or fair. Donald Trump has short-conned his way into the White House by saying what a lot of people were thinking. The people have spoken. That does not mean all the other people have to shut up.

Even on a clear day when a giant evil baby isn't trashing the system because he saw a shiny desk he wanted, representative democracy doesn't always deliver fairness and justice and a decent society. That takes a different sort of democratic work, work that does not begin and end at the ballot box, work that will resume right after we relearn how to look our friends and neighbours in the eye.

Today, all over America, black, brown and Muslim children are too frightened to go to school. Facts and figures may not win votes the way feelings do, but today's polls tell us that this election was not just about class, gender or partisan positioning. This election was, more than anything, about race. It was about white resentment, which is now among the greatest threats to global security. It was about white rage, and there are a lot of us who need to own that inconvenient truth today lest it own us all tomorrow.

When they told liberals and journalists and policymakers, and anyone with the cheek to suggest that maybe immigrants weren't the problem, that we weren't listening to 'ordinary people', they meant we weren't listening to white people. When they told us we didn't pay enough attention to 'real Americans', they meant to white Americans. When they told us that we didn't take their concerns seriously, they meant that we didn't agree with them. 'White working-class' voters have been given plenty of airtime in this election, just as they were in the EU Referendum, including in the mainstream press that they claim to despise, because sober facts don't sell advertisements like a mean-drunk playing with matches next to an arsenal of incoherent rage.

The time for complacency is long gone. So too is the time for bowing to the hurt feelings of those who were willing to fire at the elite directly through the stomachs of their neighbours. Every effort has been made to sympathise with their distress at a perceived loss of privilege that is felt, wrongly, as prejudice. The media on both sides of the pond has fallen over itself to consider whether the boiling bigotry on display might somehow conceal 'legitimate concerns'. Somehow, the concerns of working-class people are only considered legitimate when they reflect a reactionary strain that does not threaten vested interests. Somehow, the concerns of working-class women who want basic reproductive rights, the concerns of working-class people of colour who want the police to stop shooting them with impunity, the concerns of working-class trans people who don't want to be beaten up in public toilets, have been landscaped into the territory of the 'liberal elite'. That rubbish needs to stop right now. If you're angry and upset, that does not make you out of touch. If you suspect that a great wrong has been done today, that does not make you a bourgeois shill. It makes you sensible.

Today, hundreds of millions of people in America and around the world have woken up afraid – for themselves, for their children, for the future of a planet where an authoritarian psychopath has his hands on the nuclear codes and the fate of a burning world waiting on his pleasure. Those people are being told that they are sore losers. That they should shut up and accept it. That their fear is somehow funny. Laughing at the pain of the most vulnerable. Squealing with glee when the bully lands a blow. That's the world millions of notionally decent human beings voted for, and don't tell me for a second they didn't know what they were choosing.

The president-elect told us who he was right from the get-go. If the lacquered, lying sack of personality disorders that is Donald Trump has any redeeming feature, that is it. He made no attempt to hide his narcissism, his hard-on for dictators, his vision of the entire damn world as the next acquisition in his dodgy property portfolio. During the campaign he was openly racist, sexist, xenophobic and openly willing to become more so as long as it played well with the crabbed, frightened part of his base that just wants to know someone else is hurting worse. He has vowed to jail his political and personal opponents, destroy freedom of the press, deport Muslims and give his donors free rein to frack as they please so he can carry on gaslighting the world. This is the man America elected. This, today, is what Democracy looks like. If you're disgusted, that doesn't mean you hate freedom.

It is not elitist to look fascism in the face and reject it. It is not anti-democratic to carry on believing in a society where there is space for everyone. Fighting for tolerance, justice and dignity for women, queer people and people of colour is not frivolous or vain. Who decided that it was? Who decided that only those who place fear over faith in their fellow human beings are real, legitimate citizens whose voices matter? That's not a rhetorical question. I want to know. Give me names.

This election was phrased as a populist revolt against a nebulous and nefarious 'elite' which somehow also included the parts of society that have had the least for the longest. Resentment against the political class is real, and it was fatally underestimated by those within the Democratic machine who were determined to have their anointed successor at any cost. It was decreed that the only alternative to naked screaming fascism was the status quo. Despite her gender, Hillary Clinton was the status quo candidate, the legacy candidate, the dynasty candidate. She also looks like what she is – a woman in politics – and that enraged as many people as it inspired.

It is hard enough to tell an exciting story about the status quo at the best of times, and these are not the best of times. These are anxious, febrile times where millions see their future closing down around them like a great dark mouth. The status quo is a roll-call of vacillating neoliberal technocrats who are unable to offer any alternative to kamikaze capitalism and its discontents. It was hard to cheer unequivocally for Clinton, just as it was hard for conscientious British progressives to bang the drum for the European Union. But the actual elite – the people with real money and power – are not the ones struggling to retain their breakfasts today.

I happen to be in a conference room with a few hundred of them right now, at a tech convention bustling with lobbyists, businessmen and venture capitalists. I'm looking around me, and they're still making deals over finger-food. If they've been vanquished, they don't seem to have caught on just yet. The elites are going to be fine.

America has always transposed its class tensions into cultural violence, and that, more than anything, is how racism and xenophobia serve the same 'corrupt elite' that Trump voters claim today to have trampled. Donald Trump is still a reality TV star, and he knew just how to rig the glittering gameshow of American realpolitik to his advantage, and now we all get to see what we've won. Let me give you a clue: it isn't money.

It is no longer accurate to speak of dog-whistle racism. The whistle is now audible to everyone, and it's a screaming air-raid siren, and there aren't enough shelters to run to. A number of people have taken the time to let me know, on this day of all days, that despite voting for the preferred candidate of every neo-fascist with a network connection, despite voting for a man who has whipped up a wave of racial hatred and surfed it all the way to the White House, they do not feel that they are racist, and would prefer that nobody said so. They didn't put it delicately, and nor will I; I am done caring what the people prefer.

I am done listening to my liberal friends contort themselves to take into account the notional opinions of the 'white working class'. What does that even mean? How did we come to the craven consensus that the 'white working class' is a homogenous mass of blustering bigots who must be pandered to as one might pander to a toddler having a tantrum at the edge of a cliff? A great many white people who are far from wealthy take issue with that particular patronising strain of self-scourgery on the left. They manage not to blame all their problems on feminazis, immigrants and their black and brown neighbours. Those people are real Americans, too.

So, no more of this nonsense. I'm done. I am done pretending that the good intentions of white patriarchy are more important than the consequences enacted on the bodies of others. Good intentions aren't the issue here. Feel free to be as racist as you like in the privacy of your own heart, if you can live with yourself, but not – and this is very important – in the privacy of your own house.

I understand that a great many people are aggrieved that women, migrants and people of colour no longer seem to know their proper place. I understand that a great many otherwise decent humans believe that more rights for black, brown and female people mean fewer rights for 'ordinary people', by which they mean white people. But just because you're angry doesn't mean you're right. Just because you feel bad doesn't mean you are allowed to break things to make yourself feel better. It's okay to be annoyed that you didn't get a seat on the bus. What's not okay is to lash out, trash the seats, smash the windows, snatch the wheel and steer the whole damn bus off a bridge along with yourself and everyone you know.

Because let's be very clear: this was a revolt by white Americans and their allies, but it is not going to be a victory for most of them. In the extended chuckle of smuggery that passed for an acceptance speech, Trump promised his supporters that all of them would get the chance to realise their dreams, even and especially the weird angry horny dreams that don't make sense when you explain them. He promised to double growth, even as stock markets tumbled around the world. Those promises will not be delivered upon. The moment when that becomes clear is not the moment when Trump and his followers get humble. It's the moment when people start looking for scapegoats.

It's also the moment when we get serious. The rest of us, I mean. Because there are a lot of us, and we're 'the people', too. Now is when we get serious. Not right now, obviously. Speaking personally, the end of this chapter is all that stands between me and the bottle of vodka in my immediate future, but that is not a sound long-term strategy for dealing with the days ahead. Now is when we get together and get to work, because the bullies have been given a licence to act, and that cannot go unanswered. I understand if you want to shout at a few friends right now. I know I do, although I haven't yet. But be ready to reach out to them tomorrow, because the fight against despair continues, and alliances matter, and so does basic self-care. We need to be serious. I need to be serious, and I'm sorry about that. I'm sorry that the time for witty barbs about the president-elect, his hands, his hair and the howling ideological void of opportunistic narcissism behind his megalomaniac clown-mask is over, because inappropriate as those witty barbs are right now, they will probably be actively illegal before long. Now, we need to be serious. Some of us worked very hard to turn this ship around. Now we need to work even harder to stop it sinking.

I'm not going to give you any fluff about hope at this point in history. Hope is possible, and necessary, and remarkably tenacious, but in the meantime there is always spite. We can carry on living, carry on looking after one another, carry on working towards a world beyond this burning pile of rubbish to spite those who want to see everyone who looks and thinks differently from them cowed and silent. We can carry on to spite them, and in spite of them.

The bullies have won today. They will not win for ever, unless we let them into our hearts and souls as well as the seat of government of the nominally free world, and that is something I am not prepared to countenance. 'The people' have spoken. 'The people' will continue to speak. But if freedom means a thing any more, the other people – all of the other people, all those inconvenient millions of us all over America and all over the world – cannot and will not be silent.

## AGAINST BARGAINING

*Late November 2016*

What does it mean to be mentally healthy in a world gone mad? Sirens are blaring, lights are flashing, and we have been whisked out of the territory of metaphor on to the hard ground of fact. The rise to power and election of Donald J. Trump is the sick recrimination of a society shrivelled by anger and anxiety, and the response from deep within the psyche of the same society has been various degrees of panic, depression and grief. Illinois suicide hotlines have been overwhelmed since the election, with calls up 200 per cent, according to Chicago public health officials. A mental health asteroid has smashed into the carapace of a culture already calcified with anxiety and ambient dread. Major newsrooms are rumoured to have hired in therapists so their journalists can continue to work. Everyone is wondering what this crisis will mean for their future, for their families, trying to work out how they'll cope. Some coping strategies, however, are more dangerous than others.

The first time I suspected that Donald Trump might become president, I was at the back of the convention hall in Cleveland, watching the reality TV tycoon accept the nomination at the climax of a shindig that was somewhere between the Eurovision Song Contest and the Nuremberg Rally. I listened to the delegates in front of me whoop and scream and earnestly debate whether Barack Obama would be among the Muslims forcibly deported from the United States, and I thought to myself: these people love him for all the reasons my people hate him. We've underestimated the ignorance, the hate, the showmanship. This guy might win.

I should mention at this point that I have an anxiety disorder. As I staggered out into the soupy Cleveland night, I felt the familiar rats-in-the-belly squirm, the tightness of breath that precedes a full-blown panic attack. And so I did what I have learned to do to manage anxiety. I calmed myself down. I took some deep breaths, had some sugary tea, turned off social media and told myself that I was over-reacting. Millions of Americans couldn't possibly be that stupid. It would be okay. That was a big mistake. Yuge, as a certain someone would put it. I should have sat with that panic attack. I should have listened to what that legitimate anxiety was trying to tell me. It turns out that you cannot stop fascism by turning off Facebook and doing some deep breathing. All you can do is make yourself feel better, and there are limits to how much better it's safe to feel right now.

There are none so blind as those who won't see – specifically, those who have been conditioned through generations of history lessons and Hollywood propaganda to be suspicious of authoritarian strongmen and yet still refuse to recognise an actual fascist when he struts into the White House with a suicide squad of goons. I studied Hitler's rise to power almost every year at secondary school. You may well have done the same. Thinking back through those textbooks I memorised, though, one question was always glossed over: what was it actually like to be an ordinary German in 1933? What were people feeling, listening to the state wireless whine out the workings of the new world order? How many were pleased to see the blackshirts on their streets – and how many were simply keeping their heads down, telling themselves that they'd been through worse, that they should give the new guys a chance and see if they really meant what they said? How many tried to normalise the utterly unconscionable, because the alternative was despair?

As I write, fascism is being normalised on every uplit screen and white liberals are turning away to gaze pointedly at their own navels. Asking how much of this is our fault is more comfortable than asking what the hell we do now, because it's a question with an easy answer. 'All of it was our fault' is the easy answer. It's the wrong answer, but it's the easy answer, because if you can persuade yourself that it's your fault, that means you still have control.

At times of turmoil, your brain plays tricks on you. Normalisation is not just a thing people do because they secretly like fascism and want it to win. Well, not all of them. Normalisation is also psychic armour. It is a way of making the intolerable tolerable. It is a survival strategy, and like many such strategies, it is largely available to those with least to lose. Most black and LGBT Americans, along with anyone else who grew up feeling unsafe in America, moved through the stages of grief for a culture that cared about their lives long ago. For everyone else, the same grief is sore and shocking, and it's causing some strange behaviour.

The trouble with the five stages of grief is that one of them is bargaining. As a rogue's gallery of far-right ideologues, white supremacists and howling authoritarian sociopaths line up to take control of the White House, bargaining is what well-meaning liberals have spent all week doing – at least, those who have not already been personally threatened into silence. They've hopped from denying a Trump win was possible to telling themselves and each other that maybe it'll be all right, just as you might soothe a child in a storm shelter. Maybe the federal government will save us, or moderate conservatives, or Jesus. Maybe there's something reasonable in the rage of disinherited white Americans who rolled Orange Hitler into the Oval Office. Maybe we should have listened to them more, had more empathy, even as Trump voters deny any possibility of empathy for those whose beliefs, nationality or skin colour happens to differ from their own. Maybe we shouldn't have called their behaviour racist, misogynist, extremist. Maybe it was us, we say, rearranging the traditional post-crisis leftist firing squad into a perfect circle. Maybe we had this coming.

This, of course, is an internalisation of the language of abusers everywhere. Look what you made us do. We wouldn't have hurt you if you hadn't provoked us. If you're quieter, nicer and better behaved from now on we can put this behind us – although we'll have to punish you first. The people who have taken power in the mightiest nation on earth are native speakers of the language of abuse. They live and breathe the rhetoric of control, of gaslighting, of shame. This is how abuse works: not just overtly, but insidiously. It claims territory in your heart. It colonises your mind until it becomes comfortable. Until it becomes something you can live with, or at least survive.

So you tell yourself that you survived Bush and Blair. Surely you can survive this, too. If you keep your head down. If you give the new order a chance. If you don't make any strong statements. If you trust the government not to run the train off the rails. There will be attempts to reason with the abuser. To make him less of an abuser, because it is in fact hard to accept yourself as a victim. In the face of a sea-change in the socio-political order, you shut yourself tight in your shell and seal yourself off against everything that disturbs you. This might be thought of as the clam before the storm. And this is how it happens. This is how the bad guys win. This is how a 'white supremacist' becomes a 'controversial Breitbart executive' becomes a 'White House senior counsellor'.

This is also how life has changed in the United Kingdom since June, when the Brexit vote plunged the country into economic, cultural and constitutional disaster. A slow, chilling creep of normalisation of language and policies that would, scant years ago, have been the preserve of extremists. As the Overton window lurched to the right and the new, wholly unelected prime minister declared that 'ordinary, decent people' were right to fear immigrants, the millions of abnormal, indecent people who did not vote for Brexit – 48 per cent of the population who turned out to vote – curled into themselves with horror. The political left immediately started tearing itself apart, and those of us not wedded to the Labour party watched in alarm as the very people who were supposed to stand up for human decency and workers' rights took a wildly mistimed sabbatical to attack one another in public. Paranoia and conspiracy theories ran rife through the news, the tabloids abandoned any pretence at having moved on from their storied history of supporting fascists, and those who were clinging on to hope with their fingertips began to lose their grip.

As the Trump ascendancy became inescapable, therapists and psychiatrists across America were unsure how to treat a surge in patients presenting with symptoms of anxiety and depression. Psychiatric orthodoxy envisions anxiety as an individual problem, a maladaptive response to everyday conditions. There is nothing everyday, however, about Donald Trump and his march to the presidency on a carpet of hate – and to feel anxiety in response is anything but ill-adjusted. It is a survival instinct for the millions of Americans who really are directly threatened, physically threatened, by the new power agenda: their bodies make them targets. The traditional understanding of anxiety, despair, paranoia and hopelessness assumes some element of delusion or overreaction. But the white supremacists in the White House are very real. A vengeful, sociopathic narcissist who has been accused of sexual assault and has threatened to deport and incarcerate millions of black, brown and Muslim Americans will now have control of nuclear weapons and access to the most extensive surveillance network ever envisioned. Anxiety and despair are not irrational in this context. They are, in fact, the only rational response.

Months ago, thousands of 'citizen therapists', mental health professionals in the United States, produced a manifesto airing their concerns about what 'Trumpism' was doing to the American psyche:

> The public rhetoric of Trumpism normalizes what therapists work against in our work: the tendency to blame others in our lives for our personal fears and insecurities and then battle these others instead of taking the healthier but more difficult path of

> self-awareness and self-responsibility. It also normalizes a kind of hyper-masculinity that is antithetical to the examined life and healthy relationships that psychotherapy helps people achieve. Simply stated, Trumpism is inconsistent with emotionally healthy living – and we have to say so publicly.*

Sanity is socially and politically determined; and when politics change, the definition of who is well and unwell, who is sane and who is sick, tends to change with it. The traits of good mental health, of the supposedly well-balanced individual, are often suspiciously similar to those of the compliant citizen, the obedient worker, the dutiful woman – whatever those traits might be, depending on the mood of the world and the whims of the powerful. Those who oppose the existing order can count on being labelled as deranged, as irrational, especially if they make the mistake of showing emotion in a power regime that considers all emotions weakness, all feelings laughable – except the rage of the 'white working class', as long as this is properly harnessed in the service of vested interests. What happens, then, when an attitude of outrage, of resistance, becomes reclassified as mental illness?

Just look at what happened to Kevin Allred. When the Rutgers University lecturer posed a question about

*http://citizentherapists.com/manifesto/

the Second Amendment (the right to bear arms) for his students online this week, he was not expecting to be forced into a psychiatric hospital. Hours after he posted, according to his own report, he found the police at his door, telling him he had to go with them to Bellevue hospital. He was declared sane by a number of baffled in-house medical professionals, but diagnosis is no longer simply a medical issue. It is also a political one. A president-elect who has threatened to jail his opponent and refused to decry racist violence done in his name is considered mentally well by virtue of the position he holds. A precarious academic who raises an issue about the Second Amendment online is subject to mandatory psychiatric treatment.

Popular politics are no longer simply post-truth – they are post-reason. When working-class people vote against their own interests, they are usually dismissed as irrational. The Clinton campaign, much like the Remain campaign in Britain, worked on the basis that people would vote with their reason, rather than with their feelings – forgetting that white men in the West have always been encouraged to believe that it is their feelings that matter more than anyone else's, and that a unilateral response to those feelings is justified. That's what Trump voters, Brexiteers and their ilk have done and continue to do as the everyday violence against women, queer people, black, brown and Muslim citizens escalates across the Western world. They have interpreted their own feelings as an excuse for bigotry and a licence to abuse. They have allowed these feelings to be exploited by a venal salesman with a vicious agenda. They have allowed these same feelings to be put to work for the very people who caused so much of the mess. As above, so below: hurt people hurt people. Just because it's comprehensible does not make it okay. Just because your feelings are injured, this does not give you licence to injure others in turn.

This, again, is the logic of abuse: I have been hurt by life, and therefore I am entitled to take my feelings out on other people. I have no doubt that millions of those who voted for Trump have been deeply wounded by life. I have no doubt that those people feel that the hard-won ascendancy of women and people of colour to a slightly more equitable social position is a direct identity threat. I am sure those feelings are genuine and profound. That's fine. It's fine to have feelings. It's not fine to place those feelings at the wheel of the ship of government and steer it into a damn iceberg.

Let me break it down for those of you fortunate enough not to have lived in fear of this sort of abuse. The people who propelled Trump to victory and are now celebrating have been stalking and harassing women, people of colour, Jews, Muslims and LGBT citizens online and in the flesh for years. They have been stalking and harassing these citizens and calling it good fun. When those of us who were targeted spoke out, we were told that the abuse was not real. That they didn't really mean it when they leaked our addresses online and sent death threats to our families. That we provoked it, brought it on ourselves. That we should laugh it off and get off the Internet. Close your computer. Be quieter. Behave.

We tried to raise the alarm. We tried to make it clear that these people were serious, that they meant business, that they were doing harm. Now these people are seizing power across the Western world, and bringing with them all the tools of psychological warfare that they have used with impunity for so long.

Do not doubt that this is a war of nerves as much as a war of resources. Systematic psychological abuse is a favourite tactic of the alt-right, and was an election strategy for Trump. Identify an enemy by name or aspect, grind them down with threats and harassment, do your best not just to dehumanise them in the eyes of others but to undermine their own sense of human worth. Hours after Donald Trump declared victory, forum members from one of the many neo-Nazi outlets that stumped for the president-elect were cackling over the misery of frightened women, people of colour and LGBT citizens terrified for their families and communities. Andrew Anglin, publisher of the *Daily Stormer*, urged his followers to double down on the abuse: 'You can troll these people and definitely get some of them to kill themselves,' Anglin wrote. 'Just be like "it's the only way you can prove to the racists that Hillary was right all along".'*

Anglin egged on his tame troll army, reassuring them that headlines announcing a rash of suicides would further demoralise the left. Read that back to yourself. Understand that these are words of war. Understand that rational as despair may be, there are those who would count your pain a victory.

They would be wrong on that count. Because the new right, the alt-right, all these new permutations of old bigotry, consider every emotion weakness if it isn't ballistic spite. They adhere to a cult of toxic masculinity that deems evidence of feeling a defeat. That is why they are so fixated on 'triggering' their opponents, why they are obsessed with the notion of 'safe spaces', why the worst possible thing you can be is a 'snowflake', oversensitive, convinced of your worth as a human in a humane society. They believe that compassion is maladaptive, that liberalism is a disorder. They are wrong. Having feelings does not make a person weak. Allowing those feelings to control your behaviour is what makes monsters.

*https://www.google.co.uk/amp/s/www.washingtonpost.com/amphtml/news/morning-mix/wp/2016/11/11/get-some-of-them-to-kill-themselves-popular-neo-nazi-site-urges-readers-to-troll-liberals-into-suicide/?client=safari

We all know people who are not managing, people who we're actively checking in on. In the days since the result – which, however the embarrassed commentariat scrambles to recapture the narrative, was and remains a profound shock – I have fielded calls from friends, relatives and strangers driven to the point of despair. People who were already precarious and vulnerable and now have to imagine the prospect of four years of swivel-eyed authoritarian rule that may push the entire species to the point of habitat collapse. Then, as if things weren't bad enough, Leonard Cohen died. I found myself torn between sadness and real worry that millions of people around the world who were barely coping as it was were suddenly listening to *Various Positions*.

It is, perhaps, no surprise that the people who seem to be managing best out of the at-risk citizens I know are almost all survivors of some sort of sustained abuse: domestic violence, child abuse, the historic abuse enacted by grim and sordid definition on marginalised and minority groups, or all three. Some of the most vulnerable people I know are also the best in a crisis, because they kick immediately into survivor mode. One of my most fragile friends has spent the past few days making some of the fiercest political art of her life; another has put together quick, comprehensible reading lists for strategies of resistance; another is fundraising like mad for abortion rights charities and bringing networks together to keep up the momentum. This doesn't mean they're grieving any less, nor that those of us still pinned to our beds with panic are poor soldiers in this war in which we find ourselves conscripts. It means that the strategies that will sustain us all in the coming weeks and months are exactly the strategies that have always allowed human beings to survive abuse and intimate terrorism. They are strategies for practical survival that are also emotional armour.

In the coming months and years those of us who still believe in a better world will need to guard the most important frontline: the one in the head. Trump and his team may be about to inflict horrors on the world – not unimaginable horrors, more's the pity, but horribly imaginable ones. We must find a way to maintain our outrage, our shock, our refusal to accept the new power order as legitimate, while guarding our emotional resolves. Normalisation and passive acceptance are an easy sourcc of comfort but they are just about the worst coping strategies imaginable for living under an authoritarian, racist regime, so we must find others. Resistance is, and will remain, exhausting. Can we continue to treat toxic masculinity, aggression, bullying, misogyny and othering as dangerous and unhealthy when their very personification sits in the Oval Office? Can we hang on to our sense of what is right and just and necessary even as the definition of decency, of normality, is twisted and tortured into a new and violent shape? We can, and we must.

That doesn't mean we have to be happy about it. Personally, I spent the three days after the election weeping, writing and trying to force food down myself as I rearranged every plan I had made to step away and rest for a while after seven years of exhausting journalistic work. Donald Trump has really messed with my life plan. This is far and away not the worst thing he has done, but it makes it a bit more personal. I was planning to go away for a while and write a novel. I was planning to have an actual holiday for the first time in my adult life. It was a nice plan. God knows, I need a rest. For now, basic self-care will have to do.

Nothing I've done or not done has ever kept or will ever keep me safe from those who mean harm to me and to those more vulnerable than me. However dicey it might be for my mental health to stand in opposition to these people, it is more dangerous to do nothing. Comfort now comes at the cost of calamity later. I'm not going to take silly risks. I'm going to make sure I have a day off now and then, and a ready supply of tea. I am going to spend time with my face in my mum's dog's fur. But to normalise this crisis, to rationalise it, to slink away and make a nice safe life for myself while I can, would be to betray everyone I know who doesn't get that option.

Normalisation is psychic armour. But so is resistance. In the coming weeks and months and years we must navigate a course between the exhaustion of perpetual outrage and the numbness of normalisation. That means taking care of ourselves and of one another. It means practising a sort of emotional intelligence that the new power order lacks the capacity to imagine, an emotional intelligence that is all that stands between us and fascism with a cartoon face. It's also called courage. If standing up to bullies was cost-free, we'd have a different world. If enough of us do it anyway, we can still make one.

# 2

# Love and Other Chores

> That's one career all females have in common whether we like it or not. Being a woman. Sooner or later, we've got to work at it.
>
> Margo Channing, *All About Eve*

> Do you wanna be somebody, or somebody's?
>
> Angel Haze

## NO, YOU CAN'T HAVE IT ALL

Can women have it all? That this is still a major ethical dilemma of mainstream feminism shows how far we've still got to go. Yes, even though they've taken the nudes out of *Playboy*. The answer is less important than the fact that the question is vapid. Here's a better one: when did the message that 'girls can do anything' get twisted into the edict: 'girls must do everything?'

Anne-Marie Slaughter's book *Unfinished Business* claims to solve the problem of 'work–life balance', extrapolating from Slaughter's much-discussed article in *The Atlantic*, where she revealed why she quit a prestigious Washington career to spend more time with her two sons. The piece was titled 'Why women still can't have it all'. 'Having it all', to be clear, does not mean 'time to write a book, the total destruction of capitalist patriarchy and my very own puppy', which is what I'd have if I had everything I wanted. No, the 'it all' that every girl is supposed to want has a very specific meaning: it means the ability to simultaneously meet the demands of marriage, children and a high-powered career.

Slaughter fails to ask whether this is what all women do want, or should want – but even within such a narrow scope, her solutions are timid.

The message of *Unfinished Business* is that in order to keep everyone happy, you must simply try harder. It's difficult to please your boss, your husband and your kids all at once, so you must think harder about how you're going to do it without dissolving into a tangle of shredded nerves in a crumpled skirt-suit. All of this is just an updated version of what we have been told for centuries: women are supposed to work twice as hard as men, for half the reward, a saying I've always understood as a coded threat.

Somehow, modern women have allowed ourselves to be convinced that the right to work outside 'the home' is the only liberation that matters – never mind that working-class women and women of colour have always worked outside the home.

Slaughter isn't really talking to them, a fact that she acknowledges in three lines in the introduction, before going back to reframe the debate towards those women lucky enough to have a supportive partner, a lucrative career and the option to pay other people to look after their kids sometimes. Note that nobody is asking whether the nanny can have it all, even if she wants it.

For those few women who might be able to have 'it all', the programme sounds utterly exhausting. As I toiled through the latter chapters of career advice, wondering exactly when this notional working mother is meant to sleep, I realised with horror that Slaughter is talking to me. Specifically to me, and to people like me – middle-class, largely white women in professional careers who are at the stage of thinking seriously about how we might manage to juggle work and children. We're not supposed to ask if we want to do that, only how we'll manage.

I'm twenty-nine years old. It is possible that my biological clock is ticking, but I don't know, because I can't hear it over the racket of propaganda from the media, the movies, friends and relatives, all of it exhorting me and every other woman of so-called 'childbearing age' to settle down and make babies before it's too late.

Actually, I'd love to have a child someday. But in this unequal world, my circumstances seem to be aligning so that what I would have to sacrifice in order to make that happen is more than I'm able or willing to give. That's not an admission of weakness. It's a statement of priorities of the kind that women and girls are encouraged not to make in public. Instead, we are supposed to hoard up our guilt in private – whatever it is we eventually choose. If we put our careers first, we're selfish. If we devote ourselves to children and care work, we're lazy, or we're spoiled. If we try to juggle both at once, we're unable to give either our full attention. The engine of capitalist patriarchy runs on the dirty fuel of women's shame, so whatever we choose, the important thing is that we blame ourselves. That way, we don't blame the system.

Little boys don't get sold this nonsense. They're not encouraged to worry about how they'll balance their roles as husbands and fathers with paid work. Family life, for men, is not supposed to involve a surrendering of the self, as it is for women. Young men rarely worry about how they will achieve a 'work–life' balance, nor does the 'life' aspect of that equation translate to 'partnership and childcare'. Not for men.

It's not that I don't respect the choice to devote yourself to raising children. On the contrary – I can't stand the overplayed phobia of maternity that has become fashionable among parts of the young left, the sneering at 'mummy clothes' and avoidance of 'nappy valley'. The more of my friends and colleagues have children, the more I respect the enormity of the project, the tremendous efforts and risks involved. Childcare is vital, demanding work, work that we urgently need to stop devaluing – and we can only do that when we start giving women and girls real alternatives.

More than anything, Slaughter's book is a missed opportunity. The radical truth at the core of her story is that even a woman with all of her privilege – a lucrative, prestigious career, a loving, supportive husband and a boss who happened to be Hillary Clinton – even she could not make it work. She could not 'have it all'. The obvious conclusion ought to be that the 'work–life balance' is a lie of leviathan proportions. Instead, Slaughter falls back on a type of magical thinking, at once tragic and predictable: we can achieve 'work–life balance' *if we just work harder*.

There was, until quite recently, a powerful movement within women's liberation to acknowledge enforced 'reproductive labour' – childcare, housework and caring for husbands and elderly relatives – as a source of women's oppression. There was a demand, in Judith Butler's words, not just for equal work for equal pay, 'but for equal work itself'. It is not these words that spring to mind, however, so much as the mantra of Bartleby the Scrivener, the stubborn clerk in Herman Melville's famous story of workplace dissent. Whenever he is asked to perform a routine task, Bartleby replies: 'I would prefer not to.'

At a time when womanhood is still presumed to involve endless, exhausting work, it strikes me that the young women of the twenty-first century need to rediscover our inner Bartleby. Every page of *Unfinished Business* makes me think: I would prefer not to. Spend eighteen years raddled with guilt and exhaustion, trying to fulfil all the expectations of paid work and motherhood at once? I would prefer not to. I've got things to do. I still haven't finished season five of *Battlestar Galactica*! I still haven't been rascally drunk in a Moscow gay bar! I've got books to read! Adventures to have! And sure, I could do some of that while balancing a baby on one knee and a briefcase on the other . . . but I would prefer not to.

The truth about 'work–life balance' is that it doesn't exist. It never has existed, and unless we radically rethink our attitude to work and care, it never will. There it is. That's the truth nobody wants to acknowledge. You can't 'have it all', not even if you're in the lucky minority who can afford to pay someone else to take care of your kids, so stop trying and stop blaming yourself. There. Now we've got that sorted out, it's time to think about other options.

This is still an unequal world. But women are freer than we've ever been to build independent lives, to refuse to be bullied or shamed into lives we did not choose. We can't 'have it all' when the system is broken. It's time and beyond time for women to start asking what else we want – starting, perhaps, with a fairer deal.

## MAYBE YOU SHOULD JUST BE SINGLE

Mid-February is the most frigid time of year, so it's always seemed apt that this is when people choose to hold the highest holy day of the cult of coupledom.

If you're reading this, there's a not insignificant chance that you are one or several of the following: a) young, b) female, c) single or d) nauseated by the sheer volume of saccharine romantic propaganda sloshing around the public sphere at this particular time of year. But none of us live outside culture, and feeling frustrated on Valentine's Day doesn't make you stupid or duped or a mindless drone for the greetings-card industry.

With that in mind, it's time, as the Americans say, for some real talk.

Anti-Valentine's rants are almost as clichéd as the hearts-and-flowers parade. I have too much respect for you to subject you to yet another list of reasons to enjoy being single, or things to do while you wait for your soulmate to arrive. In practice, these mostly seem to involve wearing pyjamas, applying face-masks and modelling for stock photos. But Valentine's Day marks a point in the calendar when people start asking the Internet for love advice, so here's mine.

I think that it's usually better for women to be single. Particularly young women. Particularly straight young women. Not just 'all right', not just 'bearable' – actively better.

I have spent most of my twenties single, sometimes by choice, and sometimes because I was dating men and unable to locate one of those who didn't try to hold me back or squash me down. I spent quite a lot of time being sad about that, even though my life was full of friends, fulfilling work, interesting lovers and overseas adventures. Looking back, though, staying single was probably the best decision I made, in terms of my career, my dedication to my work and activism, and the lessons I learned about how to care for myself and other people.

It's not that I didn't get upset and frustrated. There were times when I badly wanted a partner, and for much of that time, I felt like I had to choose between having one and being my best self. That self, the self that was dedicated to writing, travelling and politics, that had many outside interests and more intense friendships, was not something men seemed to value or desire – at least not in that way. I don't mean to suggest that I don't also have gigantic, awkward flaws that make me largely unbearable to be with – just that boys rarely stuck around long enough to find that out. Plenty of them were perfectly happy to sleep with me, but after a little while, when I became a real person to them, when it became more than just sex, they turned mean or walked away.

That was hard. There were weeks when I walked around like I'd been kicked in the chest, wishing like hell that I had the ability to be someone else, someone more stereotypically lovable. With hindsight, though, I'm glad that I've never been willing or able to narrow my horizons for a man. It didn't turn out to be half as scary, or a fraction as lonely, as I'd been told. And, you know, I had a bunch of fun and got a buggerload of writing done.

I'm not single right now. It's sad that I felt I had to wait until that was the case before writing an essay like this. Part of me, I suspect, wanted to justify myself, to prove to you that I could gain the love of a man-shaped human, and thereby be an acceptable female. I wanted to wait and see if I felt the same way from the other side of five years without a primary partner. It turns out that I do.

You see, I don't believe that my relationship constitutes a happy ending. I don't want a happy ending. I don't want an ending at all, particularly not while I'm still in my goddamn twenties – I want a long life full of work and adventure. I absolutely don't see partnership as the end of that adventure. And I still believe that being single is the right choice for a great many young women.

Nothing frustrates me so much as watching young women at the start of their lives wasting years in succession on lacklustre, unappreciative, boring child-men who were only ever looking for a magic girl to show off to their friends, a girl who would in private be both surrogate mother and sex partner. I've been that girl. It's no fun being that girl.

That girl doesn't get to have the kind of adventures you really ought to be having in your teens and twenties. It's not that her dreams and plans don't matter, but they tend to matter slightly less than the boy's, because that's what boys are taught to expect: that their girlfriend is there to play a supporting role in their life.

You see them everywhere – exhausted young women pouring all their spare energy into organising, encouraging and taking care of young men who resent them for doing it but resent them even harder when they don't. You see them cringing for every crumb of affection before someone cracks and it all goes wrong and the grim cycle starts again. You can fritter away the whole of your youth that way. I know women who have.

What I'm trying to say is that there are a lot of things that are much worse than being single under modern patriarchy. The feminists of the late twentieth century were often single by choice, and they're mocked for it now by those who like to forget that they had good reason for it. It was better to be alone than to make the sort of grim bargains marriage or partnership required and still requires of heterosexual people who happened to be female.

It just wasn't worth it. Sometimes it still isn't worth it. For those of us who mostly or exclusively date the so-called 'opposite' gender, romantic love really can be a battlefield. It's where politics play out intimately and, often, painfully. We're not supposed to acknowledge that love is political. But how can it be otherwise? How can it be anything but political, when relationships with men are so often where women experience gendered violence, where differences in pay and privilege hit home, where we do all the work of caring and cleaning and soothing and placating that patriarchy expects us to do endlessly and for free?

Buried under the avalanche of hearts and flowers is an uncomfortable fact: romantic partnership is, and always has been, on one level, an economic arrangement. The economics may have changed in recent decades, as many women have gained more financial independence, but it's still about the money. It's about who does the domestic labour, the emotional labour, the work of healing the walking wounded of late capitalism. It's about organising people into isolated, efficient, self-reproducing units and making them feel bad when it either fails to happen or fails to bring them happiness.

Today, whatever else we are, women are still taught that we have failed if we are not loved by men. I've lost count of the men who seem to believe that the trump card they hold in any debate is 'but you're unattractive'. 'But I wouldn't date you.' How we feel about them doesn't matter. Young women are meant to prioritise men's romantic approval, and young men often struggle to imagine a world in which we might have other priorities.

The trouble is that in order to win that approval, we are supposed to lessen our power in every other aspect of life. We are supposed to downplay our intelligence, to worry if we have more financial or professional success than our partner. We can be creative and ambitious, but never more so than the men in our lives, lest we threaten them. And there are so few men that are worth making that sort of sacrifice for.

'In patriarchal culture,' as bell hooks observes in *All About Love: New Visions*, 'men are especially inclined to see love as something they should receive without expending effort. More often than not they do not want to do the work that love demands.' Even the very best and sweetest of men have too often been raised with the expectation that once a woman is in their lives romantically, they will no longer have to do most of the basic chores involved in taking care of themselves.

When I've spoken critically about this monolithic ideal of romantic love in the past, most of the pushback I've received has been from men, some of it violent, and no wonder. Men usually have far more to gain from this sort of traditional arrangement. Men are allowed to think of romantic love as a feeling, an experience, a gift that they expect to be given as a reward for being their awesome selves. That sounds like a great deal to me. I wouldn't want that challenged.

Women, by contrast, learn from an early age that love is work. That in order to be loved, we will need to work hard, and if we want to stay loved we will need to work harder. We take care of people, soothe hurt feelings, organise chaotic lives and care for men who never learned to care for themselves, regardless of whether or not we're constitutionally suited for such work. We do this because we are told that if we don't, we will die alone and nobody will find us until an army of cats has eaten all the skin off our faces.

Little boys are told they should 'get' girlfriends, but they are not encouraged to seriously consider their future roles as boyfriends and husbands. Coupledom, for men, is not supposed to involve a surrendering of the self, as it is for women.

Young men do not worry about how they will achieve a 'work–life balance', nor does the 'life' aspect of that equation translate to 'partnership and childcare'. When commentators speak of women's 'work–life balance', they're not talking about how much time a woman will have, at the end of the day, to work on her memoirs, or travel the world, or spend time with her friends. 'Life', for women, is envisioned as a long trajectory towards marriage. 'Life', for men, is meant to be bigger than that.

No wonder single girls are stigmatised, expected at every turn to explain their life choices. No wonder spinsterhood is supposed to be the worst fate that can befall a woman. 'Spinster' is still an insult, whereas young men get to be fun-loving bachelors, players and studs. There would be serious social consequences if we collectively refused to do the emotional management that being a wife or girlfriend usually involves – so it's important that we're bullied into it, made to feel like we're unworthy and unlovable unless we're somebody's girl. Today, we're even expected to deliver the girlfriend experience in the workplace, as 'affective labour' – the daily slog of keeping people happy – becomes a necessary part of the low-waged, customer-facing, service-level jobs in which women and girls are over-represented.

That's an ideological reason to be single. Now here's a practical one. The truth is that most men in their teens and twenties have not yet learned to treat women like human beings, and some never do. It's not entirely their fault. It's how this culture trains them to behave, and in spite of it all, there are a few decent, kind and progressive young men out there who are looking for truly equal partnerships with women.

The trouble is that there aren't enough of them for all the brilliant, beautiful, fiercely compassionate women and girls out there who could really do with someone like that in their lives. Those men are like unicorns. If you meet one, that's great. You might think you've met one already – I've often thought so – but evidence and experience suggest that a great many unicorns are, in fact, just horses with unconvincing horns. If you don't manage to catch a real unicorn, it doesn't mean there's anything wrong with you. Either way, you should have a plan B.

Not everyone has that choice. Many young women are already parents or carers. The global movement against welfare affects women more than any other group, since women do the majority of caring labour, forcing them back into dependence on partners, primarily men, unless they are privately wealthy.

Austerity and anti-welfarism are an attack on women's independence under capitalism. This is why agitating for economic change, such as the institution of a guaranteed minimum income, should be one of feminism's core projects.

In the meantime, however, we have to organise where we are. That's why it's so critical that women with the ability to do so – particularly women and girls at the beginning of their adult lives – prioritise their financial and emotional independence, including from men.

Rejecting that sort of partnership doesn't mean rejecting the whole notion of love. On the contrary: it means demanding more of love. I'm a gigantic squishy romantic at heart. It's just that I think compulsory heterosexual monogamy is the least romantic idea since standardised testing, and I don't see why our best ideals of love and lust and passion and dedication need to be boxed into it.

The worst thing about traditional romantic love is that it's supposed to be the end of the story – if you're a girl. The music swells, the curtain drops as you fall into his arms, and then you're done. You get to drift off into a life of quiet bliss and baby-making. Isn't that what every girl really wants?

It is not, nor should it be. There are many different routes to a life of love and adventure and personally, I don't intend to travel down any one of them in the sidecar. So we need to start telling stories about singleness – and coupled independence – that are about more than manicures and frantic day-drinking. We need to start remembering all of the women down the centuries who chose to remain unpartnered so that they could make art and change history without a man hanging around expecting dinner and a smile. We need to start remembering that the modern equivalents of these women are all around us, and little girls need not be terrified of becoming them.

More than half of women over eighteen are unmarried. More than half of marriages end in divorce. It is well past time to abandon the idea that a single woman has failed in life.

Even supposedly empowering stories of singleness, from *Sex and the City* to Kate Bolick's recent book

*Spinster*, seem to end with the protagonist finding her soulmate just when she's given up hope. That's not where my story ends. I'm enjoying the novelty of not being single, but it's bloody hard work.

Any dedicated love relationship is hard work, even when you're big and ugly and lucky enough to be able to negotiate your own boundaries and insist on your independence. It's work I only just manage to find time in the day for. It's work I definitely would not have had time for two or three years ago, when I was completely absorbed with churning out three books at once while simultaneously trying to become a better human being. And it's work I'd advise most young women not to be bothered with, in the knowledge that their human value is not and never will be contingent on being someone's girlfriend.

It's just not worth it.

We have to get on with saving the world, after all, and we can't do it one man at a time.

## FOR BETTER, FOR WORSE

Susan B. Anthony never married. The suffragist, abolitionist and civil rights campaigner foresaw in 1877 that 'in women's transition from the position of subject to sovereign, there must needs be an era of self-sustained, self-supported homes', leading, 'inevitably, to an epoch of single women'. Seven generations later, we may have finally arrived. More women are living alone or without a partner than ever before, and the question on the table once again is not how to have a better marriage, but whether to have one at all.

Two recent books by American journalists have blown air on the dying coals of the long-sidelined debate over marriage, partnership, the sheer amount of work involved in the whole business, and whether it's worth it for women who value their personal autonomy over the vanishing amount of security offered by coupledom. Rebecca Traister's *All the Single Ladies* draws attention to the growing power of uncoupled women in the United States, and the threat this poses to the socio-economic status quo. Moira Weigel's *Labor of Love*, meanwhile, focuses on the fact that for many women, what has been called love and phrased as destiny is in fact work – hard work, endless work, organisational and domestic and emotional work without boundary and reward – and much more optional than society would have us believe. 'Single female life is not prescription,' Traister writes, 'but its opposite: liberation.'

These books could not have arrived on my doorstep at a better time. I had been struggling to find language for my growing anxiety over the fact that, at almost thirty, I still have no desire to settle down and form a traditional family. I've been waiting, as open-mindedly as possible, for a sudden neo-Darwinian impulse to pair up and reproduce. And yet here I am, and it hasn't happened. Despite no small amount of social pressure, I am happy as I am.

I am quite content with the fact that my work, my politics, my community and my books are just as important to me as anyone I happen to be dating. I love babies, but not enough to make the work, the pain, the worry and the lost opportunities involved worth it for me – not right now, and maybe not ever. I live in a commune, I date multiple people, and I'm focused on my career. I'd always assumed, because I'd always been told, that this was a phase I was going through. Reading these two books has helped me be honest about the fact that marriage and babies have always been way down my list of priorities, and they're close to being nudged right off. There's too much else I want to do. I've made the same choice that men my age have been able to make for centuries without being scolded by society, or even having to think about it too much – and in and of itself, that's not radical. The possibility of millions of women making the same decision, en masse, however, is an entirely more threatening prospect.

As women writers around the world open up, for the first time in generations, about the regrets they have nursed in private over marriage and motherhood, the work involved in both is finally becoming visible. The key phrase here is 'emotional labour'. Emotional labour, Weigel reminds us, is not just the cleaning and the cooking and the wiping of snotty noses, but the organisation of households and relationships, the planning of marriage and fertility, the attention paid to birthdays and anniversaries, the soothing of stress, the remembering of food allergies – all the work, in short, that goes into keeping human beings happy on an intimate level. Someone has to do it, and the burden has fallen on women to such an extent that it has been naturalised, made invisible by the assumption that women and girls are just built to take care of all this stuff, if not by God then by nature, with a great deal of pseudo-scientific hand-waving over the specifics. The idea that we might not be, and that we might furthermore be fed up of doing so thanklessly and for free, is profoundly threatening to the smooth running of society as we know it.

It is more than possible for those who perform emotional and domestic labour to be alienated from the products of that labour, especially when so little recompense is on offer. Emotional and domestic labour is work, and women have been putting up with terrible working conditions for far too long.

I knew that the discussion of emotional labour had gone mainstream when I saw it plastered across the front cover of a women's glossy not generally known as a radical feminist recruiting tract. 'Who does the work in your relationship?' asks *Psychologies*, alongside a picture of Beyoncé, who recently dropped an album demanding that her husband do better 'or you're gonna lose your wife' alongside coded threats to bring down the government. Bey has come a long way from 'put a ring on it', and so have the rest of us.

'The revolution,' Traister declares, 'is in the expansion of options, the lifting of the imperative that for centuries hustled nearly all (non-enslaved) women . . . down a single highway towards early heterosexual marriage and motherhood.' The reframing of marriage and partnership not just as work, but as optional work, raises real questions for women and girls thinking about 'settling down'. Is it worth it? Is signing up for what might turn out, even if you're lucky, to be a lifetime of domestic management too high a price to pay for limited reward? Do you actually want to spend years taking care of children and a partner when it's hard enough taking care of yourself? Not so long ago, marriage was most women's only option if they wanted financial security, children who would be considered legitimate, social status and semi-regular sex. Our foremothers fought for the right to all of those things outside the confines of partnership, and today the benefits of marriage and monogamy are increasingly outweighed by the costs.

Study after study has shown that it is men, not women, who benefit most from marriage and long-term partnership. Men who marry are, on the whole, healthier and happier than single men. Married women, by contrast, were no better off than their single counterparts. Men who divorced are twice as likely to want to get married again, whereas women more often wanted out of the whole business. This might explain why it is women, not men, who must be steered and conditioned towards partnership from childhood.

It is little girls, and not little boys, who are taught to prepare for marriage, to imagine their future roles as wives and mothers, to fear being 'left on the shelf'. 'Bachelor' is a term of respect, but 'spinster' is a term of abuse, and it is women, not men, to whom the propaganda of romance is directed. From Hollywood to reality television to the comment desks of broadsheets, it is a truth universally acknowledged that a single woman, no matter what resources she may possess, must be in want of a man.

Or must she? I had always scorned Jane Austen, whose most famous aphorism I just bastardised, until I found myself on a train last year with nothing to read but *Emma*. I realised something I'd never considered as a literature student: that Austen's famous novels of shrubbery romance in stately homes and claustrophobic marriage plotting make a lot more sense once you realise that all her protagonists are profoundly depressed and economically desperate. The reason that her middle-class heroines are so singularly fixated on marriage is that they have no meaningful alternatives: without a suitable mate, they face poverty, shame and social isolation. They are not romances. They are horror stories. I was hooked, and ploughed through the entire collection in three weeks.

Jane Austen's books are still read and re-imagined as silly, frivolous stories for and about silly, frivolous women, but there are desperate stakes on the table. Austen, who never married herself, writes about women living in cages built by men, trying to survive as best they can, which is precisely what makes the stories so exciting and, to me at least, so frightening. Women's real fears and concerns about marriage and cohabitation have always been dismissed in exactly the same way, as trivial issues unworthy of consideration in the public sphere. But there are vital, visceral matters of work and power at play – and that's still true today, in a world where most women, thankfully, have a few more options than we did in the 1810s.

Today, single women have more power and presence than ever before; but there's still a price to pay for choosing not to pair up. It's not just about the stress of steering a life in unnavigated waters and unlearning decades of conditioning that lodges the notion that life without a partner leads to misery in the malleable parts of our hearts. It's also about the money. Over half of Americans earning minimum wage or below are single women, and single mothers are five times as likely to live in poverty as married ones. This has been taken as proof that marriage is better for women, when it should, in fact, be a sign that society must do more, and better, to support women's choices as men have been supported for centuries.

If women reject marriage and partnership en masse, the economic and social functioning of modern society will be shaken to its core. It has already been shaken. Capitalism has managed to incorporate the mass entrance of women into the traditionally male workplace by depressing wages, but the question of how households will be formed and children raised is still unsolved. Public anxiety over the low fertility rate among middle-class white women is matched only by the modern hysteria about working-class, black and migrant women having 'too many' babies – the attempts by neoconservatives to bully, threaten and cajole wealthy white women back to the kitchen and nursery are as much about racist panic as they are about reinstituting a social order that only ever worked for men. 'Single women are taking up space in a world that was not built for them,' Traister concludes. 'If we are to flourish, we must make room for free women, must adjust our economic and social systems, the ones that are built around the presumption that no woman really counts unless she is married.' Traister is relaxed about the prospect of single women asking that the support a husband might once have provided be publicly available. 'In looking to the government to support their ambitions, choices and independence through better policy,' she writes, 'single women are asserting themselves as citizens in ways that American men have for generations.' The same is true across the world: the liberation of women from mandatory domestic and emotional labour is a prospect of freedom that previous generations could only have imagined, and we owe it to them to take it seriously.

With all these options available, what about those who still choose marriage or partnership? They can couple up in the knowledge that their choices are made freely. When partnership ceases to be mandatory, it only becomes more special. Not long ago, one of my partners got married. I went to his stag night as part of the groom's party. I'm happy for him, and for his fiancée, whose permission I got before mentioning her in this piece. I love weddings. I love watching people

I'm fond of build a future together, however they choose to organise it, and I also love getting dressed up and drunk on cheap champagne with their mad relatives. There's not a lot I'd rather do than be a wedding guest for a weekend; it's just that I also happen to believe in dismantling the social and economic institutions of marriage and family.

I believe in all of that not despite my squishy, tender heart, but because of it. I'm a romantic. I think love needs to be freed from the confines of the traditional, monogamous, nuclear family – and so do women. I think wrapping up the most intimate, exhausting aspects of human labour in a saccharine slip of hearts and flowers, calling it love and expecting women to do it thanklessly and for free is a profoundly unromantic idea. In the real world, love is perhaps the one truly infinite, renewable resource we have – and it's beyond time that we had more options. I want more options for myself, and I want them for all of us, not just as a feminist, but as a romantic, too, because it's the only chance we have of one day, at last, meeting and mating as true equals.

The personal, however, remains political. Women refusing the traditional demands of love and marriage is not just a lifestyle issue, it's a labour issue. It is not beyond the bounds of possibility that, realising how terrible their working conditions are and have always been, women everywhere are simply going on strike, and it is a strike the like of which society has barely contemplated. It is distributed and dispersed, and the picket lines begin at the door of every household and the threshold of every human heart. Like any labour strike, it requires the raising of consciousness and a certain amount of solidarity between strikers, and it is not without costs. But this is how freedom is won.

## LET'S NOT ABOLISH SEX WORK; LET'S ABOLISH ALL WORK.

Is sex work 'a job like any other' – and is that a good thing? On 26 May 2016 Amnesty International officially adopted a policy recommending the decriminalisation of sex work around the world as the best way to reduce violence in the industry and safeguard both workers and those who are trafficked into prostitution.

'Sex workers are at heightened risk of a whole host of human rights abuses including rape, violence, extortion and discrimination,' said Tawanda Mutasah, Amnesty International's senior director for law and policy. 'Our policy outlines how governments must do more to protect sex workers from violations and abuse.

'We want laws to be refocused on making sex workers' lives safer and improving the relationship they have with the police while addressing the very real issue of exploitation,' said Mutasah, emphasising the organisation's policy that forced labour, child sexual exploitation and human trafficking are human rights abuses which, under international law, must be criminalised in every country. 'We want governments to make sure no one is coerced to sell sex, or is unable to leave sex work if they choose to.'

The proposal from the world's best-known human rights organisation has caused uproar, particularly from some feminist campaigners who believe that decriminalisation will 'legitimise' an industry that is uniquely harmful to women and girls.

As sex workers around the world rally for better working conditions and legal protections, more and more countries are adopting versions of the 'Nordic Model' – attempting to crack down on sex work by criminalising the buyers of commercial sex, most of whom are men. Amnesty, along with many sex workers' rights organisations, claims that the 'Nordic Model' in fact forces the industry underground and does little to protect sex workers from discrimination and abuse.

The battle lines have been drawn, and the 'feminist sex wars' of the 1980s are under way again. Gloria Steinem, who opposes Amnesty's move, is one of many campaigners who believe the very phrase 'sex work' is damaging. '"Sex work" may have been invented in the US in all goodwill, but it has been a dangerous phrase – even allowing home governments to withhold unemployment and other help from those who refuse it,' Steinem wrote on Facebook in 2015. 'Obviously, we are free to call ourselves anything we wish, but in describing others, anything that requires body invasion – whether prostitution, organ transplant, or gestational surrogacy – must not be compelled.' She wanted the UN to replace the phrase 'sex work' with 'prostituted women, children, or people'.

The debate over sex work is the only place where you can find modern liberals seriously discussing whether work itself is an unequivocal social good. The phrase 'sex work' is essential precisely because it makes that question visible. Take the open letter recently published by former prostitute 'Rae', now a committed member of the abolitionist camp, in which she concludes: 'Having to manifest sexual activity due to desperation is not consent. Utilising a poor woman for intimate gratification – with the sole knowledge that you are only being engaged with because she needs the money – is not a neutral, amoral act.'

I agree with this absolutely. The question of whether a person desperate for cash can meaningfully consent to work is vital. And that's precisely why the term 'sex work' is essential. It makes it clear that the problem is not sex, but work itself, carried out within a culture of patriarchal violence that demeans workers in general and women in particular.

To describe sex work as 'a job like any other job' is only a positive reframing if you consider a 'job' to be a good thing by definition. In the real world, people do all sorts of horrible things they'd rather not do, out of desperation, for cash and survival. People do things that they find boring, or disgusting, or soul-crushing, because they cannot meaningfully make any other choice. We are encouraged not to think about this too hard, but to accept these conditions as simply 'the way of the world'.

The feminist philosopher Kathi Weeks calls this universal depoliticisation of work 'the work society': an ideology under whose terms it is taken as a given that work of any kind is liberating, healthy and 'empowering'. This is why the 'work' aspect of 'sex work' causes problems for conservatives and radical feminists alike. 'Oppression or profession?' is the question posed by a subtitle on Emily Bazelon's excellent feature on the issue for the *New York Times*. But why can't selling sex be both?

Liberal feminists have tried to square this circle by insisting that sex work is not 'a job like any other', equating all sold sex, in Steinem's words, with 'commercial rape' – and obscuring any possibility of agitating within the industry for better workers' rights.

The question of whether sex workers can meaningfully give consent can be asked of any worker in any industry, unless he or she is independently wealthy. The choice between sex work and starvation is not a perfectly free choice – but neither is the choice between street cleaning and starvation, or waitressing and penury. Of course, every worker in this precarious economy is obliged to pretend that they want nothing more than to pick up rubbish or pour lattes for exhausted office workers or whatever it is that pays the bills. It is not enough to show up and do a job: we must perform existential subservience to the work society every day.

In the weary, decades-long 'feminist sex wars', the definitional choice apparently on offer is between a radically conservative vision of commercial sexuality – that any transaction involving sex must be not only immoral and harmful, but uniquely so – and a version of sex work in which we must think of the profession as 'empowering' precisely because neoliberal orthodoxy holds that all work is empowering and life-affirming.

That binary often can leave sex workers feeling as if they are unable to complain about their working conditions if they want to argue for more rights. Most sex workers I have known and interviewed, of every class and background, just want to be able to earn a living without being hassled, hurt or bullied by the state. They want the basic protections that other workers enjoy on the job – protection from abuse, from wage theft, from extortion and coercion.

A false binary is often drawn between warring camps of 'sex-positive' and 'sex-negative' feminism. Personally, I'm neither sex-positive nor sex-negative: I'm sex-critical and work-negative.

Take Steinem's concern that if 'sex work' becomes the accepted terminology, states might require people to do it in order to access welfare services. Of course, this is a monstrous idea – but it assumes a laid-back attitude to states forcing people to do other work they have not chosen in order to access benefits. When did that become normal? Why is it only horrifying and degrading when the work up for discussion is sexual labour?

I support the abolition of sex work – but only in so far as I support the abolition of work in general, where 'work' is understood as 'the economic and moral obligation to sell your labour to survive'. I don't believe that forcing people to spend most of their lives doing work that demeans, sickens and exhausts them for the privilege of having a dry place to sleep and food to lift to their lips is a 'morally neutral act'.

As more and more jobs are automated away and still more become underpaid and insecure, the left is rediscovering anti-work politics: a politics that demands not just the right to 'better' work, but the right, if conditions allow, to work less. This, too, is a feminist issue.

Understood through the lens of anti-work politics, the legalisation of sex work is about harm reduction within a system that is always already oppressive. It's the beginning, rather than the end, of a conversation about what it is moral to oblige human beings to do with the labour of their bodies and the finite time they have to spend on Earth.

Sex work should be legal as part of the process by which we come to understand that the work-society itself is harmful. The liberal feminist insistence on the uniquely exploitative character of sex work obscures the exploitative character of all waged and precarious labour – but it doesn't have to.

Perhaps if we start truly listening to sex workers, as Amnesty has done, we can slow down at that painful, problematic place, and speak about exploitation more honestly – not just within the sex industry, but within every industry.

## LOVE, UNLIMITED

Polyamory, if you believe the newspapers, is the hot new lifestyle option for affectless hipsters with alarming haircuts, or a sex cult, or both. A wave of trend articles and documentaries has thrown new light on the practice, also known as 'ethical non-monogamy' – a technical term for any arrangement in which you're allowed to date and snuggle and sleep with whomever you want, as long as everyone involved is happy. Responses to this idea range from parental concern to outright panic. Sleeping around is all well and good, but do we have to talk about it? Have we no shame? What's wrong, after all, with good old-fashioned adultery?

Having been polyamorous for almost a decade, I spend a good deal of time explaining what it all means. When I told my magazine editor that I wanted to write about polyamory, she adjusted her monocle, puffed on her pipe and said, 'In my day, young lady, we just called it shagging around.' So I consider it my duty to her and the rest of the unenlightened to explain what it is that's different about how the kids are doing it these days.

The short answer is: it's not the shagging around that's new. There's nothing new about shagging around. I hear that it has been popular since at least 1963. What's new is talking about it like grown-ups. It's the conversations. It's the texts with your girlfriend's boyfriend about what to get her for her birthday. It's sharing your Google Calendars to make sure nobody feels neglected.

The *Daily Mail* would have you believe that polyamory is all wild orgies full of rainbow-haired hedonists rhythmically thrusting aside common decency and battering sexual continence into submission with suspicious bits of rubber. And there's some truth to that. But far more of my polyamorous life involves making tea and talking sensibly about boundaries, safe sex and whose turn it is to do the washing-up.

Over the past ten years, I have been a 'single poly' with no main partner; I have been in three-person relationships; I have had open relationships and dated people in open marriages. The best parts of those experiences have overwhelmingly been clothed ones.

There's something profoundly millennial about polyamory, something quintessentially bound up with my fearful, frustrated, over-examined generation, with our swollen sense of consequence, our need to balance instant gratification with the impulse to do good in a world gone mad. We want the sexual adventure and the free love that our parents, at least in theory, got to enjoy, but we also have a greater understanding of what could go wrong. We want fun and freedom, but we also want a good mark on the test. We want to do the right thing.

All of this makes polyamory sound a bit nerdy, a bit swotty – and it is. I find myself bewildered when online trend pieces going for titillation clicks present polyamory as gruesomely hip or freakishly fashionable. Polyamory is a great many things, but it is not cool. Talking honestly about feelings will never be cool. Spending time discussing interpersonal boundaries and setting realistic expectations wasn't cool in the 1970s, and it isn't cool now. It is, however, necessary.

There is so little that makes ethical sense in the lives of young and youngish people today. If there is an economic type that is over-represented among the poly people I have encountered, it is members of the precariat: what Paul Mason memorably called the middle-class 'graduate with no future'. Even the limited social and economic certainties that our parents grew up with are unavailable to us. We are told, especially if we are women, that the answer to loneliness and frustration is to find that one, ideal partner who will fulfil all our emotional, financial, domestic and sexual needs. We are told this even though we know full well that it doesn't work out for a lot of people. Almost half of all marriages end in divorce.

Paradoxically, as the moral grip of religious patriarchy has loosened its hold in the West, the doctrine of monogamous romance has become ever more entrenched. Marriage was once understood as a practical, domestic arrangement that involved a certain amount of self-denial. Now your life partner is also supposed to answer your every intimate and practical need, from orgasms to organising the school run.

Polyamory is a response to the understanding that, for a great many of us, that ideal is impractical, if not an active source of unhappiness. People have all sorts of needs at different times in their lives – for love, companionship, care and intimacy, sexual adventure and self-expression – and expecting one person to be able to meet them all is not just unrealistic, it's unreasonable. Women in particular, who often end up doing the bulk of the emotional labour in traditional, monogamous, heterosexual relationships, don't have the energy to be anyone's everything.

I don't expect anyone to be everything to me. I want my freedom, and I want to be ethical, and I also want care and affection and pleasure in my life. I guess I'm greedy. I guess I'm a woman who wants to have it all. It's just that my version of 'having it all' is a little different from the picture of marriage, mortgage and monogamy to which I was raised to aspire.

Not all polyamorous relationships work out – and nor do all conventional relationships. We're making it up as we go along. It would be helpful to be able to do that without also having to deal with prejudice and suspicion.

It's easy to see where the suspicion comes from. The idea of desire without bounds or limits is threatening. It is a threat to a social order that exerts control by putting fences around our fantasies and making it wicked to want anything unsanctioned. It is a threat to a society that has developed around the idea of mandatory heterosexual partnership as a way to organise households. It is threatening because it is utopian in a culture whose imagination is dystopian, because it is about pleasure and abundance in a culture that imposes scarcity and self-denial. Freedom is often frightening – and polyamory is about balancing freedom with mutual care. In this atomised society, that's still a radical idea.

# 3

# Culture

> There is no greater agony than bearing an untold story inside you.
>
> Maya Angelou

> We were the people who were not in the papers. We lived in the blank white spaces at the edges of print. It gave us more freedom.
> We lived in the gaps between the stories.
>
> Margaret Atwood, *The Handmaid's Tale*

## CHANGE THE STORY, CHANGE THE WORLD

I saw *Star Wars* the week it was released, like everyone else, and yes, it was madly entertaining, and no, it wasn't perfect, and if I want to see a film that's deeply iconoclastic and challenges all my cultural preconceptions I will see something that isn't *Star Wars*. The part that had my heart in my teeth, though, wasn't the part I'm not supposed to tell you about. It came a little bit later. It was when Rey, the techie scavenger girl, picks up the lightsaber to fight the bad guy as an equal.

And the music swells. The same old theme and a new kind of hero on a new kind of journey. The same old story made stunning in its sudden familiarity for every girl who ever dreamed of being more than a princess. Rey picks up her weapon, and everything changes.

In a box-office-pulverising film whose gorgeous effects and point-perfect pacing leave their fingerprints on the back of your eyeballs for days, it says something that the most dazzling feature of all is the female protagonist and her love interest (possibly). Stories about outliers and unexpected heroes have always been around – the difference is that being a woman, a person of colour, a queer person, or some shocking combination of the three does not make you an outlier in quite the same way any more.

We're allowed stories now that aren't just 'look what she did, despite what she is'. Our heroism is no longer quite so unexpected. And that's as thrilling as it is threatening to those who are used to a single story about white boys winning the day.

The way we tell stories is changing. The change is creeping slow and political as hell. Just look at the diverse stories we've had this year, none of them perfect, all of them groundbreaking in the simplest and most shocking of ways.

It's *Jessica Jones* and *Kimmy Schmidt*. It's *Steven Universe*. It's *Orange Is the New Black* and *How To Get Away With Murder*. It's black Hermione and female Ghostbusters. It's *Transparent* and *Welcome To Night Vale*. It's Gamergate and the Hugo Awards. It's *Mad Max*. It's *Star Wars*. Diversity shouldn't be exciting by now, but it is. And of course, the backlash is on.

People who are quite happy to suspend disbelief in superpowers, summoning spells, dragons, aliens, planet-destroying starbases and Mark Hamill's acting abilities somehow find the idea of, for example, a black Hermione a bit too much and react with death threats and hate-mobs. This week, when the Internet learned that a black woman had been cast in a new play billed as the 'next instalment' in the Harry Potter series, author J. K. Rowling reacted perfectly, reminding fans: 'Canon: brown eyes, frizzy hair and very clever. White skin was never specified. Rowling loves black Hermione.'

Was Rowling imagining a black girl when she sat down to write that book in the mid-1990s? Probably not. But she knows, like the best storytellers, that books are hands held out to lonely children of every age, and not all those lonely children are white boys, and those stories change lives in ways even their authors cannot guess. So it matters. It matters that the 'brightest witch of her generation', the bookish heroine of a generation's definitive fairy tale, doesn't have to be white every time.

Let's not get carried away here. These stories and retellings are still exceptions. Women are still paid less, respected less and promoted less at almost every level of every creative industry. For every Jessica Jones there's a Daredevil, whose female characters exist solely to get rescued, provide the protagonists with some pneumatic exposition, or both. For every *Orphan Black* there's *Mr Robot* and *Narcos* and you know, sometimes I wonder if perhaps I watch too much television. The point is that what we have right now isn't equality yet. It's nothing like equality. But it's still enough to enrage the old guard because when you've been used to privilege, equality feels like prejudice.

The rage that white men have been expressing, loudly, violently, over the very idea that they might find themselves identifying with characters who are not white men, the very idea that heroism might not be particular to one race or one gender, the basic idea that the human story is vast and various and we all get to contribute a page – that rage is petty. It is aware of its own pettiness. Like a screaming toddler denied a sweet, it becomes more righteous the more it reminds itself that after all, it's only a story.

Only a story. Only the things we tell to keep out the darkness. Only the myths and fables that save us from despair, to establish power and destroy it, to teach each other how to be good, to describe the limits of desire, to keep us breathing and fighting and yearning and striving when it'd be so much easier to give in. Only the constituent ingredients of every human society since the Stone Age.

Only a story. Only the most important thing in the whole world.

The people who are upset that the faces of fiction are changing are right to worry. It's a fundamental challenge to a worldview that's been too comfortable for too long. The part of our cultural imagination that places white Western men at the centre of every story is the same part that legitimises racism and sexism. The part of our collective mythos that encourages every girl and brown boy to identify and empathise with white male heroes is the same part that reacts with rage when white boys are asked to imagine themselves in anyone else's shoes.

The problem – as River Song puts it – is that 'men will believe any story they're hero of', and until recently that's all they've been asked to do. The original *Star Wars* was famously based on Joseph Campbell's 'Hero's Journey', the 'monomyth' that was supposed to run through every important legend from the beginning of time. But it turned out that women had no place in that monomyth, which has formed the basis of lazy storytelling for two or three generations: Campbell reportedly told his students that 'women don't need to make the journey. In the whole mythological journey, the woman is there. All she has to do is realise that she's the place that people are trying to get to.'

Which is narratologist for 'get back to the kitchen' and arrant bullshit besides. It's not enough to be a destination, a prop in someone else's story. Now women and other cultural outsiders are kicking back and demanding a multiplicity of myths. Stories in which there are new heroes making new journeys. This isn't just good news for steely eyed social justice warriors like me. It also means that the easily bored among us might not have to sit through the same dull story structure as imagined by some dude in the 1970s until we die.

What does it mean to be a white cis boy reading these books and watching these new shows? The same thing it has meant for everyone else to watch every other show that's ever been made. It means identifying with people who don't look like you, talk like you or fuck like you. It's a challenge, and it's as radical and useful for white cis boys as it is for the rest of us – because stories are mirrors, but they are also windows.

They let you see yourself transfigured, but they also let you live lives you haven't had the chance to imagine, as many other lives as there are stories yet to be told, without once leaving your chair.

This isn't just about 'role models'. Readers who are female, queer or of colour have been allowed role models before. What we haven't been allowed is to see our experience reflected, to see our lives mirrored and magnified and made magical by culture. We haven't been allowed to see ourselves as anything other than the exception. If we made it into the story, we were standing alone, and we were constantly reminded how miraculous it was that we had saved the day even though we were just a woman. Or just a black kid. Or just – or just, whatever it was that made us less than those boys who were just born to be heroes.

The people who get angry that Hermione is black, that Rey is a woman, that Furiosa is more of a hero than Mad Max, I understand their anger. Anyone who has ever felt shut out of a story by virtue of their sex or skin colour has felt that anger. Imagine that anger multiplied a hundredfold, imagine feeling it every time you read or watched or heard or played through a story. Imagine how over time that rage would harden into bewilderment and, finally, mute acceptance that people like you were never going to get to be the hero, not really.

Then imagine that suddenly starting to change. Imagine letting out a breath you'd held between your teeth so long you'd forgotten the taste of air.

Capitalism is just a story. Religion is just a story. Patriarchy and white supremacy are just stories. They are the great organising myths that define our societies and determine our futures, and I believe – I hope – that a great rewriting is slowly, surely under way. We can only become what we can imagine, and right now our imagination is being stretched in new ways. We're learning, as a culture, that heroes aren't always white guys, that life and love and villainy and victory might look a little different depending on who's telling it.

That's a good thing. It's not easy – but nobody ever said that changing the world was going to be easy.

I learned that from Harry Potter.

## THE VIEW FROM SOMEWHERE

There's no such thing as a view from nowhere. One night in May 2012, I stayed up until dawn waiting for the night coach to Chicago with a busload of young Occupy activists headed to the G20 conference. I shared a smoke with a gang of lads who weren't more than twenty, whipping out the recorder from time to time to collect quotes for the piece I was writing. I began to ask them about their politics, their understanding of economics, when one of them, an eighteen-year-old high-school dropout called Sean, whipped out a dollar bill from his pocket, set light to it and used it to light his cigarette. 'That's debt, and that's what we do with it,' he said. He wasn't a rich kid, not by anyone's standards. He owned the clothes he was standing in, a rucksack full of random belongings and half a cigarette. He needed that dollar. But he burned it anyway.

I keep coming back to this moment every time somebody asks how I can possibly claim to be objective when covering radical politics and youth movements as I have been for the past few years. Little Sean burning his money on a Manhattan street corner at two in the morning. His friends laughing and whooping, and me knowing that there's no way they'd have done that if I hadn't been there.

Every reporter changes the story. In this case, I was wearing my second-nicest tights and a bit of makeup and holding a recorder, and hence appeared old enough and professionally polished enough to be someone they felt the need to impress – but not so much older and more polished that they didn't suspect there might be an outside chance of me shagging one of them in the hostel bathrooms later on. I eventually gave up the attempt to disabuse them of this notion and simply watched the peacocking until it became dull.

In fact, a fair few articles I've filed from the front-lines of the global protest movements over the past few years have featured young men at moments of crisis and violence lighting up cigarettes dramatically, exhaling meaningfully and saying something cheesy and rousing. This is not a coincidence. This is because, at moments of social interest and in the presence of an averagely attractive woman who seems suddenly very interested in their ideas, your garden-variety young male activist, anarchist or student trouble-maker has the tendency to produce a cigarette, light it dramatically and say something they think is deep. They do this because it makes them look cool and sometimes gets them laid. I promise you, I've seen it happen. Meanwhile, my straight, male, suit-wearing colleagues, brandishing exactly the same recorder in front of exactly the same interviewees, often come away with suspicious grunts and stock quotes.

I'm only telling you this to make it clear that there's no such thing as a 'view from nowhere' – that weird mainstream media orthodoxy that holds that the perfect journalist, the ideal journalist, can only discover truth by adopting a posture of invisibility, that the perfect journalist should be little more than a human recorder himself – always himself, because this perfect reporter is invariably imagined as male, usually as a middle-class white dude from an English-speaking country. Those are the only people whose race and class and gender and nationality ever get to be 'invisible', whose views get to be from 'nowhere', because they are everywhere.

That's just one of the reasons that in-the-field investigative journalism jobs are still given mostly to white men: even if they've never visited the country in question and don't speak the language, editors still trust those people to tell the story over and above local reporters. The net result of all this is that anyone who isn't a white, heteronormative Western man has to fight doubly hard not to get stuck in an office rewriting press releases . . . on this, trust me.

The whole notion of the 'view from nowhere', the idea of completely objective reporting that's supposed to be the gold standard of journalistic practice in America in particular, is of course utter hogwash. Every view comes from somewhere, and who you are as a writer, reporter, filmmaker or blogger changes how people behave in your presence. It changes what they say to you; it changes whether they speak to you at all. That's as true for your average white dude reporter as it is for anyone else, and it matters even if you don't care a bit about equal representation in the media industry. It matters because the fallacy of bland and faceless reporting hurts journalism, by allowing bias and prejudice to masquerade as hands-off objectivity, by giving reporters licence not to be honest about how their outlook affects their output.

When the August riots ripped through London in 2011, it was *Guardian* journalist Paul Lewis who got the story. The Orwell Prize nominee filed an unbelievable number of reports from every flashpoint in the city, following young people on every side of the fighting on Blackberry Messenger, chasing the chaos on Twitter, sleeping in snatches over those five frightening days. He went out, as he wrote in the days that followed, 'wearing a hoodie and riding a bicycle; to blend in, and because no one could have got through in a car' – and that changed the story, too. People who went out dressed as 'journalists' that day got their cameras stomped on and their teeth kicked in by kids who knew perfectly well that the vast majority of the mainstream press in Britain was going to call them thugs and hooligans, because they'd been doing so for decades under the guise of objectivity, and these kids just didn't care any more.

When you put a story together, you change the story. It doesn't matter if the report you write doesn't use a single first-person pronoun, if your face doesn't appear in the video: you're there, whether you like it or not, and the most dangerous thing any journalist, 'citizen' or otherwise, can do is buy into the myth of their own objectivity.

The idea of the standoffish white Western bloke in a tie as the universal journalistic eyepiece was able to develop because we have spent centuries seeing the world purely through the eyes of white men. Right now, that's changing. Journalism is changing, and the Internet is driving an explosion of media production from people all over the world who understand that subjectivity doesn't have to mean inaccuracy, especially when you're telling stories.

Several months after that Chicago bus trip, I saw Sean again, sleeping on the streets of New York, outside Wall Street, in the dead of winter. I remembered how I'd laughed at his trick with the dollar. I remembered how he was so pleased with himself, how he told me about the new life he was hoping to build somewhere on the West Coast where the streets were warm. I understand that for some journalists, impassivity is a virtue, but I believe one cannot maintain it and tell true human stories with any degree of justice. In these anxious times, passivity is a stance in itself – and a dangerous one.

## ON QUOTAS AND MERITOCRACY

What we measure reveals what we value. Right now, in business and politics, there's a movement to measure and promote women's participation – and an equally energetic movement against it. Much has been made of the new Labour shadow cabinet, which, for the first time in history, is over 50 per cent women. Celebration has been met with outrage: all of these diversity hires must surely be diluting the quality of the work being done. Why not just appoint the best people for the job?

The governments of Britain, America and almost every other Western nation are overwhelmingly male, and they always have been – but every time an argument is made for actively promoting women's representation, much less instituting any sort of quota system, the backlash is instant and vicious. The same thing happens wherever women and people of colour begin to take power and achieve recognition in larger numbers – from the boards of major companies to the winners of prestigious literary prizes. From fiction to finance, people with a vested interest in the status quo are fighting against diversity.

Here's what people say whenever you make a case for gender quotas: it should always be about getting 'the best person for the job'. Aren't you worried about people being promoted just because of who they are, not what they can do? Isn't that discrimination? Isn't it unfair? The answer to that is: of course it's unfair. It's extremely unfair. I'm categorically against people being parachuted into positions of power and influence just because of their gender or the colour of their skin. It's a social disease. It stops us making full use of our collective capabilities. And that's precisely why we need 'diversity hires'. That's precisely why we need quotas.

In this society, plenty of people are promoted just because of their gender and race. Almost all of those people are white men. What, you think all those Bullingdon boys in government got there by their wits alone? You think the men who make up 81 per cent of the US House of Representatives did not benefit from centuries of racism and sexism, from the promotion of men and white people at the expense of absolutely everyone else?

And yet, across the board, it is women and people of colour who are accused of using their race and gender to get ahead. Let me break it down for you: Winston Churchill used his race and gender to get ahead. Franklin D. Roosevelt used his race and gender to get ahead. So, now we come to it, has Donald Trump. All of these men may have been great at their jobs – but it doesn't hurt that every time they take the stage, they personify the image of power that still dominates the political imagination in the West and beyond. We would do well to recall that for centuries, there was a quota for representation of men in politics and the press, sometimes legally enforced, sometimes so universally accepted that it didn't have to be codified in law. The quota was 100 per cent.

We're doing better these days, but change isn't coming fast enough. It should not have taken Britain eight decades to appoint the first shadow cabinet that is not majority male. It should not have taken four generations since the first British women gained the vote in 1918 to achieve 30 per cent representation for women in parliament. Hannah Jewell at BuzzFeed estimates that at this rate, getting to equality would take another twenty-two elections – or 110 years.

Many explanations have been put forward for why women aren't achieving equality in practice when we have it on paper. But the reason that makes most logical sense is the one nobody wants to talk about. It's simple prejudice. Simple sexism.

Sometimes overt, sometimes backhanded: women of childbearing age are still seen as a 'maternity risk' by recruiters, as opposed to men, who it is assumed will be able to have a family without damaging their performance at work. Women make up over 50 per cent of graduates, and tend to match or outperform men in any test where intellect and aptitude are the only measures of success – school examinations, for example. But whenever large numbers of men are involved in the hiring or selection process, women fall behind.

Sexism is standing in the way of social change – and quotas are the only proven way to speed the progress of equality.

Time and again, however, we are told that quotas themselves are the worst form of prejudice – that they might prevent 'the best people for the job' from being hired. Let's stop right there. Let's unpack that assumption. What are you saying when you tell me that a political outfit, for example, that made a point of hiring 50 per cent women, would not be getting 'the best people for the job'?

You're saying that the best people for the job aren't women.

I repeat: if you think that a truly meritocratic society would not be one in which men and women were equally represented, from politics to pop culture, what you're saying is that men are fundamentally better than women. That might be hard to hear, but we can only confront a thing by naming it honestly. And the fact is that if you truly believe in meritocracy, you must also believe in diversity – any other position is prejudice of the most insidious sort.

The opposition to full equality runs deep. Patriarchy can cope with the notion of a few women in top positions – but not 50 per cent, or anything approaching it. That would mean that women would no longer be a special interest in politics and finance; we would have real power, and men would be obliged to share it with us. When culture reserves only a few places for women in a world of men, women are forced to compete against each other for that smaller space. I vividly remember being told that there was no more room for another young woman at one media organisation that I won't name – after all, they already had one.

The more women there are in the room, the less we'll be fighting each other for crumbs, but rather competing with everyone in the room for a fair share of the whole cake.

The backlash to the mere suggestion of a quota system is strong even when mutual interests are at stake. The notion, for example, that corporations pay financial penalties for hiring too few women was rejected by British businesses – but that notion is almost redundant, because they already do pay a penalty. Study after study has shown that firms with more diverse management perform better and deliver bigger profits for their shareholders. In four centuries of exploitation, corporations have been prepared to do anything to protect their bottom line – anything except break up the boys' club.

The truth is that equality is really scary. The truth is that promoting more women in parliament, on prestigious panels, in the pages of print magazines – anywhere in culture where the number of positions is finite – ultimately means promoting fewer men. There's no getting around it. This is the part of feminism that actively requires men to give up the special privileges they have enjoyed for centuries in the name of equality and of excellence. It means that men and boys will have to work harder and be better – at least as good as the women going for the same roles. I can understand why that's a challenging idea. Building a career in politics or the media already feels like the Hunger Games, and who wants to suddenly be competing against a whole new phalanx of contenders who have been honing their skills in adversity, who are hungrier and more determined than you because they've had to be?

When accusations of prejudice fall flat, small-c conservatives start in on the concern-trolling. Of course we all want better representation for women, they say, but might that not hurt women's self-esteem? Might it not be, as Peggy Drexler writes at the *Daily Beast*, that 'women whose hard work earns them professional success [find their] achievements are downplayed in the shadow of enforced quotas'?

It's funny that the only time conservatives concern themselves with women's self-esteem is when they're trying to hamper our progress, rather than, say, give us more power, money and influence, all of which, I hear, can be great confidence-boosters. Shall we ask all those Olivers and Marcuses who got their City internships through friends of their fathers how their self-esteem is doing? I imagine it's doing just fine.

Women are always asked to consider what men will think of us before we take any step towards freedom and justice – but that's no way to get ahead. Even with greater diversity at work and in politics, society will find a way to undermine women in the workplace; but the more women there are the harder they'll have to work at it – as well as everything else.

Ultimately, I suspect that it's not women who need to be worried that their mediocrity might be exposed. It's not women, after all, who have been over-promoted for centuries. We have been comfortable for generations with mediocre people drifting into positions of influence and power, as long as those mediocre people happen to be white, wealthy and male.

Don't get me wrong: I've met a great many white men in media and politics who are stunningly good at their jobs. But they don't always have to be in order to make the rent. And that's the difference.

In an ideal world, quotas would not be necessary. In an ideal world, a true meritocracy, the most talented people would be put forward, and that would automatically mean diversity. But quotas may be the only way of achieving, eventually, a world where quotas are obsolete.

We need diversity, and we need it now. We need the best brains and the best hearts in positions of influence to steer us through what may be the most challenging chapter in the long story of the human race. And the fact is that for thousands of years, the potential of at least half of humanity, at every level of society, has been battered by bigotry, squandered on obligatory pregnancy and domestic labour, ground down by violence. We have lost so much, as a society and as a species, by not putting women forward. It's time to make up for what we've lost. It's time for equality – by any means necessary. It's not just about fairness. It's about survival.

## THE TRAGEDY OF JAMES BOND

There is something rather tragic about James Bond. In advance of seeing *Spectre*, the latest instalment in the super-spy sex-murder franchise, I watched several of the old films again.

The experience was like having your forebrain slowly and laboriously beaten to death by a wilting erection wrapped in a copy of the Patriot Act: savage and silly and just a little bit pathetic.

James Bond is a guilty pleasure but one in which the pleasure is increasingly overwhelmed by the guilt. Even Daniel Craig seems to know this. The actor acknowledged, just before the premiere of his latest turn as Bond, that the character 'is actually a misogynist. A lot of women are drawn to him chiefly because he embodies a certain kind of danger and never sticks around for too long.' Craig, who has fronted a gender equality campaign affiliated to Amnesty International and appears to be about as unsexist as anyone who has worked in Hollywood for twenty years can be, gives us the Bond the twenty-first century needs: a character who is aware that he is both a relic and a thug and is surprised that he still gets to be the hero.

Nobody is saying that Bond isn't fun. On top of all the explosions and wacky gadgets, the Sean Connery-era Bond movies are so mind-blowingly sexist that they are hilarious. The revamped films aren't much better – the last time we saw Bond, he was watching a villain tie up his sex-slave lover, place a glass of Scotch on her head as the camera aimed at her cleavage, then shoot her just to prove how evil he was. Bond's verdict? 'Waste of good Scotch.' Again, gross enough to be funny: until you remember that this is the guy we are supposed to be rooting for. It is possible to watch the films ironically but it is hard to sustain a rigorous internal critique when the scenery is blowing up and *Dr No* must be stopped at all costs. Ultimately, it is terribly difficult to sustain an ironic erection. To do so involves a kind of anxiety that the men and boys of the twenty-first century know very well.

The new Bond films work because they tackle that anxiety head-on. The director Sam Mendes told *Empire* magazine that 2012's *Skyfall* – the highest-grossing Bond film in history – was about ageing, uncertainty and loss and that this dynamic forces itself through the action scenes, the ridiculous firefights, the awesome bit in which the train carriage packed with explosives ploughs through someone's ceiling just because they had the budget. Daniel Craig has not been given enough credit for taking a character who was a cardboard throwback even in the 1960s and playing him straight: as a wall-eyed, traumatised thug, a protagonist who is two-dimensional precisely because he is empty inside.

Craig animates the automaton that is Bond by asking just what it would take to make a person behave in this horrific way – and like any piece of well-done puppetry, the effect is sinister. Daniel Craig is the Bond we deserve, a Bond who takes seriously the job of embodying a savage yearning for a lost fantasy of the 1950s. It is about masculinity, yes, but also about Britishness, about whiteness and about heterosexuality, about the loss of certainty in all of these in a changing world.

That is why I agree with Roger Moore that Bond cannot be played by a woman or a person of colour, except in pastiche – Bond's whiteness and maleness are as much a part of who he is as the gadgets and the sharp suits and the romantic alcoholism. Indeed, these are almost all of who he is. Bond is anxious twentieth-century masculinity incarnate, a relic of twentieth-century power struggling to come to terms with its own irrelevance, still fighting cartoon Cold War villains as the planet burns – which is what gives the films their melancholy beauty.

The franchise is dripping with camp nostalgia for a time that never really was, a time when men could be real men, which meant that they were allowed to hurt whoever they wanted and still get away with it. It's right up there in the job description: licence to kill. Bond is the kind of hero he is because he is allowed to do anything he wants to anyone he likes, from harassment to outright murder, all while wearing snappy suits and driving cool cars and getting every single one of the girls, for a rather suspicious value of 'getting'. He may be a dangerous sociopath, but he's our dangerous sociopath, so of course we're rooting for him, because damn, look at the other guy. He's got an eyepatch. And a cat. And he dresses like your granddad if your granddad was the weird judge off *Project Runway*.

The 'licence to kill' thing always bothered me – on a logistical level as much as an ethical one. Before the opening credits even roll, Bond has usually caused enough mayhem to keep some poor desk clerk occupied in paperwork for a year.

Whose job is it to follow Bond around with a stack of forms and a can of disinfectant, explaining his behaviour to grieving widows and elderly parents who don't understand why their daughter has been petrified in gold paint by goons and left to die in a hotel room by some sleazeball she's just met? Presumably the job falls to Moneypenny, who seems unaccountably upset that she never gets a shot at Bond, despite the fact that 'Bond girl' is a career in which 'work–life balance' is extremely awkward to negotiate.

The problem with the way we watch Bond is not that Bond is a killer. I rather like films about serial killers, those gory thrillers that seduce you into rooting for the twisted anti-hero over the good guy. The problem with Bond is that he is supposed to be the good guy. He is a borderline rapist who is employed by the government to murder people – and yet he is not an anti-hero. He is just a hero. If your child said they wanted to grow up to be just like Hannibal Lecter, you would be worried. Somehow Bond gets a pass and, come Hallowe'en, a legion of little boys will be dressing as 007 with the full support of their doting parents. Bond is a hero for no other reason than that he is on our side, which is how most Western nations and particularly the British come to terms with their particular legacy of horror – with a quiet embarrassment that nonetheless knows how to defend itself by force.

The dilemma of James Bond is a pantomime version of the dilemma facing most men who grew up watching the films and wondering what it would be like to be that guy, whom everybody seems to love not in spite of the awful things he does but because of them. In real life, anyone who behaved even slightly like James Bond would be ostracised, arrested, or both. And that is the problem. Bond is still supposed to be a hero but if you knew him in real life, you would be warning all your friends not to invite him to their parties. That disconnect follows men home from the cinema and into their daily lives, because most of the behaviours that are supposed to make you a hero – the things you are still supposed to do if you want to be a strong, respected, manly man – also make you an unqualified arsehole.

That is why James Bond isn't evil. James Bond, more than anything, is a tragic figure and his tragedy is the tragedy of white, imperialist masculinity in the twenty-first century. It is a tragedy of irrelevance that becomes all the more poignant and painful in the retelling. It cannot last for ever and it must not last for ever – but while it does I'll thank you to pass me the popcorn.

## COMMODITY FEMINISM

In the late 1920s, not many women smoked. To do so in public was seen as unladylike, a signal of promiscuity and general naughtiness. So the American Tobacco Company hired Edward Bernays, the man now known as 'the father of public relations', to find a way of selling cigarettes to women. The first feminist wave was still in full, frilly-hatted swing and Bernays realised that women's desire for independence could be manipulated for profit.

Bernays let it be known that during the Easter Sunday Parade of 1929, a group of suffragettes would be lighting 'torches of freedom', and arranged for photographers to be on standby. On cue, in the middle of the parade, a gang of hired models produced packets of cigarettes and sparked up. The images were distributed around the world.

It worked like a dream. In 1923 women purchased only 5 per cent of all cigarettes sold but by 1935 that had increased to 18 per cent. Almost instantly, cigarettes became associated with empowerment. It was perhaps the first time feminism was appropriated to sell us things we don't need; it wouldn't be the last. I'm writing this with an e-cigarette in my hand, by the way. It isn't very empowering.

Capitalism has a way of cannibalising its own dissent. The endless weary suggestions that we need to 'rebrand' feminism miss how women's liberation – particularly when gently pried away from its more radical, anti-family, anti-racist, anti-capitalist tendencies – has long been used to sell everything from cheap perfume to vibrators. From Revlon's Charlie adverts, marketing chain-store scent to the 'new women' of the 1970s, to the more recent Dove 'Campaign for Real Beauty' (which shows how we can make ourselves feel better about the psychosocial terrorism of the beauty ideal by rubbing in a bit of body lotion), every groundswell of idealism has salesmen scampering in its wake.

Recently an advert produced by Snickers in Australia featured construction workers shouting feminist statements. 'You want to hear a filthy word?' they yell from their scaffolding. 'Gender bias!'

The advert's punchline – 'You're not yourself when you're hungry' – manages to be offensive on a number of levels, not least by implying that manual labourers in their natural state are rude, aggressive boors. As was quickly observed, if this is how men behave when they haven't eaten cheap chocolate there's a good argument for never feeding them again.

Advertising is one of the sites where profound cultural battles are played out in public. Posters selling cosmetic surgery appear far more rarely on the London Underground since they began to be defaced and stickered over with messages about sexism and self-image. Naturally, I'd never do anything like that, because that would be destruction of property. So if you're reading this and thinking of doing a bit of subvertising, I'd encourage you to scrawl slogans only over any posters you may own, any billboards you may own, and the walls of any public buildings or bus shelters you may own.

Even the most challenging advertising usually plays on trends and ideas that are current in the mainstream. The co-option of basic feminist sentiments by the hawkers of cheap chocolate and panty liners clearly demonstrates that a cultural shift has taken place – yet the stark juxtaposition of these ever-so-slightly challenging adverts with the everyday wall of airbrushed limbs draped over cars, credit cards and the telephone numbers of payday loan companies signals just how far we have to go.

The trouble is that, while progressive ideas can be used to spice up a confectionery campaign, social justice itself is a hard sell. The kind of feminist change that will make a material difference to the lives of millions, the kind of feminist change growing numbers of ordinary people are getting interested in, is about far more than body image. It's about changing the way women (and, by extension, everyone else) get to live and love and work. It's about boring, unsexy, structural problems such as domestic work and unpaid labour, racism and income inequality. It's about freeing us to live lives in which we are more than how we look, what we buy and what we have to sell.

The activists of what is now being spoken of as feminism's 'fourth wave' – digital, intersectional, globally connected and mad as hell – are good at branding, and increasingly confident in getting their message out. The iconography of injustice has altered in the Internet age and viral moments, popular hashtags, catchy videos and slogans are being used to promote ideas that are more challenging than anything mainstream advertising has yet thought of.

There is nothing wrong with a bit of showmanship. Nor is using feminist ideas to sell chocolate and cosmetics a bad thing.

But there are some ideas that will remain challenging and disturbing, however you dress them up. You can't walk into a shop and buy a torch of freedom – you can only light a fire yourself, and pass it on.

## LITTLE ORPHAN NELLIE

In 1893, the celebrated reporter Nellie Bly went to visit Emma Goldman in prison. The young anarchist provocateur was held in the first Manhattan jail to be called the Tombs; it was built on the wreck of an old swamp and stank of rot and faeces. The two women had both grown up in poverty and obscurity, and found fame, if not fortune, by writing about the conditions suffered by women and the working poor. But while Bly was lauded for circling the globe in only a fetching checked travelling cloak, Goldman was locked up for incitement to riot. Bly was one of the few journalists to show Goldman any sympathy and the first to understand her importance as a cultural figure. In Bly's piece, Goldman is permitted to speak her truth at length, along with some girly chat about clothes of the frivolous sort that Goldman would never have stooped to in her own writings. These are the details that never make it into the manifestos but nevertheless make the politics a hundred times more human.

The reporter mentions Goldman's precocious talent – she is barely twenty-five – and lists the six languages she can speak and write. We are invited to be impressed. Then Bly comes to the matter of marriage and whether Goldman believes it to be a universal good, the ultimate balm of a woman's life:

> 'I was married,' she said, with a little sigh, 'when I was scarcely seventeen. I suffered – let me say no

> more about that. I believe in the marriage of affection. That is the only true marriage. If two people care for each other they have a right to live together so long as that love exists. When it is dead what base immorality for them still to keep together! Oh, I tell you the marriage ceremony is a terrible thing!'

No counter-argument is offered, or even entertained. Bly agrees with Goldman but cannot say so directly. To do so would not have been in character, at least not the character as whom she made her living.

Some people seem born to break down walls. Nellie Bly was born Elizabeth Jane Cochran in Pennsylvania in 1864. She was the thirteenth of fifteen children and, following the early loss of her father and her mother's remarriage to, and scandalous divorce from, a mean drunk, she struggled to find teaching work. Her first break in journalism came when she sent an excoriating letter to the *Pittsburg Dispatch*, responding to an article about 'What Girls Are Good For' – marriage, motherhood and obscurity, according to the original columnist, whose name is lost to history. 'If girls were boys quickly it would be said: start them where they will, they can, if ambitious, win a name and fortune,' wrote Bly, then twenty. 'Gather up the real smart girls, pull them out of the mire, give them a shove up the ladder of life, and be amply repaid.' She signed her letter as 'Orphan Girl'.

The editor, George Madden, was so impressed that he offered her a job. Because women's writing was considered unseemly, Madden decided that Cochran should have a pen name. He took 'Nellie Bly' from a minstrel song: a white man bestowing on a white girl a name created by a white man for a fictional black serving girl. From the start, Cochran – now Bly – was caught between the stories men wanted to tell about girls and the stories girls would tell for themselves, 'given the chance'. Bly is now remembered less for the stories she wrote than for the stories that sprouted up around her. Maureen Corrigan notes in the introduction to the new Penguin edition of Bly's collected journalism that Nellie Bly has become 'a headline, not an author'. Her femaleness is phrased now, as it was in her day, as a fascination; the editorial furniture, neatly preserved in the Penguin edition, sells her in the manner in which Victorian circuses might advertise a travelling freak show: *See this Young Girl Write Hard-Hitting Stories Just Like a Man!*

Bly racked up a lot of firsts in her meteoric career. Just a year after being hired by the *Dispatch*, she had left for New York, where the first mass-circulation newspapers were being printed, wangled a job at the *World*, and made her name with 'stunt' reporting. She was to become the most celebrated reporter of her age, at a time when journalists did not expect to become household names. Bly was also the first decoy to allow the patriarchal press to feel really good about itself for allowing a little woman into the big boys' club.

'Gonzo' journalism is now read as a macho practice: turn up somewhere ripped and stoned and undercover and immerse yourself in a culture or practice, then write viscerally, from the brain and the gut. In fact, women were doing it first. Bly was just twenty-one when she got herself committed to Blackwell's Island Insane Asylum to report on the dispiriting conditions suffered by the inmates there: the beatings, the starvation, the cold. Her feature in the *World* drew public attention to the plight of the mentally unwell in the US and led to some limited reforms.

From the start, Bly is a natural writer. Her voice is caustic and confident, lilting effortlessly between the gush and private wonder of a schoolgirl's diary and the rigour of the most celebrated political reporters of her time. Bly was a celebrity, working at a time when a revolution in newspaper technology had coincided with a surge of interest in women's liberation. She was the right face for the right time. The fact that she was also tremendously talented in the literary and practical craft of journalism was at once the whole point and somewhat beside it.

By the time she headed out on her infamous round-the-world dash, attempting to circle the globe in fewer than the eighty days described in Jules Verne's novel, she was already famous. 'Strong Men Might Well

Shrink From the Fatigues and Anxieties Cheerfully Faced by This Young American Girl', cries her home paper's report, preserved in this edition, describing how the wind ruffled Bly's 'fair young cheeks'. Bly made her deadline and was greeted by cheering crowds in New York. The resulting column series, which became a book, is not about the world at all. Rather, it's about Nellie Bly, the mannish young woman, the myth. We hear more about the outfits she was wearing than her impressions of the nations she glimpses out of the dining cars of cross-country sleeper trains.

The round-the-world dash is by far the weakest part of Bly's oeuvre as presented in the Penguin collection. For a start, the speed at which the young reporter is travelling means that she barely has time to speak to anybody at all or to dig into the flesh of a place as she does in her undercover work. She is utterly focused on beating the self-imposed deadline, as if to miss it were to sacrifice her carefully built credibility. Bly sees the countries she visits mostly through train windows and the portholes of ships, and she sketches the people who actually live there in hasty and often racist caricatures.

As a young provincial reporter, Bly went to Mexico and wrote without sentiment or stereotype of the lives she saw there. In four short pages you get the starkness of inequality, the taste of a fresh tortilla, the gentleness of strangers. 'The women, like other women, sometimes cry, doubtless for very good cause, and the men stop to console them,' she observes.

On her round-the-world trip, Bly has no time for such nuance. The inhabitants of Aden, then a British colony, are simply 'black people of many different tribes' and 'little naked children' who 'ran after us for miles, touching their foreheads humbly and crying for money'. That language, like Bly's legend, is dressed in an outfit of patriotism. She is always that Plucky American Girl who can dash around the globe, trotting out the hasty racial stereotypes as well as any puffed-up British colonial officer.

The mainstream press has always been a treacherous trough to drink from. As her career continues, you can feel Bly fighting for maturity in her work against a climate that wants one thing from her and one thing only: her own story. She struggles to shake the wide-eyed excitement of the precocious girl-essayist at its proper time. It's as if Elizabeth Cochran, the anonymous Lonely Orphan Girl, is trying to write her truth, but Nellie Bly, celebrity reporter, is covering her mouth. Her struggle with persona plays out on the page. In the decades after her retirement, Nellie Bly was written about in books, taught about in schools, and memorialised in songs (she appears as a side character in the traditional 'Frankie and Johnny', which was covered by Elvis). Until now, though, almost nobody bothered to read her actual work, at least not in a systematic way. It has taken a century for Bly's journalism to be collected in print.

Bly's zeal to write about the women the world had failed, the women locked in madhouses, trapped in bad marriages and dead-end jobs in airless tenement rooms, started early. The stories she wrote received space in return for a certain imposed sensationalism. Her editors give a measured investigation into the working lives of young women in box-making factories in Manhattan the pre-clickbait title 'What It's Like to Be a White Slave'. The more Bly struggles to expose the conditions of women in the poorest parts of America, the more Bly's editors treat her as a fascinating trinket. Not only is she a young woman who can spell; she's actually talking politics.

Some of these interviews and essays are collected in the chapter 'The Woman Question', playing neatly into the notion, as popular now as it was a century ago, that there is only one. Bly had many different questions about women. She wanted to know how they lived and worked, where they were permitted to go, why they were paid so much less than men, not only in the professions to which they were slowly being admitted, but in factories, fields and farms. She wanted to know why nobody was talking about women except as 'dolls' or 'drudges'.

The prison interview with Goldman is not included in this collection, although it is among Bly's finest pieces of political writing. When Bly asks Goldman (then at the start of a long, dangerous career of exile and agitation) how she imagines her future, the political prisoner tells her: 'I cannot say. I shall live to agitate to promote our ideas. I am willing to give my liberty and my life, if necessary, to further my cause. It is my mission and I shall not falter.' Entirely unbothered by notions of journalistic objectivity, Bly ties off the piece by calling Goldman a 'modern Joan of Arc'.

Bly's rebellion could be rehabilitated; Goldman's never was. In 1893, when they could not vote, leave their husbands or own property, women could rebel but not too much. You could be the exception to the rule as long as the rule remained intact. Nellie Bly was not permitted to become the writer for the ages that she might very well have been. In the end, there was only one story that editors were interested in hearing from her, and it was not the story of the tenement box-makers or women's suffrage activists. It was the all-American story of the lonely orphan girl made good.

## NEW MEDIA, OLD RULES

One day not so long ago, I was contacted separately by two distressed friends, both writers, both women. One is famous, successful, hard as diamond under glass and trying gamely to brush off fantasies of personal and specific violence being sent to her by people nominally on the left. She is discovering that as a woman writing and speaking about serious politics in public, it's not enough just to be *good* – you also have to deal with the overheads of abuse, bullying, dismissal and disrespect, all while smiling and being nice and pretending as hard as you can that it doesn't get to you.

My other friend is just starting out, is very young and very talented. She was in tears, wondering if she should just kick it in altogether because of all the people writing in complaining that she's 'all me, me, me' and a 'careerist'. 'Careerist' is often directed as an insult against women and people of colour – the type of people in media who are not supposed to have careers. If you're Ezra Klein, careerism is fine: you're expected to be proud of your work, to promote your brand of journalism, to behave as a professional would. 'We have to work on your sense of entitlement,' I told my young friend. 'It needs to be bigger.'

Right now, there's a big global conversation going on about journalism and diversity, but we've only just started to realise the scale of violence at play.

Journalist Emily Bell observed in the *Guardian* that the hot new media startups, backed by serious investment, look suspiciously like the stale old media establishment in terms of demographics. She pointed out, quite reasonably, that the projects that have everyone talking about the 'future of journalism' – Ezra Klein's *Vox*, Nate Silver's *FiveThirtyEight* and *The Intercept*, helmed by Glenn Greenwald and Laura Poitras – have not hired very many women or people of colour. They certainly haven't been hired in huge numbers in editorial, decision-making roles. The piece prompted a great deal of impassioned response on both 'sides', the best of which has been Julia Carrie Wong's new series at *The Nation*, in which she takes apart 'Old Problems In New Media'. To my mind, the real question is: what does an organisation or individual have to do to get feted as 'the future of media'?

What gets to be a startup, and what's just one woman, or one black kid, or a whole bunch of angry queers shouting? There's a magical process whereby an individual or group of individual media workers get transformed from frightening and/or uppity women and people of colour to the next hot thing in the future of publishing. The whiter and maler you look, the more it seems the magic happens.

The magic is to do with being white and male and having various other markers of privilege while still defining yourself as a scrappy outsider, to quote Nate Silver, responding to Bell's piece: 'The phrase "clubhouse chemistry" is an allusion to baseball, but the idea that we're bro-y people just couldn't be more off. We're a bunch of weird nerds. We're outsiders, basically. And so we have people who are gay, people of different backgrounds. I don't know. I found the piece reaaaally, really frustrating. And that's as much as I'll say.'

Outsiders. That, as Zeynep Tufekci observed at *Medium*, gets to the nub of startup culture's intransigent sexism, racism and classism. Those who have the power right now, in tech but also to some extent in media, see themselves as rejects, weirdos fighting for their place, and there are reasons for that. The emotional patterning laid down in puberty is hard to shake. If you got used to being excluded, being left out, having to fight to survive because you were smart or nerdy or different or all three, that's a mentality that stays with you. That sort of trauma can be useful later in life – it gives you stamina, drive, a determination to carry your ideas through against the odds, a hunger to prove yourself, fierce dedication to your fellow oddballs and weirdos, and I could go on. But it is still trauma, and it comes with baggage. Part of which is that long after you've stopped being an outsider and instead become a privileged pillar of the new establishment, not only do you fail to notice, but when someone points it out to you, you get angry – you get reaaaally, really frustrated – because being an 'outsider' has always been a forming part of your identity, and being told there are people further out than you is hard to handle.

These, it turns out, are the kind of 'outsiders' the old guard can cope with: outsiders who look almost exactly like them, except younger and cooler. The question the media startups and most critics are still asking is: why are the new flagship organisations so lousy with white guys, whereas the more interesting question is: why do these people still get to set the terms of what 'the new media' is? Don't we live in one of the most exciting times in the history of journalism, and isn't that change being driven, out of necessity, by women and people of colour? Aren't the most popular, most viral articles on most mainstream websites – although not necessarily the most prominent or well-paid ones – consistently being written by women and people of colour? Take a glance down the top articles in the *New Statesman*, in the *Guardian*, in *Salon*, and you'll see what I mean.

My qualification to talk about all this is that I've spent eight years working, largely as a freelancer, sometimes within mainstream publications and sometimes outside them, to change how journalism and commentary was done. I've been doing this along with hundreds of women, people of colour, trans people and allies who saw a media world that was closed to them and only spoke to them to tell them lies, and thought, fuck that, we have the technology to do better. So we did. Except that when we did, we weren't called 'the future of media'. If we got hired by establishment outfits it was initially as mascots, performing seals who weren't trusted to cover 'real journalism'. I'm thinking of the newspaper that hired me on a promise that it would let me do serious long-form reporting and then pressured me to cover only 'fluffy' women's issues, sending me to cover precisely one story in nine months: the Women's Beach Volleyball at the Olympics.

*Modelview. Racialicious. Colourlines. Writers Of Colour* (now *Media Diversified*). *The Vagenda. Meta. Novara. Trans Media Watch.* Those are just the first few names I've plucked out of the air in terms of exciting new outfits that, whatever you feel about their content, are real journalism and criticism and commentary, and are undeniably startups, changing the way media is done. They're just not considered 'startups', not considered 'serious' journalism because 'objectivity' and 'seriousness' are often presumed to be a function of privilege, of whiteness, of maleness, or all three. When *Jacobin* was profiled in the *New York Times*, its founder, Bhaskar Sunkara, was rightly hailed as a representative of the future of left media. But when *The New Inquiry*, the online magazine for which I am an Editor at Large, which was founded by two women, is run by a woman and features a lode-bearing amount of serious writing by women and people of colour, was profiled in the same paper, it was relegated to the 'style' section.

There are two problems with the mainstream media for women, people of colour, poor people, disabled people, queers – well, actually, there are quite a lot more than that, but let's start with two. First, the media misrepresents us, throws out lazy stereotypes that perpetuate oppression. And then it shuts us out, denying us a voice, allowing us to speak only as token demographic representatives rather than as reporters, writers, authors, columnists, critics. The media is an industry that produces culture, and both of those elements need taking apart and ramming back together in a way that works for more of us who actually create and consume it.

As Wong writes: 'A journalism more aware of the intersections of race, class and power will be much better equipped to ask the questions that might not even occur to reporters who have never interacted with the state from a position of weakness – whether that's as a person of color subject to intense police repression or a woman whose access to reproductive health care is increasingly under attack.' And yet this is precisely the sort of journalism that is being dismissed as 'unobjective', relegated to the 'style' section, to the 'women's' section, written off as marginal because it has been pushed to the margins of an increasingly spiteful, embattled white patriarchal establishment.

This is why, whenever I am asked if I'm 'really' a journalist rather than 'just' an activist or 'just' a feminist, I never have an uncomplicated answer. Because the simple act of doing my job as a reporter, critic, commentator and author would be a feminist act even if I never wrote another word about reproductive justice or consent culture, which is not my intention. Being in the media, making media, changing media, creating culture, activism – these things are not the same, but they are part of the same sphere of activity. We are here because we have to be, and we're changing the game.

Yes, it's fucking political. For me the politics are in the stories I choose to cover, the perspective I bring, and the fight I have to engage in every single day to stay present, aware and professional while trolls and harassers attempt to bully me off the Internet just for daring to be female with a public platform. That harassment is an overhead that women and people of colour, and particularly women of colour, have to face in a quantity and quality that those who do not experience it often find difficult to comprehend, especially from their own 'side'. Whatever you think of Suey Park's work, the backlash against her has been terrifying in the scale of its racism and sexism – she told *Salon* that she has had to stop her speaking work because of the threats she's getting.

Technology was supposed to help us move beyond all of this, and it has. If there's one reason that women, people of colour, queers and everyone else on the margins of the mainstream press have been able to build their own future and set the agenda so successfully, that reason is the Internet. And the reason the Internet has become so fraught for women and people of colour attempting to carve out public careers or just do some decent journalism and criticism is that the Internet is where we've been changing the world. Challenging power.

My biggest fear is that old-school media bros, making the jump to digital-only ventures years after the rest of us set up shop here, will decide they invented it, and that everyone else will agree. That Ezra Klein, Nate Silver et al will get to be the pioneers, sticking their flags all over the vibrant existing ecosystems of online journalism. Preventing that from happening is about more than just lobbying for shiny new startups to hire more women and people of colour. It's about getting the media that women and people of colour are already making properly recognised, properly remunerated, and given the respect and credit it deserves for creating the future of journalism – because we have, and we are.

## GIRLS LIKE US

Hey girls, we're all the same, aren't we? At least, that's what they'd like us to think. We are living through an unprecedented glut of narrative richness, at a time when people from an enormous range of backgrounds, including women and people of colour, are finally beginning to share stories about their lives across boundaries of class and distance in numbers too big to ignore. But you wouldn't know it from the mainstream press, which still reserves a very few places for female creators, who are expected to represent all womankind, then excoriated when they inevitably fail to do so.

Take, for instance, the ongoing storm of publicity around the HBO show *Girls*, which follows the lives of four young white girls living in Brooklyn. I am often asked if I relate to *Girls*. Well. I'm a white, middle-class media professional in my mid-twenties living and dating in a major Western metropolis. Of course I relate to *Girls*, and I think it's smart and funny and fun, although there are still bits that don't speak to me at all. What's more important is whether or not any piece of art to which some women relate – particularly women from a certain privileged demographic – can be considered definitive.

The vivisection of *Girls*, and of its creator, Lena Dunham, has become a cultural project involving hundreds of writers, critics, blogs and TV pundits worldwide. Alongside serious issues of race and representation, there have been articles obsessing over whether Dunham's jawline was tightened in her photoshoot for *Vogue*. There have been interminable debates over the nudity in the show, and whether it's necessary. There has been barely disguised rage that a woman who isn't a standard Hollywood beauty is allowed to display her body in public, to place her less-than-perfect flesh at the centre of her show, to play a character who sleeps with good-looking men.

The popular blog *Jezebel* offered $10,000 for un-airbrushed images of the *Vogue* photoshoot, as if having one's hips narrowed in post-production were hard evidence of betraying the sisterhood, of not being that perfect poster girl for global feminism who has, to the best of my knowledge, never existed, and who would need to be destroyed if she did. As Dunham told the *Huffington Post* in 2012: 'The idea that I could speak for everyone is so absurd.' But the reactionary trend of taking any rich young white girl's story and making it a totem for young womanhood everywhere is bigger than Dunham, and it's a brutal beast to battle.

Nobody is saying that Lena Dunham doesn't deserve critique. Debate and discussion is part of the life of a piece of art, particularly when it comes to episodic television, which has replaced film as the dominant medium of collective storytelling. What is curious is that no male showrunner has ever been subject to quite this sort of intense personal scrutiny, this who-are-you-and-how-dare-you. No male showrunner has ever been asked to speak to a universal male experience in the same way, because 'man' is still a synonym for 'human being' in a way that 'woman' is not.

Men do not experience the personal being made universal. When men direct honest, funny television shows about young men living their lives, it's not 'television that defines the young male experience', it's just television. When men write 'confessional literature', it's just 'literature'. Male artists and writers produce deeply personal content all the time, but as Sarah Menkedick once wrote at *Velamag*, for them 'it's called "criticism" or "putting yourself in the story" or "voice-driven" or "narrative" or "travelogue" or "history" or "new journalism" or simply a "literary journey"'.

Forbidding any woman simply to be an artist, forbidding us from speaking about our experience without having it universalised and trivialised, is the sort of broad-brush benevolent sexism that undermines the real threat that a multitude of female voices might otherwise pose. It comes from a culture that puts up endless barriers to prevent women and girls expressing ourselves honestly in public and then treats us like fascinating freaks when we do. It is still so rare, so unbelievably, fist-clenchingly rare, to see young women depicted in the mainstream media with anything like accuracy, as human beings rather than pretty punctuations in somebody else's story, that as soon as it happens we want it to be more than it is. So *Girls* is asked to speak for every young woman everywhere, and then torn apart when it inevitably fails to do so, because nobody can, because nobody ever could. And that's the problem.

In 2012 Kendra James, a black writer with a similar social and educational background to Dunham, wrote a heartfelt piece entitled simply 'Dear Lena Dunham: I Exist', in which she asked 'why are the only lives that can be mined for "universal experiences" the lives of white women?' Why, indeed? In mainstream culture, white, straight, middle-class women don't get to speak about their experience without having it universalised and made meaningless in the process – but black women, poor women and queer women usually don't get to speak about their experience at all. In 2013, only one black female director released a major film. Essentialism is as racist and classist as it is sexist. It is always reactionary. The idea of girlhood as a universal story is a great way to stop individual women's stories being heard. And it's treacherous territory to negotiate.

The mainstream media still tells a single story about what women are and what they do. The Internet, by contrast, allows us to tell many stories. My own work and writing comes out of the blogosphere, out of LiveJournal and blogspot and status updates, and my first jobs in journalism were for small, independent publications. Sometimes I forget that writing for publications like the *New Statesman* and the *Guardian* comes with very different overtones – the attitudes of the mainstream press are changing, especially online – but for a lot of people they still represent a culture whose idea of femininity is horribly monolithic.

The telling of many stories, the sharing of different experiences, is part of what's creating a sea change in our cultural understanding of gender and power. I see that happening everywhere. But sometimes just seeing isn't enough. The politics of cultural representation are riven by rage for good reason. This is still a sexist, racist society, one that reserves a very limited number of places for female writers and artists – fewer still for women who are not white, straight and middle-class – and then demands that they speak as women first and as human beings second. Those who by chance or privilege manage to attain those few, totemic positions become lightning rods for the understandable anger of those who were not chosen, who do not see big-budget dramas made about their lives, who are only called on, if at all, to describe what it is like to live as 'other'.

Only white, straight, cis girls get to be Everygirl. That's just one more reason that the idea of Everygirl is bullshit. It hurts every real person trying to live her own story within the limits of imagination permitted to us.

Feminism will have achieved something huge when one artist isn't expected to stand in for every young woman everywhere. We will be on the cusp of something magical when women are actually permitted to be artists, to create fiction, to make mistakes, to grow up, to be flawed and human in public. If there's one thing about the phenomenon of *Girls* that *does* speak to a universal female experience, it's the spectacle of being crushed by impossibly high expectations.

The really scary truth about the universal girl experience is that there isn't one. The truth about young women that nobody wants to acknowledge is that we are all unique, and the number of stories that haven't been told about our lives is vast, particularly if we are poor, or queer, or if we are not white. It is the telling of many diverse stories, rather than the search for the perfect archetype, that will really challenge the narrative of patriarchy, and I want to see more women's stories told, not just online, but in mainstream, high-stakes media. I resolve in future to be a more useful part of that great retelling.

To paraphrase Bakunin, there is no such thing as a perfect poster girl for feminism – and if there was, we'd probably have to destroy her.

## WHAT WE TALK ABOUT WHEN WE TALK ABOUT TRIGGER WARNINGS

In the mainstream press, it is common for newscasters to warn viewers if they are about to see 'potentially distressing' content. So why is there such resistance to trigger warnings, which encourage openness and honesty rather than shutting down debate?

There's a whole lot of outrage swilling around about trigger warnings. It came in response to a *New York Times* report on the request, by a small number of students at American universities, that teachers put 'trigger warnings' on potentially disturbing texts – reading material that might, for example, contain graphic descriptions of violence against women. The objection seems to be that since so much classic literature involves violent misogyny, racism and brutality towards minorities, whinging leftists should pipe down and read without questioning, analysing or reacting to the canon. This appears to me, as a literature graduate, to be a rather odd proposal for university teaching, and I'm extremely glad that conservative commentators are not, as yet, in charge of the syllabus.

I believe the discussion about trigger warnings is being had in bad faith. I believe it is being used as a stand-in to falsely imply a terrifying leftist censoriousness, by people who don't understand where the term comes from and don't want to. As Soraya

Chemaly notes at the *Huffington Post*, stern dismissal of trigger warnings has become a proxy for dismissing women, people of colour, queer people and trauma survivors as readers. It is saying that our experiences do not matter – that we should calm down and 'grow a thicker skin'.

It says that any attempt to acknowledge or accommodate readers with difficult experiences is tantamount to Stalinism. Someone is being told to shut up here, but it's not F. Scott Fitzgerald.

So let's calm down and talk clearly about what a trigger warning is and is not. A trigger warning is a simple, empathic shorthand designed to facilitate discussions of taboo topics in safe spaces. What it absolutely is not is a demand that all literature be censored to ensure that moaning feminists and leftists are not 'offended'.

I'm not saying that I've never seen people try to shout one another down by demanding trigger warnings, but it's a lot less common than has been implied, and when it does happen, it's usually missing the point. I have almost never seen the shorthand attached to films or literature, and nobody is suggesting a scenario where you won't be able to walk into a bookshop without being told what is and is not sexist. It's about knowing and respecting your audience; crucially, it is about context. In 'safe spaces' like feminist discussion forums, mental health and survivors' groups, trigger warnings are the very opposite of censorship. They allow discussions of traumatic and difficult issues to be had in an upfront manner. Rather than editing the subject material to avoid upset, group members are treated like adults and allowed to make their own decisions about what they can handle on any given day.

If you want to get angry about censorship on school and college campuses, take a trip to the state of Texas, where not too long ago the Board of Education approved a curriculum designed to emphasise Republican political philosophies and 'stress the superiority of American capitalism', among over 100 right-wing amendments to the curriculum. Attempts to include more Latino figures as historical role models for the many Hispanic children attending Texas schools were consistently quashed.

Or have a word with Michael Gove, who spent his time as Education Secretary reworking the British history syllabus to emphasise the positive side of Empire. If you're angry about censorship of classic literature, visit any of the hundreds of American school libraries where parents have lobbied to have books withdrawn from school libraries for their sexual or controversial content – books like *To Kill a Mockingbird* and *The Color Purple*.

Censorship of literature is not to be tolerated. But it isn't the online social justice crowd who are lobbying for such censorship. Asking that classes and discussion spaces take the possible experiences of their members into account in those discussions isn't just a different ballpark – it's a different game entirely.

A trigger warning is not a rule, it's a tool. It does not demand that we withdraw from topics that are taboo or traumatic, but rather suggests that we approach such topics with greater empathy, greater awareness that not everyone reads the same way.

There is some debate over where precisely the term 'trigger warning' entered common parlance. I first encountered it on LiveJournal and in related online communities that were sensitive to mental health issues; mental health bloggers in particular used the term to signal that what was about to be discussed or described might be harrowing for those with PTSD.

One of the many crucial things that has been missed, deliberately or otherwise, is that trigger warnings, at least initially, were almost always attached to personal narratives. They became a way to share stories of trauma, anger and extreme experience while preserving a space which did not alienate the vulnerable.

In those spaces online, we spoke about rape and abuse, racism and gendered violence, discrimination and frightening mental health experiences, but these discussions were not designed to shock – indeed, part of the point of the discussion was that these things happened so often that they should not be shocking; they happened to so many of us that there needed to be a way to talk about them. I honed my own writing in exactly those forums, discursive spaces where the personal and the political were raw and real, and trigger warnings were just a part of the shorthand I grew up with – and I may have got this entirely wrong, but I'm not known as a delicate, retiring person who's reticent about speaking her mind.

My previous book, *Unspeakable Things*, touched on all sorts of potentially traumatic issues, the reason being that if you want to do transformative feminist politics properly you have to be willing to engage with rage and pain. It was not published plastered in trigger warnings, and I wouldn't have wanted it to be, but when I sent out draft chapters to friends for comment, I told them straight up: this might be triggery. Perhaps if you're having a bad head day for body issues you might not want to read the eating disorders chapter. If I were ever so lucky as to see it discussed in a university class, I'd have no objection to teachers letting their students know that there are some difficult passages.

Trigger warnings are fundamentally about empathy. They are a polite plea for more openness, not less; for more truth, not less. They allow taboo topics and the experience of hurt and pain, often by marginalised people, to be spoken of frankly. They are the opposite of censorship.

In the mainstream press, it is common for newscasters to warn viewers if they are about to see 'potentially distressing' content, but it is more common still for reports and narratives to be censored for the benefit of the delicate.

Instead of hearing what precisely a famous publicist did to an underage girl in his car, writers simply tell us that he 'abused' her. Instead of hearing exactly what a famous comedian said about Asian people, or black people, we are told that he used 'offensive language'.

And in all the coverage of the trigger warning phenomenon, what I can't help but pick up on is bristling outrage at the very idea that alternative readings of culture might have to be taken into account. Outrage that there might be different ways of telling stories, different experiences that have hitherto been silenced but are now being voiced en masse, different outlooks that are being introduced to culture and literature by readers, writers and creators who have grown up expecting to suffer trauma but not to speak of it. Trigger warnings are not about censorship – they are about openness, and that's what's really threatening.

## BARBIE'S BODY

So, Barbie has curves now. Sort of. In an effort to revive their flagging brand, Mattel, makers of the iconic doll fashioned after a German sex aid in the 1950s, have released a limited run of four new body shapes: skeletal, tall and skeletal, short and skeletal, and ever so slightly less skeletal. This grudging nod to the zeitgeist, at least a decade too late, has been lavishly covered across the international press – including on the cover of *Time* magazine. You'd think the last Rubicon of women's liberation was Barbie's thigh gap.

Small reforms, of course, can be useful signposts to broader change. If nothing else, the new line is a clear signal that commercial manufacturers have started to pay minimal attention to gender equality – just like television and film companies, and for the same reason. A reputation for sexism now hurts a firm's bottom line. Mattel's spokespeople have been explicit that this is the reason for their rebrand – Barbie wasn't working for Millennial mothers.

The drive for more options for girls is steamrolling through popular culture. Barbie really can't do a lot more than smile, look pretty and bend at the waist – she can't even stand on her own two feet, which are permanently moulded to fit into tiny stilettos, meaning she needs to be propped up or held.

Barbie's profits had been falling for years, and she was losing out to Lego Friends, which lets little girls actually build things, and figurines of Disney's Princess Elsa – heroine of the most feminist kids' film to hit the mainstream in living memory. Something had to be done.

Next to Elsa, let alone fully jointed, realistically proportioned dolls like the Lammily range, Mattel's new range still looks dated. The new Barbies come in various shades of gorgeous, but they all have perfect skin, perfect hair, perfect outfits and the same creepy rictus grin, like members of some terrible high-fashion death cult, dosed up to the unblinking plastic eyeballs on faux-feminist platitudes and diet drugs. I wouldn't want them on my bedroom shelf. They look like they're about to go for your neck.

A Barbie doll with a slightly reduced waist to hip ratio is not the feminist cultural revolution it's being sold as – sold being the operative word, the millimetres of plastic flesh measured precisely in pounds and dollars. This is because a feminist cultural revolution would involve, at minimum, a massive restructuring of what society believes women are, what they do and what they deserve. Let me give you a hint: it's more than the right to stand very still, smiling and looking pretty, with thighs that happen to meet in the middle.

It's not that there's no value in challenging beauty standards. On the contrary. The perception, for example, that whiteness equates to beauty which equates to social value has long been a vector for the oppression of women of colour around the world. It's rather telling that the press coverage of the new Barbie range makes far more of the four different body types available than the seven different skin tones, and the fact that one has what appears to be a natural Afro.

The weaponisation of beauty by queer and feminist subcultures is an important trend. There's a world of difference, though, between bloggers from the fat-positivity movement redefining beauty standards and toy companies telling us we ought to be grateful that after six decades they've finally produced a doll that doesn't look like she's about to die of starvation. But redefining beauty can only go so far.

The bigger lesson, the one some little girls go to their graves not knowing, is that beauty is not mandatory. Some of us will never be beautiful, and none of us will be beautiful for ever, at least not by society's standards, and that's okay. Beauty is not the only or the most important measure of a person's worth if she is female.

The cult of thinness is a particular assault on the mental and physical health of women and girls. Beauty, though, as Naomi Wolf observed in *The Beauty Myth*, is always about 'prescribing behaviour and not appearance'. It's why we train little girls in shame and self-repression just when we should be letting their imaginations run riot. It's about teaching little girls to control their bodies, and thereby their destinies. And that's what makes Barbie a relic – not just her unattainable proportions or the way she smiles all the time despite having no genitals, no nipples and no room in her torso to fit internal organs. Barbie is a relic because girls and their parents are no longer quite so interested in that sort of doll. They don't want to buy it, and they don't want to be it, because it's boring. They're far more interested in Mattel's other line, Monster High, where the dolls come with blue and green skin, fangs, fins, horns and tentacles. I may or may not have ordered the zombie-unicorn doll, purely for research purposes.

What toy manufacturers, along with almost every other industry that markets to women and girls, has not understood is that women want more than to be told we're pretty. We want power. We want respect. We want control over our bodies and ownership over our desires. We want to be valued as human beings, whatever we look like, whatever we do for a living. We want the same basic rights to autonomy and agency that men have always enjoyed. And that's just for starters.

There is nothing particularly revolutionary about suggesting different models for sexual objectification. Beauty standards have shifted over the centuries, as a quick walk around any national gallery will remind you, but the duty to be beautiful at all costs is the real obstacle to women's health and well-being. The idea that girls can be beautiful at an apparently gargantuan size eight is small, positive reform – but the real change will come when they realise they don't need to be.

Girls do not owe the world a pretty face and a plastic smile, and they won't be fobbed off with yesterday's toys.

## FAME UNDER PATRIARCHY

I am often asked what I think of 'celebrity feminism'. Specifically, when I talk to young people, I'm asked what I think of various famous women and their followers who have taken up the F-word since the whole concept became cool a few years ago. In one week alone I was asked to judge Emma Watson, Beyoncé and Kesha, the pop star whose public fight with her record company for the right not to make music with her alleged rapist has mobilised an army of online support around the world.

You know, I thought feminism was about supporting women fighting structural misogyny in every industry and none. Apparently I was wrong. What it's really about is determining which women are most politically pure and ranking them accordingly, after we've finished judging them on their hairstyles and sexual choices.

Feminism has hit the mainstream in a serious way, and that's causing a bit of an identity crisis. Can we still be radical when pop stars proudly use the F-word? Can we still fight for unglamorous things such as maternity leave and abortion rights when Chanel is marching models down the runway dressed as banner-waving feminist protesters? Can you maintain a critique of capitalist patriarchy if you bought the 'feminist' slogan T-shirt?

Celebrity feminists make it easy to fall back on purity politics, because celebrity feminists always fail: partly because they're mostly young, creative women living under the sort of relentless public scrutiny that makes Airstrip One look like a yoga retreat. The latest to mess up in public is Emma Watson, the young actress and UN goodwill ambassador best known for playing Hermione Granger, 'the brightest witch of her age', in the Harry Potter films.

Let's make no bones about it: it was a big mistake for Watson to lend her face to a Lancôme 'skin brightening' cream in 2013. Never mind the question of whether someone with a passion for equality should be shilling for the beauty industry at all – it was distinctly un-Hermione-like behaviour. The whole thing was a sad-trombone moment, not least because it cried out for some catty writer to describe Watson as 'the whitest witch of her age'.

You see? I was mean just then and I'm not proud of it, and patriarchy remains unshaken. I'd like to apologise to Emma Watson. I remember when I used to spot her sitting at the bus stop in Oxford by herself. She probably can't take the bus any more, because when she's not being harassed by the hordes of sexist photographers and creepy fans who've followed her around since her teens, she has to deal with snobby feminists like me getting all superior because we were reading theory while she was quite busy being a child star.

Just because I was a feminist before it was cool doesn't mean I have to be a snooty hipster about it. I think Watson's analysis is pretty basic, but in this messed-up world someone's got to put on a pretty frock and make the bare argument that women are human so that the rest of us can get on with undermining the gender binary and destroying the wage gap. Trying to develop your politics in the public eye is like being forced to sight-read a sheet of music in front of an audience of thousands, half of whom are screaming insults at you from every side.

Yes, Emma Watson messed up, and she has since apologised for hawking products 'which do not always reflect the diverse beauty of all women', and so she should. Yet if this is the feminist hunger games, we should remember who the real enemy is: it's the companies that make money by telling us we all need to be thinner, prettier and whiter.

Sure, I'd like Emma Watson to do better. I'd like Lena Dunham to do better. I'd like to do better myself. We could all do better – within the women's movement, within the left – but we never will if we make witch-burning part of our political practice, or judge ourselves too harshly when we wear an outfit or make a decision that doesn't seem 'correctly feminist'. It's the same broken logic of blame that insists that you can't be anti-capitalist if you own a smartphone, or have ever, in a moment of weakness, let a drop of imperialist chain cappuccino pass your sinful lips.

Celebrity women, too, are living in a patriarchy, compromising to survive, and working within a system whose rules they did not choose. Many of them are young and vulnerable. Patriarchy holds women to impossible standards and shames them when inevitably they fail to meet these. Feminism must not do the same.

# 4

# Gender

> only through new words might new worlds be called into order . . .
>
> Saul Williams, *Said the Shotgun to the Head*

> People have the right to call themselves whatever they like. That doesn't bother me. It's other people doing the calling that bothers me.
>
> Octavia Butler

## HOW TO BE A GENDERQUEER FEMINIST

I've never felt quite like a woman, but I've never wanted to be a man, either. For as long as I can remember, I've wanted to be something in between. To quote Ruby Rose: I called myself a girl, but only because my options were limited. I always assumed that everyone felt that way.

I discovered my mistake one day in junior school, when a few of the girls in my class were chatting about what boys they fancied. I wasn't often invited to participate in these sorts of secret female chats.

Even back then, there was something odd about me, a strangeness that was partly about identity but also about the fact that I wore shapeless black smocks, rarely brushed my hair and tended to jump when anyone spoke to me. I couldn't think of anything to say that would be both interesting and true. So I mentioned that I often felt like I was a gay boy in a girl's body. Just like everyone else, right?

I could tell from their faces that this was not right. It was very, very wrong.

This was a time before Tumblr, when very few teenagers were talking about being genderqueer or transmasculine. The women I'd heard of who were allowed to dress and talk and behave like boys were all lesbians. I often wished I was a lesbian. But I almost always fancied boys, and if you fancied boys, you had to behave like a girl. And behaving like a girl was the one subject, apart from sports, that I always failed.

It was around this time that I first read second-wave feminist Germaine Greer. She seemed to explain fundamental truths that every other adult in my small universe of school, home and the library seemed equally anxious to ignore, and it helped that there were also dirty jokes. I clung to *The Female Eunuch* with the zeal of a convert and the obsession of a prepubescent nerd. I wrote Greer a letter with my very favourite pens and almost imploded with excitement when she wrote back, on a postcard that had koalas on it. I resolved right then and there that one day I would be a feminist and a writer just like her.

According to Greer, liberation meant understanding that whatever you were in life, you were a woman first. Her writing helped me understand how society saw me – and every other female person I'd ever met. We were not human beings first: we were just girls. Looking back, though, that militant insistence on womanhood before everything is part of the reason it's taken me a decade to admit that, in addition to being a feminist, I'm genderqueer. That I'm here to fight for women's rights, that I play for the girls' team, but I have never felt like much of a woman at all.

I grew up on second-wave feminism, but that didn't stop me starving myself. I was anorexic for large parts of my childhood and for many complex, painful, altogether common reasons, of which gender dysphoria was just one. I felt trapped by the femaleness of my body, by my growing breasts and curves. Not eating made my periods stop. It made my breasts disappear. On the downside, it also turned me into a manic, suicidal mess, forced me to drop out of school and traumatised my entire family. At seventeen, I wound up in hospital, in an acute eating disorders ward, where I stayed for six months.

The window in my hospital room did not open more than a crack. Just wide enough to sniff a ration of fresh air before I got weighed in the morning. I turned up with all my curves starved away, with my hair cropped close to the bones of my skull, androgynous as a skeleton, insisting that people call me not Laura, but Laurie – a boy's name in England. I was too unwell to be pleased that I finally looked as genderless as I felt.

At that point, I just wanted to die. Mostly of shame.

Long story short: I didn't die. I got better. But not before I let some well-meaning medical professionals bully me back on to the right side of the gender binary.

Psychiatric orthodoxy tends to lag behind social norms, and doctors are very busy people. So it's not their fault that, less than twenty years after homosexuality was removed from the official list of mental disorders, the doctors treating me took one look at my short hair and baggy clothes and feminist posters and decided that I was a repressed homosexual and coming out as gay would magically make me start eating again. Like I said, they were trying.

There was only one problem. I wasn't gay. I was sure about that. I was bisexual, and I was very much hoping that one day when I wasn't quite so weird and sad I'd be able to test the theory in practice. It took a long time to persuade the doctors of that. I can't remember how, and I'm not sure I want to. I think diagrams may have been involved. It was a very dark time. I was too unwell to enjoy looking as genderless as I felt.

Anyway. Eventually they gave up trying to make me come out and decided to make me go back in. If you weren't a lesbian, the route to good mental health was to 'accept your femininity'. You needed to grow your hair and wear dresses and stop being so angry all the time. You needed to accept the gender and sex you had been assigned, along with all the unspoken rules of behaviour involved. You needed to get a steady boyfriend and smile nicely and work hard. I repeat: these people didn't mean to do me or anyone else lasting psychological damage. Just like every other institution through the centuries that has tried to force queer and deviant people to be normal for their own good, they truly were trying to help.

For five years, I struggled to recover. I tried hard to be a good girl. I tried to stick to the dresses, the makeup, the not being quite so strange and cross and curious all the time. For five years, I shoved my queerness deep, deep down into a private, frightened place where it only emerged in exceptional circumstances, like a bottle of cheap vodka, or a showing of *The Rocky Horror Picture Show*, or both. But being a good girl didn't work out very well, so I cut the difference, cut my hair short, and went back to being an angry feminist.

And feminism saved my life. I got better. I wrote, and I had adventures, and I returned to politics, and I made friends. I left the trauma of the hospital far behind me and tried to cover up my past with skirts and makeup.

Today, I'm a feminist and a writer, but I no longer valorise Germaine Greer so blindly. For one thing, Greer is one of many feminists, some of them well respected, who believe transgender people are dangerous to their movement. Their argument is pretty simple. It boils down to the idea that trans people reinforce binary thinking about gender when they choose to join the other team instead of challenging what it means to be a man or a woman. Greer has called trans women a 'ghastly parody' of femaleness.

Greer's comments about trans women exemplify the generational strife between second-wave feminists who sought to expand the definition of 'woman' and the younger feminists who are looking for new gender categories altogether. This tension has been cruel to trans women, who have been cast as men trying to infiltrate women's spaces. But it's alienating to all corners of the LGBT community.

By the time I was well enough to consider swapping the skirts for cargo pants, changing my pronouns and the way I walked through the world, I'd become well known as, among other things, a feminist writer.

At twenty-four, I wrote columns about abortion rights and sexual liberation, and books about how to live and love under capitalist patriarchy. In response, young women wrote to me on a regular basis telling me that my work helped inspire them to live more freely in their femaleness. They admired me because I was a 'strong woman'. Would I be betraying those girls if I admitted that half the time, I didn't feel like a woman at all?

So I hoarded up my excuses for not coming out. I carefully described myself as 'a person with cis privilege' rather than 'a cis person' when the conversation came up. I decided that the daily emotional overheads of being a feminist writer on the Internet were enough for now.

And I waited.

Over the past few years, more and more of my friends and comrades have come out as trans. I've been privileged to be part of a strong and supportive queer community, and it has helped that a great many of my close friends are both trans and feminist. For them, there doesn't seem to be a problem with fighting for gender equality while fighting transphobia – which sometimes, sadly, means that they're also fighting feminists.

Many of the critiques of trans politics from feminists through the decades have been openly bigoted, the sort of self-justifying theories that let people feel okay about driving other, more vulnerable people out of their jobs, outing them to their families and welfare advisers, and putting them in danger.

Buried under the bullshit, though, are some reasonable critiques. One is that people who claim a trans identity are only doing so because gender roles are so restrictive and oppressive in the first place. Sadly, many trans people are forced to play into tired gender stereotypes in order to 'prove' their identity to everyone from strangers to medical gatekeepers – not long ago, one friend of mine was queried at a gender clinic because she showed up to her appointment in baggy jeans, which was evidence of her 'lack of commitment' to life as a woman. I repeat: even trousers are political.

I regret that there wasn't more language, dialogue and support for trans and genderqueer kids when I was a teenager and needed it most. I regret that by the time I had found that community and that language, I was too traumatised by hospital, by prejudice, and by the daily pressures of living and working in a frenzied, wearily misogynist media landscape to take advantage of the freedoms on offer. I regret the fear that kept me from coming out for so many years. Would I betray the girls who looked up to me if I admitted that I didn't feel like a woman at all?

When I say I regret those things, I mean that I try not to think about them too much, because the knowledge of how different things could have been if I'd known as a teenager that I wasn't alone, the thought of how else I might have lived and loved and dated if I'd had the words and the community I have now just a little sooner, opens cold fingers of longing somewhere in my stomach and squeezes tight. But when they let go, I'm also glad.

The journey I took as I came to terms with my own identity – the journey that will continue as long as I live – all of that has led me to where I am now.

More than anything, I'm excited. I'm excited to see how life is going to be different for the queer, trans and even cis kids too, growing up in a world that has more language for gender variance. I'm excited to find out what sort of lives they will lead, from the genderqueer activists in the audience at my last reading to the barista with the orange mohawk who handed me the cup of tea I'm clutching for dear life as I write alone in this cafe, trying to believe that writing this piece is something other than gross self-indulgence.

The barista is wearing two name badges. One says their name; the other one says, in thick chalk capitals, *I am not a girl. My pronouns are They/Them.*

So here it is. I consider 'woman' to be a made-up category, an intangible, constantly changing idea with as many different definitions as there are cultures on Earth. You could say the same thing about 'justice' or 'money' or 'democracy' – these are made-up ideas, stories we tell ourselves about the shape of our lives, and yet they are ideas with enormous real-world consequences. Saying that gender is fluid doesn't mean that we have to ignore sexism. In fact, it's the opposite.

Of course gender norms play into the trans experience. How can they not? But being trans or genderqueer, even for cis-passing people like me, is not about playing into those norms. It's about throwing them out. Some 'radical' feminists argue that trans and genderqueer people actually shore up the gender binary by seeking to cross or straddle it rather than setting it on fire. To which I'd say: it is possible to jump over a burning binary. Just watch me.

Only when we recognise that 'manhood' and 'womanhood' are made-up categories, invented to control human beings and violently imposed, can we truly understand the nature of sexism, of misogyny, of the way we are all worked over by gender in the end.

Coming out is an individual journey, but it is a collective weapon. Questioning gender – whether that means straddling the gender binary, crossing it, or breaking down its assumptions wherever you happen to stand – is an essential part of the feminism that has sustained me through two decades of personal and political struggle. In the end, feminists and the LGBT community have this in common: we're all gender traitors. We have broken the rules of good behaviour assigned to us at birth, and we have all suffered for it.

But here's one big way I differ from a lot of my genderqueer friends: I still identify, politically, as a woman. My identity is more complex than simply female or male, but as long as women's reproductive freedom is under assault, sex is also a political category, and politically, I'm still on the girls' team.

I don't think that everyone who was dumped into the 'female' category at birth has a duty to identify as a woman, politically or otherwise. Because identity policing, if you'll indulge me in a moment of high theoretical language, is fucked up and bullshit. This is just how it happens to work for me.

We're all gender traitors.

In a perfect world, perhaps I'd be telling a different story. I'm never going to be able to say for sure whether in that perfect world, that world without sexism and gender oppression, that world without violence or abuse, where kittens dance on rainbows and nobody has ever heard of Donald Trump, I would feel the need to call myself genderqueer. My hunch is that I would; and all I've got for you is that hunch, along with a stack of feminist theory books and a pretty nice collection of flat caps.

I am a woman, politically, because that's how people see me and that's how the state treats me. And sometimes I'm also a boy. Gender is something I perform, just like everyone else, when I put on my binder or paint my nails. When I walk down the street. When I talk to my boss. When I kiss my partner in their makeup and high heels.

I don't want to see a world without gender. I want to see a world where gender is not oppressive or enforced, where there are as many ways to express and perform and relate to your own identity as there are people on Earth. I want a world where gender is not painful, but joyful.

But until then, we've got this one. And for as long as we all have to navigate a gender binary that's fundamentally broken and a sex class system that seeks to break us, I'm happy to be a gender traitor.

I'm a genderqueer woman, and a feminist. My preferred pronouns are 'she' or 'they'. I believe we're on our way to a better world. And you can call me Laurie.

## UNNATURAL BEAUTY

Body image is big business. In 2013, the Brazilian modelling agency Star Models launched a graphic campaign with the intention of showing young women how horrific acute anorexia is. It shows models photoshopped to the proportions of fashion sketches – spindly legs, twig-like arms, wobbling lollipop heads.

Given the high-profile deaths of two South American models from anorexia – one of whom, Luisel Ramos, dropped dead of heart failure at a catwalk show – one might interpret this as a way for the agency to detoxify its brand while drumming up a little publicity. But that would be too cynical; the global fashion industry really cares about young women's health now. That's why model agencies were recently discovered recruiting outside Swedish eating disorder clinics.

Elsewhere, a new campaign video by Dove uses facial composite drawing to demonstrate how women underestimate their own looks. Dove is owned by Unilever, a multibillion-pound company that seems to have little problem using sexism and body fascism to advertise other products: it also manufactures Lynx, of the 'fire a bullet at a pretty girl to make her clothes fall off' campaign, the Slim-Fast fake-food range, and more than one brand of the bleach sold to women of colour to burn their skin 'whiter'.

The fashion, beauty and cosmetics industries have no interest in improving women's body image. Playing on women's insecurities to create a buzz and push products is an old trick but there's a cynical new trend in advertising that peddles distressing stereotypes with one hand and ways to combat that distress with the other. *We're not like all the rest*, it whispers. *We think you're pretty just as you are. Now buy our skin grease and smile*. The message, either way, is that before we can be happy, women have to feel 'beautiful', which preferably starts with being 'beautiful'.

Let's get one thing straight: women don't develop eating disorders, don't self-harm and have other issues with our body image because we're stupid. Beauty and body fascism aren't just in our heads – they affect our lives every day, whatever our age, whatever we look like, and not just when we happen to open a glossy magazine.

We love to talk, as a society, about beauty and body weight – indeed, many women writers are encouraged to talk about little else. What we seldom mention are the basic, punishing double standards of physical appearance that are used to keep women of all ages and backgrounds in our place. For a bloke, putting on a half-decent suit and shaving with a new razor is enough to count as 'making an effort'. For women, it's an expensive, time-consuming and painful rigmarole of cutting, bleaching, dyeing, shaving, plucking, starving, exercising and picking out clothes that send the right message without making you look like a shop-window dress-up dolly.

Eating disorders such as anorexia and bulimia are severe mental illnesses but they exist at the extreme end of a scale of trauma in which millions of women and girls struggle for much of their lives. The fashion, diet and beauty industries exploit and exaggerate existing social prejudice, encouraging women to starve ourselves, to burn time and money and energy in a frantic, self-defeating struggle to resemble a stereotype of 'beauty' that is narrowing every year.

Studies have shown that, across the pay grades, women who weigh less are paid more for the same work and have a better chance of promotion than those who are heavier. In politics, in business and in the arts, accomplished and powerful men are free to get fat and sloppy, but women can expect to be judged for their looks if they dare to have a high-profile job: we're either too unattractive to be tolerated or too pretty to have anything worth saying. Beauty is about class, money, power and privilege – and it always has been. Women and girls are taught that being thin and pretty is the only sure way to get ahead in life, even though this is manifestly not the case.

Those few young women who have fought their way to public acclaim despite lacking the proportions of catwalk models are expected to account for themselves in interviews, from the Oscar-winning singer Adele to the only-ever-so-slightly-plump Lena Dunham.

It's hard to feel all right about yourself in this sort of toxic beauty culture: as long as 'fat' is the worst thing you can possibly call a woman, any of us who dares to speak up or out about what is happening will be called fat, whether or not we are.

'Fat' is subjective and socially situated, and it's the slur most commonly directed at any girl or woman who asserts herself, whether physically or politically. Even the most stereotypically thin and beautiful woman will find herself dismissed as unattractive if what comes out of her mouth happens to threaten male privilege, which is why feminists of all stripes continue to be labelled 'fat and ugly'. This culture would still prefer women to take up as little space as possible.

Rather than fighting for every woman's right to feel beautiful, I would like to see the return of a kind of feminism that tells women and girls everywhere that maybe it's all right not to be pretty and perfectly well behaved. That maybe women who are plain, or large, or old, or differently abled, or who simply don't give a damn what they look like because they're too busy saving the world or rearranging their sock drawer, have as much right to take up space as anyone else.

I think if we want to take care of the next generation of girls we should reassure them that power, strength and character are more important than beauty and always will be, and that even if they aren't thin and pretty, they are still worthy of respect. That feeling is the birthright of men everywhere. It's about time we claimed it for ourselves.

## GIRL TROUBLE

Another week, another frenzy of concern-fapping over teenage girls. In late 2013, I was invited on to Channel 4 News to discuss a new report detailing how young people, much like not-young people, misunderstand consent and blame girls for rape. The presenter tried to orchestrate a fight between myself and the other guest, Labour MP Luciana Berger, because it's not TV feminism unless two women shout at each other.

As we approached the six-minute, time-for-some-last-words mark, the presenter Matt Frei was clearly floundering. It turns out that even respected broadcasters with years of experience have no idea how to handle the twisted narrative about girls and sex, and how adults feel about girls having sex, and what precisely it is about all of this that constitutes news. He turned to Berger and said (I quote): 'Miley Cyrus – should we just ignore her? Is she good or is she bad? What's your judgement on her?'

When the off-air lights blinked, I felt like I'd just gone through a Shakespearean shadow-play of the public conversation about young women right now, and it scared me. Berger and I had both come on to the programme to talk seriously about agency, about education and the importance of respecting young people, and instead we stumbled from slut-shaming to pat ten-second pronouncements about sexual violence to manufactured controversy to worrying about the age of consent to deciding whether Miley Cyrus is empowered or exploited or both in the space of six minutes and twelve seconds exactly. Clearly, teenage girls aren't the only ones who are confused.

Teenage girls, however, don't get to put down their presenting notes on that painful, awkward confusion and switch to the next topic. They don't get to change the channel. Moral panic is the register in which young women are spoken to and about – always.

It should be no big shocker, then, that a report by the charity Girlguiding suggests that girls' self-esteem is not just low but also falling, year-on-year. As with any sociological study, the nature of the questions being asked – how much do girls care about makeup? How many wear nail polish, push-up bras, high heels? – reveals as much as the answers do, in this case about our priorities around girls and the women they're becoming. When we cannot help mustering our masturbatory outrage over whether or not young girls are wearing push-up bras – always with the padded bras – we should perhaps be less surprised to learn that '87 per cent of girls aged 11–21 think women are judged more on their appearance than on their ability'.

The tone of the reports on girls' lack of confidence, on the persistence of myths of ignorance about rape and sexual violence, is as patronising as ever. The implication is that girls fret about their appearance, are confused about sex and consent, and worried about the future because they are variously frivolous or stupid.

They aren't. They know perfectly well what's going on, and why. It is not silly for girls to believe, for example, that society judges them on their appearance when it manifestly does and will continue to do so when they have become adult women unless we bring down patriarchy first.

The Girlguiding report finds that, as well as being miserable, self-hating and cynical about the prospect of equality, young women are terrifically ambitious. They work hard, and they want to do well in their careers. This is not a contradiction. Ambition is demanded of us because we know mediocrity is not an option. When society tells women that if we are just averagely good-looking, or averagely smart, or reasonably high-achieving, we will never be loved and safe, perfectionism is an adaptive strategy. We learn that if we want love and security, we have to be perfect, and if it doesn't work out, well, that means we just weren't good enough. And we know it probably won't work out well. Girls aren't fools. They know what is being done to them. They know what that means for their futures in terms of money and power.

Girls get it. An under-reported, crucial facet of the study is the extent and cynicism of girls' concerns about economic equality and unpaid work. A full 65 per cent of girls aged eleven to twenty-one are worried about the cost of childcare, and while 58 per cent say they 'would like to become a leader in their chosen profession', 46 per cent of them worry that having children will negatively affect their career.

Girls know perfectly well that structural sexism means they can't have everything they're being told they must have. They are striving to have it all every way, to have everything and be everything like good girls are supposed to, and it hasn't broken them yet, for good or ill. That is one reason young women still do so well in school and at college despite our good grades not translating to real-world success. It's one reason we're so good at getting those entry-level service jobs: we are not burdened by the excess of ego, the desire to be treated like a human being first, that prevents many young men from engaging proactively with an economy that just wants self-effacing drones trained to smile till it hurts.

The press just loves to act concerned about half-naked young ladies, preferably with illustrations to facilitate the concern. Somehow nothing changes. And maybe that's the point. Maybe part of the function of the constant stream of news about young girls hurting and hating themselves isn't to raise awareness.

Maybe part of it is designed to be reassuring. It must be comforting, if you're invested in the status quo, to hear that young women are punished and made miserable when they misbehave.

For all those knuckle-clutching articles about how girls everywhere are about to pirouette into twerking, puking, self-hating whorishness, we do not actually care about young women – not, that is, about female people who happen to be young. Instead, we care about Young Women (TM), fantasy Young Women as a semiotic skip for all our cultural anxieties. We value girls as commodities without paying them the respect that both their youth and their personhood deserve. Being fifteen is fucked up enough already without having the expectations, moral neuroses and guilty lusts of an entire culture projected on to this perfect empty shell you're somehow supposed to be. Hollow yourself out and starve yourself down until you can swallow the shame of the world.

And Miley Cyrus. Ah, Miley. The Zaphod Beeblebrox of 2013, distracting attention away from power with choreographed hammer-humping. The way Miley Cyrus has been allowed to dominate months of necessary discussion about young women and what they do, about sex and celebrity and the pounding synthetic intersection of the two which is pop music, is the ultimate example of our guilty, horny fascination with young girls' sexual self-exploitation. We have discussed Miley Cyrus as a cipher for precarious womanhood everywhere to the extent that she has functionally become one. Miley is not the only very young woman doing bold, original or shocking things in public right now, but she's the one who gets to stand in for all girls everywhere.

Of course, young trans women and women of colour, however heroic, could never be Everygirl. That's why Rihanna only gets to be a 'bad influence' on girls, but Miley somehow *is* all girls. She is the way we want to imagine all girls – slender young white innocence forever being corrupted, allowing us to stroke out another horrified concerngasm.

In the real world, girls are not all the same. Attempting to make any one woman stand in for all women everywhere is demeaning to every woman anywhere. It tells us that we are all alike, that for all society's fascination with our feelings and fragility we are considered of a kind, replaceable. We're all the same, and we're all supposed to have the same problems. And that's the problem.

I've fought for years, since I was a messed-up schoolgirl myself, for a world in which women could be treated like human beings, and sometimes it seems like nothing's changed. It is as fucked-up and torturous to be a teenage girl now as it ever was, maybe more so. I am angry because in that time I have seen countless miserable, self-hating, brilliant girls become miserable, self-hating, brilliant women who have somehow managed to survive and scrape through the shitty, sexist slimepile of rules and threats and contradictions to claw out a sense of self they could live with.

Well, most of them managed to survive. Not all of them. And not all of the ones who did grew up to thrive. I have seen such pain and wasted potential over these years that I could cry, and sometimes, when I'm tired, I do. The emotional violence this society does to teenage girls and young women makes us all suffer in the end.

So please, just stop it. Stop telling girls contradictory things. Stop telling them that they're worthless if they're not sexy, beautiful and willing and then shaming them into believing that if they were raped, it must have been their fault for dressing like sluts. Stop telling them they have to be high-achieving and independent and not rely on a man and then hating them for any freedom they manage to hold on to.

Stop teaching young women to hate themselves. Stop it. Because let me tell you something else about young women today. I'm going to say it slowly and clearly so it doesn't get forgotten quite so fast. Young women today are brilliant. They. Are. Brilliant.

If you are not stunned by how smart, how fearless, how fucking fantastic young women and girls are right now then maybe you've been watching too many twerking videos, or only paying attention to the news coverage that reassures us that yes, young girls are miserable, as they deserve to be. But you'd have to be glued to *Bangerz* pretty consistently not to notice how bloody great this generation is.

Really, they're great. They know the challenges in front of them and they are determined to overcome them. They're as bright and ambitious as Millennials, except that they grew up with the Internet and they have no illusions that good behaviour will get them everywhere. I don't mean to essentialise; I've met some brutal, boring teenage girls in my time, too. But the cohort is shaping up to be just about as spectacular as it's going to have to be to fix the mess their parents made.

I believe that today's young women might yet grow up to save this vicious world. But if we abuse that promise, if we carry on hurting them and insulting them and treating them as trash symbols of our own shame, then maybe we don't deserve to be saved.

## IT'S THE LITTLE THINGS

It's always the little things. In the midst of a welter of unutterably depressing news about welfare and political turmoil, the great controversy is, yet again, the stunning fact that women are human beings with bodies that grow hair, eat, sweat and shit.

First, a spectacularly misogynist and homophobic (and now withdrawn) advert from Veet, manufacturers of hair-removing goo, claimed that failing to remove your leg-hair with the help of Veet products will turn you into an actual bloke. Then there was the equally repugnant site set up to shame 'Women Eating on the Tube', featuring non-consensual pictures of women doing just that, because there's nothing worse a female person could possibly do than demonstrate in public that she has a body that gets hungry.

Now, in eight years of feminist blogging I have avoided weighing in on the body hair debate for two reasons, the first of which is political. I've always been faintly distrustful of the school of feminism that advocates a return to 'natural' womanhood as a political statement, because as far as I'm concerned, there's no such thing. There is something a tiny bit reactionary about the plea for nature as opposed to liberated modernity; it runs uncomfortably close to the rhetoric of those social conservatives who would prefer women to be 'natural' when it comes to being submissive to a male provider and hogtied by their own reproductive capacities, but to continue the decidedly unnatural practices of bleaching, waxing and taking a bath more than once a year. The problem arises when any behaviour, however private and personal, is socially enforced. The problem arises when, according to the language of Veet, you have to go through the expensive and time-consuming rigmarole of shaving to prove that you are a proper, well-behaved woman and therefore worthy of the kisses of easily shocked men with boring haircuts. And the problem arises when this sort of pop controversy is used as a decoy, distracting us from structural arguments about class, power and privilege. Body hair, in particular, has become an obstructive stereotype when it comes to feminist history – sexist commenters speak of 'hairy-legged feminists' when what they really mean to say is that women who do not conform, women who refuse to perform the rituals of good feminine behaviour, are a deeply fearful prospect.

The second reason is a bit more personal. According to the accepted way this sort of article is supposed to go, now is when I'm supposed to tell you exactly what I do with my own body hair and why and how it's always been a problem.

Unfortunately, I am personally exempt from this particular dilemma by virtue of being a human axolotl who doesn't grow much hair anywhere. I am literally unable to be the furry-legged, forest-crotched feminist hellwraith I often find myself accused of being. This makes shaving a largely academic issue, and puts me in precisely no position to judge any woman for her intimate topiary decisions, and I wish my friends would stop asking me to validate theirs. Seriously. Do what you want. I just want you to be happy.

As a teenager, though, I used to shave anyway – gamely saving up my pocket money for popular brand equipment I really had no use for – because I wanted to be part of that secret club of skin nicks and ritual complaints about razor burn. Did you shave, sugar or wax? Did you remove the hair up to the top of your shortest gym skirt, or all the way up, implying arcane and enviable sluttery? I remember these conversations as among the few times I was permitted, as a nerdy, nervous, weird-looking kid, to chat to the cool girls. The pain, expense and wasted time of womanhood was something we were all supposed to share. Few of us had the language of feminism – this was before Tumblr, Twitter and Internet activism brought gender politics into every schoolgirl's back pocket. We complained about shaving and straightening and eyelash-curling because that sort of complaining was a safe, accepted way to express discomfort with the basic fact that, in Simone de Beauvoir's words, 'one is not born, but rather becomes a woman'.

Gender policing is all about the little things. It's the daily, intimate terrorism of beauty and dress and behaviour. In this as in so much else, feminists who are not transsexual can learn a great deal from trans writers and activists. I'm indebted to the work of Charlie Jane Anders and Julia Serano, both of whom talk about how femininity gets captured by capitalism, and how that homogenous, compulsory performance of femininity becomes a scapegoat for all society's bad feelings about women in general and trans women in particular. So it is not enough to feel that you are a woman – you have to prove it with a hundred daily conformities and capitulations. The reason the Veet advert is so hurtful, the reason the 'Women Eating on the Tube' site and its backlash went so viral, is that they both spell out gender policing at its simplest level: behave, be quiet and pretty and compliant, control your messy, hairy, hungry self, or you are not a woman at all.

None of which is to say that girliness can't be a good time. Dressing up, playing with makeup, fashion – all of that is a lot of fun right up until it becomes compulsory, until you have to do it to prove you're a real woman, a good employee, a person worthy of love and affection. The same goes for all of the bizarre rules that go along with being female in this society, the rules you have to engage with whether or not you choose to follow them: be pretty. Be nice. Be thin. Try to look as young and fragile as possible. Be sexy, but not overtly sexual. Don't eat in public. Don't eat at all. Your body is all wrong: shave it down, starve it smaller, take up less space, be less physical, be less.

The little things turn out to be about the big things. They're about race, class and gender status. For trans women, or women of black, Middle Eastern or Mediterranean heritage, the question of body hair is extra fraught, because 'passing' as a woman these days turns out to mean looking as much like a nubile white cissexual supermodel as possible. Shaving or waxing is an ongoing expense, even if you do it yourself at home; getting hair removed professionally or lasered away permanently can run to thousands of dollars over a lifetime.

The same principle applies to eating on public transport: doing so is not considered 'classy'. 'Real ladies' conceal their bodily functions from the world as much as possible. 'Real ladies' are blank, smooth, pale slates, with nothing inside, no guts, no gore, no appetite, no personality.

Cultural disgust for the female body is deeply political. It is tied into reproductive and social control, which affects all female-identified people, whether or not we plan to have children or are biologically capable of pregnancy. Gender policing is about making sure that women don't get above ourselves, that we can be seen as less than human, with no real interiority, without real bodies that eat and shit and hurt and die. If the female body remains a beautiful mystery, if it retains an ethereal, abstract quantity, you don't have to feel so bad when you do bad things to it.

How and where we choose to eat lunch. What we do with our hair in the morning and our pubes at night. Whether and when we wear makeup. Whether we wear jeans or a skirt. All of these things are intimate, everyday decisions that wouldn't matter if we didn't spend thousands of hours and a great deal of money fretting about them over the course of the short time we get to spend on this planet. We experience all of this on an intimate, everyday level, and it seems like it shouldn't matter, but it does. The little indignities, the little restrictions, they matter so much. And if we're smart and pay attention, they give us a language to talk about the big ones. The world in which we fritter away our energies worrying about body hair and eating on public transport is the same world in which the British government has just appointed a Minister for Women who is against both abortion rights and gay marriage. It is the same world in which people on welfare have just taken another hammering, being painted as scroungers even as the outgoing Minister for Women gets to keep almost £44,000 in wrongly claimed expenses. It is the same world in which women are indefinitely detained and then threatened with deportation for being born queer in the wrong country and wanting to live and love in peace.

And the little capitulations wear us down. They soften us up for the big capitulations. Any good dictator knows that, which is why Kim Jong Un has just made it mandatory for every male student in North Korea to emulate his slightly odd haircut.

Ultimately, being a 'good woman' isn't just about shaving and whether you eat crisps on the bus. It's about how silent you're prepared to be in the face of social injustice.

## WORD GAMES

Language matters. It defines the limits of our imagination. You don't have to be a gender theorist to understand that if we have only two ways of referring to human beings – 'he' or 'she' – we will grow up thinking of people as divisible into those two categories and nothing more. So it is significant that, in late August, OxfordDictionaries.com – an online resource created by the publishers of the *Oxford English Dictionary* – added an entry for the gender-neutral title 'Mx'.

This is how it's defined: 'a title used before a person's surname or full name by those who wish to avoid specifying their gender or by those who prefer not to identify themselves as male or female'. In 2015, the *OED* added to its lexicon the word 'cisgender', meaning 'not transsexual'. That matters, too, because without a word for it, you were either 'trans' or you were 'normal'.

Sweden has also recently added the gender-neutral pronoun '*hen*' to its dictionary. Pronouns such as 'xe' and 'they' (used to refer to a singular subject) are already in use in English as alternatives to 'he' and 'she'. Many conservatives and professional pedants are furious – it's fussy, it's far too politically correct and how are you supposed to pronounce 'Mx', anyway? So whose side should we be on?

By some accident of serendipity, the day I found out about all of this was also the day I met the feminist linguist Dale Spender. At seventy-one, when I met her, she was small and delicate and dangerous, like a cupcake full of razors. She was dressed from head to toe in purple: a lilac handbag, bright violet shoes, an elegant silk dress in swirls of fuchsia and lavender. The activist and author of *Man Made Language* could be the embodiment of Jenny Joseph's poem 'Warning' ('When I am an old woman I shall wear purple . . .') but Spender has worn the colour every day for decades, in honour of the suffragettes.

Swallowing my hero worship together with a lukewarm coffee backstage at a writer's festival, I asked Spender what she thought, as someone who has long pioneered the politics of women's language, about the recent push towards a more gender-neutral vocabulary.

'It's the same argument we had in the 1970s, when we started using "Ms",' Spender told me. The title 'Ms' was promoted by feminists and widely adopted as an alternative to 'Mrs' or 'Miss' – the idea being that there was more to a woman's life than her marital status. 'So many of us were getting divorced and leaving bad marriages and we didn't know how to refer to ourselves,' Spender said. 'I wasn't a "Miss" any more but I definitely wasn't a "Mrs". They said the same thing back then – that "Ms" was clumsy, that people didn't know how to pronounce it. But how about "Mrs" or "Mr"? They're hardly obvious!'

Spender reminded me that the *Oxford English Dictionary* has always been run by men and that mainstream lexicography had a male bias; it wasn't until 1976 that 'lesbian' got an entry in what the feminist Mary Daly dubbed the 'dick-tionary'.

Spender is dismayed to see this kind of linguistic activism falling out of fashion – 'We used to spend days coming up with new words for concepts that needed to be talked about' – and she was delighted that Internet culture had brought it back with gusto.

'I love the word "mansplaining",' Spender said. 'It's perfect. You know instantly what it means. And "manspreading", "manterrupting" – did you know that in mixed-gender conversations, most interruptions are by men?'

There is nothing new about activists working to move language forward to create cultural change but it is easy to underestimate the effects of that change over time. Listening to Spender talk about the importance of 'Ms' reminded me how radical a proposition it once was for women to claim their own names and titles after marriage. My mother retained what is still referred to as her 'maiden' surname, Penny, and always used 'Ms'. I remember asking as a child why she wasn't a 'Miss' or a 'Mrs' and being told that she didn't want the first thing people knew about her to be whether or not she was married. That seemed fair enough. Why would a woman want to go around with a label on them that described who they belonged to – like a dog tag – when men didn't have to? That didn't seem fair. Also, Penny was a much nicer surname and I made a note to adopt it myself when I was older.

Now that I'm the age my mother was when she had me, I am beginning to understand what an impression that simple, powerful statement made. I always understood that Mum was her own person first and a wife second and that I could be, too. My relationships with men didn't have to be the core of my identity. The feminists of the 1970s and 1980s had to fight to make that possible but I grew up with that assumption, partly because of a simple act of linguistic activism.

Perhaps the generation being born today will grow up with different assumptions: not just that women should be equal to men but that gender might not be the most important part of your identity. That's an uncomfortable idea for a great many people, and that discomfort is at the heart of the predictable pedantry over 'Mx', 'xe' and 'they'.

We can only become what we can imagine and we can only imagine what we can articulate. That's why language matters to our lives; that's why little changes in grammar and vocabulary can affect the entire architecture of our political imagination.

Today, signing 'Mx' on an application form or an electricity bill is an act of linguistic rebellion but tomorrow it could be ordinary. And that is how you change the world.

## TRANSPHOBIC THROWBACKS

In early 2013, columnist Julie Burchill used her platform in the *Observer* to launch what may be the most disgusting piece of hate-speech printed in a liberal newspaper in recent years. I'm not the only reader who was shocked to the core at her smug attack on transsexual women as 'screaming mimis in bad wigs', 'a bunch of dicks in chicks' clothing' and other playground insults too vile to repeat. Burchill claimed to be protecting a friend, which is a noble thing to do, but I suspect that the friend in question, the writer Suzanne Moore, who penned a far less vituperative article on the same subject, would rather she hadn't been associated with the popping of this particular pustule of prejudice.

Burchill's article is an embarrassment to the British press, an embarrassment to feminist writing and a shameful exploitation of a public platform to abuse a vulnerable minority. The *Observer* has now issued an apology, and rightly so, although I believe the decision to depublish the piece is not wrong so much as bizarre, since Google Cache never forgets.

It's even more dispiriting to see other mainstream media outlets, including the *Telegraph*, rally around Burchill's ignorant screed as a 'free speech' issue, as if the right to free speech and the right to publication in a major national newspaper were the same thing at all in the age of Tumblr.

But let us get back to the issues. I'm partly writing this piece out of selfishness. I want to make it clear to the readers around the world who were rightly disgusted by the *Observer* column that Burchill and Moore do not speak for all British feminists, and that not every British columnist is prepared to rally the waggons around bigotry. A young, powerful feminist movement with transsexual and queer people at the heart of the debate is gathering in strength in this country and across the world, and we know that gender essentialism and bigotry hurt all of us, cis and trans, men and women.

Transphobic men and women who promote prejudice in the name of feminism, including writers like Sheila Jeffreys, Germaine Greer, Julie Bindel and now Julie Burchill, are on the wrong side of history. For far too long, a small, vocal cadre of the women's movement has claimed that transsexuals, and in particular transsexual women, are not just irrelevant to feminism but actively damaging to the cause of women's liberation. Their arguments are illogical, divisive and hateful, and sometimes just plain bonkers. I've been to meetings where transphobic feminists have argued that if they don't keep a lookout, horrible sexist men will try to sneak into their meetings, marches and seminars in disguise in order to disrupt proceedings.

What precise form the disruption is supposed to take has not been explained, partly because it has never happened, ever. If Jeremy Clarkson or Bill O'Reilly ever decide to try it, I can assure you that they will be spotted and stopped – but right now, the feminist movement needs no help from fictional men in petticoats to damage our hopes of winning the wider war on women's freedom. Far more insidious is the insistence by some feminists on mocking transsexual women and denying their existence.

The word that annoys these so-called feminists most is 'cis', or 'cissexual'. This is a term coined in recent years to refer to people who are not transsexual. The response is instant and vicious: 'we're not cissexual, we're normal – we don't want to be associated with you freaks!' Funnily enough, that's just the kind of pissing and whining that a lot of straight people came out with when the term 'heterosexual' first began to be used as an antonym of 'homosexual'. Don't call us 'heterosexuals', they said – we're normal, and you don't belong.

To learn that the world is not divided into 'normal' people and 'freaks' with you on the safe side is uncomfortable. To admit that gender identity, like sexual orientation, exists on a spectrum, and not as a binary, is to challenge every social stereotype about men and women and their roles in society.

Good. Those stereotypes need to be challenged. That's why the trans movement is so important for feminism today.

Thanks to a global surge in acceptance and discussion of a spectrum of gender identity, trans people are becoming more and more visible, more angry and more open about their experiences. The world is changing, and those of us fortunate enough to be born in a body that suits our felt gender identity are going to have to accept that being cissexual, just like being heterosexual, isn't 'normal', merely common.

Transphobic articles in high-profile publications are not harmless. They cause active, quantifiable damage. They justify the ongoing persecution of transsexual people by the medical and legal establishment; they destroy solidarity within political and social circles; they hurt people who are used to hearing such slurs shouted at them in the street, and do not need to hear them from so-called progressives. Worse, they make it seem to the average reader, who might be a friend or relative of a trans person, that the rights of transsexual people to be treated in a humane way are still a subject for reasonable debate.

Some conservative feminists claim that arguing about trans issues is counter-productive to the wider struggle against austerity and sexual violence. They are right about that. Feminism is meant to be about defending women against violence, prejudice and structural, economic disadvantage – all women, not just the ones self-appointed spokespeople decide count, and at this time of crisis, we need to be standing together to defend women who are poor, marginalised and live in fear of violence. We cannot do that if we exclude trans and queer women, who are more than usually vulnerable to gendered violence and discrimination. Entry to feminist spaces should not be conditional on having one's genitals checked over by Julie Burchill, Julie Bindel or their representatives.

It comes down to essentialism, and essentialism, as Suzanne Moore rightly pointed out in her *Guardian* column, is always conservative. Stubborn gender essentialism – the belief that your body and your hormones should define everything about your life – is what women have been fighting since the first suffragettes unrolled their green and purple sashes. For transphobic feminists, though, it all seems to boil down to an obsession with what precisely is inside a person's underpants, which is at best intellectually vapid and at worst rather creepy.

In fact, as Simone de Beauvoir once noted, nobody on Earth is born a woman. Julie Burchill was not born a woman, unless her mother is a hitherto unheralded miracle of medical science. Just over half of us grow up to become women, and the process is a muddle of blood and hormones and angst and pressure and pain and contradiction. Transsexual women know just as well, and sometimes better than cissexual women, what it is to be punished for your felt and lived gender, what it is to fear violence and rape, to be reduced to your body, to be made to feel ashamed, to have to put up with prejudice and lazy stereotypes.

Personally, if I thought that my vagina, which I've had since I was born, was my most important feminist accessory, I would let it speak for itself. Unfortunately it hasn't read much feminist history, and neither, it seems, have transphobic bigots. If they had, they'd understand that taking a stand against violence and gender essentialism is what feminism is all about, and that's precisely why solidarity with trans people should be the radical heart of the modern women's movement.

A tipping point has been reached. All over the world, online and in local communities, transsexual men and women are finding their voices, and finding each other. Their struggle for acceptance in a society that still hates and fears those who are different, those who don't follow the rules of gender and sexuality, is vital to the modern feminist movement. Young activists understand that that's what feminism is all about, for all of us, men and women, cissexual, transsexual and genderqueer: the fight for equality and freedom of expression in a society that still believes that the arrangement of your genitals at birth should dictate the course of your life. It's time for cissexual feminists to put hate aside and stand with transsexual women in solidarity.

## BEYOND BINARIES

When April Ashley, who in 1960 became one of the first Britons to have sex-reassignment surgery, was asked by reporters if she was born a man or a woman, her answer was always the same: 'I was born a baby.' For the full effect, imagine Ashley saying this with a little smile on her perfectly pencilled lips, dignified and demure in the face of the fusillade of stupid questions she has been fielding for more than fifty years. Sadly, Ashley's point – that not all babies fit into the pink or blue box they were assigned at birth – is taking a long time to sink in.

Now, Germany has announced legislation to allow parents not to record the gender of their newborn if, as is surprisingly often the case, doctors cannot instantly determine what biological sex the wriggling, squalling bundle of growth hormones is.

There are many conditions that can cause a person to be biologically intersex. Stories about the 'third gender', about gods and humans who weren't quite men or women, have been with us for millennia, but there has long been pressure on doctors and parents to 'fix' any baby who isn't obviously either a boy or a girl. This often entails intimate surgery that is performed when the child is too young to consent. Traumatic reports about the effect this sort of procedure can have on kids when they grow up appear routinely in the tabloids – but the question of why, precisely, it is considered so urgent that every child be forced to behave like a 'normal' boy or girl is rarely discussed.

Germany's law, which came into force in late 2013, is just a small step in the long march to equal rights and recognition for intersex, transsexual and transgender people in Europe, a trudge that is beset by bigots on one side and bureaucrats on the other.

The main detractors of the German law oppose the move not on moral grounds but because of the paperwork involved – and look at me not resorting to any national stereotypes about managerial dourness to finish this sentence . . . but what if the paperwork is the problem? What if you're somcone who is literally written out of every form and official document, every passport and bank account application, because society refuses to recognise there are more than two genders?

One in 2,000 babies, or 0.05 per cent of the world population, is estimated to be intersex. That's 3.5 million people across the globe. That, in case you were wondering, is ten times the population of Iceland. And those 3.5 million are just those who are visibly intersex at birth: some estimates suggest that the correct proportion of human beings whose bodies differ in some way from 'normal' male or female, either hormonally or genetically, could be as high as 1 per cent.

Some of those people prefer to identify simply as men or as women, but many do not.

The German law will give the right to 'leave the box blank' only to those born intersex – but gender identity is about more than biology. According to a 2012 Scottish trans mental health study, about a quarter of transsexual and transgender people do not identify as male or female, and prefer to present as nonbinary, gender-fluid or agendered.

So why aren't we talking about this more? Why isn't there a bigger public conversation about intersexuality and life outside the pink and blue binary? I don't mean drooling 'true stories' – I mean level-headed discussion that understands that intersex, transgender and androgynous people are 'normal' humans, too, who spend as much time stuck on trains or waiting for trashy crime shows to download as they do considering the contents of their underpants. Why are these matters so rarely taught in schools? Why do so many children – including intersex and transgender kids – grow up believing you have to be a girl or a boy and that there are no other options?

Unfortunately, I know the answer. We don't talk about it because questioning something as culturally fundamental as the gender binary is risky. It makes people confused and it makes them angry.

For some, the notion of large numbers of people not living as men or women doesn't morally compute, objective fact and conservative morality never having been the most snuggly of bedfellows. These are often the same people who can be found quoting dubious evolutionary 'studies' suggesting there are prehistoric reasons why 'some girls just like pink', possibly involving cavewomen and colourful fruit, even though the practice of dressing girls in pink is barely a century old.

The idea that there are only two possible genders and that those genders are rigid and fixed is an organising principle of life in most modern societies. It affects everything, from how we dress to whom we can marry and what work we get to do and whether or not we will be paid for that work. Discussion of conditions such as intersexuality threatens all that. It gives the lie to the gender binary, exposing it as not just flawed, but scientifically inaccurate. And so we carry on shoving intersex and transgender folk to one side and forcing everyone who isn't 'normal' to damn well act that way or face harassment, discrimination and violence, from the playground to the pulpit. Concerned parents of confused children are coerced into picking a sex and sticking to it – but is that for their own good, or for the good of a society wedded to a simple understanding of gender?

To anyone reading this who is intersex – and I know that there will be at least a few – I apologise for how basic this must sound. My sincere hope is that in ten years' time articles such as this one will look outdated to the point of offence, rather like a column from the 1960s making the stunning observation that, gosh, some men fancy other men and might even like to marry them.

The journey from here to there will probably involve a lot of paperwork – but for millions of people across the world, it'll be worth it.

## ON THE 'TRANS TIPPING POINT'

I have a colouring book in front of me. It's called *Finding Gender*, and it was sent to me by an activist who knows how much I love social justice and felt-tip pens. In the book, a small child and a robot go on marvellous adventures, and children and nostalgic adults get to scribble on their clothes and costumes, their hair and toys. It's an ordinary colouring book in every respect, apart from the fact that the child isn't identifiably male or female. Neither is the robot. The person with the crayons gets to decide what they're wearing, whether they're boys or girls, or both or neither.

This is how it happens. From dinner-table conversations to children's books, the lines of gender are being redrawn. Suddenly, transsexual and transgender people – those who do not identify with the sex they were assigned at birth – are everywhere in popular culture. Suddenly, people who are transitioning from male to female, or from female to male, or who choose to live outside the gender binary entirely, are no longer universally portrayed as freaks to be gawped at or figures of fun, but as exactly what they have been throughout human history – real, flesh-and-breath people with feelings and dreams that matter.

In 2014, *Time* magazine published a cover story titled 'The Transgender Tipping Point'. The trend-hungry American press is toppling over with spurious tipping points, but this one is real, and it's important. Centuries of marginalisation mean that the statistics are still shaky, but it is estimated that between 0.1 and 5 per cent of the population of Earth is trans, genderqueer or intersex. Whichever way you slice it, that's millions of human beings. As a species, we have come up with space travel, antibiotics, and search engines so it seems rather archaic that so much of our culture, from money and fashion, love and family is still ordered around the idea that people come in two kinds based roughly on what's in their knickers.

Something enormous is happening in our culture. In the past three years, and especially in the past twelve months, a great many transsexual celebrities, actors and activists have exploded into the public sphere. Some have taken the brave step of disclosing their trans status after they were already household names, like American presenter Janet Mock, rock star Laura Jane Grace, athlete Fallon Fox, Oscar-winning director Lana Wachowski or activist and former soldier Chelsea Manning. Others have simply become successful without hiding or apologising for their trans status, like sassy British columnist Paris Lees, or actress Laverne Cox, star of *Orange Is the New Black*, who graced the *Time* cover as one of a new generation of breakout trans stars.

At the same time, the Internet is making it easier for members of a previously isolated section of the population to find and support one another. Until recently, the threat of violence, coupled with the relatively small visible number of trans people, meant that coming out was a fraught, complicated process. It often meant moving away from your hometown, finding a community in a city, changing your job, your school. Transgender people in isolated or rural areas found it very difficult to make connections with others who might be able to understand their situation and offer advice. A great many trans people waited decades before deciding to transition in public – and some attempted to keep that part of their lives secret for ever, at great personal cost.

The Internet changed all that. Partly because of the Internet, and partly because of a new wave of transgender role models, more and more people are coming out as trans, and they are doing so younger, and their friends and families now have the language to understand what that means. As celebrated trans author Julia Serano told me, 'The truth is that trans people exist and our lives are fairly mundane. In the US, the number of transsexuals is roughly equivalent to the number of Certified Public Accountants. Nobody views accountants as exotic or scandalous!'

If gender identity is no longer a fixed commodity, that affects everybody. Not just those who are transsexual, their friends, families and colleagues, but everybody else, too. If gender identity is fluid – if anyone can change their gender identity, decide to live as a man, a woman, or something else entirely, as it suits them – then we have to question every assumption about gender and sex roles we've had drummed into us since the moment the doctors handed us to our panting mothers and declared us a boy or a girl. That's an enormous prospect to consider, and some people find it scary.

Changing words changes the world. The word 'cis' is both necessary and challenging, because previously, people who weren't transsexual were used to thinking of themselves simply as 'normal'. If being cis, in Dorothy Parker's terminology, isn't normal but merely common, that changes everyone's understanding of how gender shapes our lives, individually and collectively.

Of course, 'cis' covers a lot of bases. A great many cis people experience gender dysphoria to some degree, and a great many women, in particular, experience the socially imposed category of 'womanhood' as oppressive. I'm one of them, and that's why I believe trans rights are so important to feminism – and why it's so dispiriting that some feminists have been actively fighting against the inclusion of trans people in anti-patriarchal and LGBT politics. The notion that biology is not destiny has always been at the heart of radical feminism. Trans activists and feminists should be natural allies.

It is increasingly clear that gender is not a binary. Unfortunately, we're living in society which has organised itself for centuries on the principle that it is, and that everyone who disagrees should be shouted down, beaten up or locked away.

For centuries, it was standard practice to compel anyone who didn't conform to the rigid roles set out for their sex – from gay and transgender people to women who were too promiscuous, angry or 'mannish' – to do so by force and medical intervention. Generations of activism have fought this type of gender policing, but for the transgender and transsexual community, that sort of bullying is still an everyday reality. Trans people are more likely to be victims of murder and assault than any other minority group – recent studies suggest that 25 per cent of trans people have been physically attacked because of their gender status, and hundreds of trans people are murdered every year. Up to 50 per cent of transgender teenagers attempt suicide. That, of course, is what violence and prejudice are designed to do. They're designed to make people hate and hurt themselves, to frighten them out of being different, to bully and brutalise any perceived threat to the social order out of existence.

Explaining why this is so significant is hard for me, because I'm about as close as you can get to the trans rights movement without being trans yourself. I've been associated with trans activism for years, and while I don't know what it's like to be harassed, threatened or abandoned for being transsexual, most of my close friends do. Right now, I'm watching the rest of the world begin to understand the community that has become my home, and it is incredibly exciting – but it's frightening, too, because the backlash is on.

Even as reports come in that the Southern Baptist Convention, an influential American religious lobby, has made it official policy to oppose trans rights, even as the anti-trans opinion pieces mount up, I'm watching my trans friends and colleagues attacked and harassed online, made to fear for their jobs and their safety. With greater visibility, the stakes are even higher – and sadly, some sections of the left, including feminists like Sheila Jeffreys and Janice Raymond, have allied with social conservatives to attack trans people as deranged.

*Time* magazine is correct to call this the 'new civil rights frontier'. The cultural Right has largely lost the argument on homosexuality. Those who argue against gay marriage and gay adoption are increasingly at odds with social norms, and the type of popular pseudo-religious homophobia that was common in the days of Section 28 sounds more and more frothingly bigoted. But gender and sexuality still need to be policed – and if you can no longer call gay people sinful and expect to be taken seriously, someone else has to be the scapegoat, the 'other' against which 'normality' is defined.

The time is coming when everyone who believes in equality and social justice must decide where they stand on the issue of trans rights – whether that be the right to equal opportunities at work, or simply the right to walk down the street dressed in a way that makes you comfortable. Those are rights that the feminist and gay liberation movements have fought for for generations, and those who have made gains have a responsibility to stand up for those who have yet to be accepted. If we believe in social justice, we must support the trans community as it makes its way proudly into the mainstream.

# 5

# Agency

> You gave up being good when you declared a state of war
>
> Grimes

## IF MEN GOT PREGNANT

The seahorse is a fascinating creature. Aside from being evidence that whatever god of creation may have existed was on some truly excellent hallucinogens, seahorses – *Hippocampus hippocampus* – are a species where the male gets pregnant. Life would be a lot more interesting if human beings had to breed like seahorses. For a start, I highly suspect that the right to terminate a pregnancy would not be under violent attack across the Western world.

In late 2015, an armed misogynist broke into a Planned Parenthood clinic in Colorado Springs and killed three people after a stand-off with police. PP is the biggest organisation offering abortion, contraception and sexual health services in the US, and it has been under sustained attack from conservative activists and politicians who will not rest until abortion is illegal.

Just a few days after that attack, a high court judge in Belfast ruled that abortion might just be permissible in cases of rape, incest or foetal abnormality, which is a huge step forward, considering that women across Ireland are forced to carry unwanted pregnancies to term in all circumstances. Those who commit the grievous sin of having consensual sex, however, are still on their own, unless they have the funds to travel to England.

There is a pattern here. The concept of women having actual goddamned agency over their lives and bodies, the idea that we might get to decide when, whether and how to have children, is still a threat to the status quo. We grudgingly allow women to make decisions related to sex and reproduction as long as they feel an appropriate degree of guilt, and hoard that guilt away in private. Have an abortion? You'd better be sorry about it for the rest of your life. Get pregnant without a partner? Be prepared to spend eighteen years explaining yourself. Leave paid work to have a child? You're lazy, spoiled and frivolous. Carry on working after your kids are born? You're cold, selfish. Get sterilised? You're an unfeeling, unnatural monster. Whoever you are, if you have a uterus and dare to make a decision about what comes out of it, shame on you. Shame is the overarching theme here, shame and scorn for anyone with the temerity to behave as if their own humanity is important.

I am sick of explaining to misogynists that women are people whose choices and autonomy matter. Instead, let's go back to considering the seahorse. Consider how different the world would be if the people with the capacity to bear children were the people society already considered fully human. Consider what would happen if men got pregnant.

If men got pregnant, abortion would be available free of charge and without restriction in every town and city on Earth. No man would be expected to justify his decision to terminate an unwanted pregnancy. It would be enough for him to say, 'I don't want to have this baby.'

If men got pregnant, then pregnancy, labour and childcare would immediately be recognised as work and compensated as such. The entire economic basis of global capitalism would be upended overnight. After the ensuing bloodless revolution, the phrase 'work–life balance' would disappear from the lexicon, along with the line, 'I don't do condoms, babe.'

If men got pregnant, 'pro-life activists' would be called 'forced-birth extremists', and reviled as such by liberals, libertarians and every political movement with a claim on human freedom.

If men got pregnant, they would be considered not mere vessels for potential human life, but human beings whose agency ought to be inviolable. Men would not stand for having their basic rights to sexual freedom and personal autonomy confiscated, even if in some people's opinion they might be committing murder. Men are often prepared to commit murder for reasons far less egregious than the occupation of their bodies by a foreign invader. There is a sizeable lobby in the United States right now that believes that people should have the right to slaughter anyone who breaks into their home, or looks the wrong way at a police officer, or does almost anything that might conceivably be considered suspicious while also being black.

If men got pregnant, they would never be told that if they did not want to conceive, they should not have sex. Major world religions would rush to reinterpret their scripture; any verses appearing to condemn abortion or contraception would be considered in the same light as those dooming wearers of mixed fabrics to fiery damnation eternal.

If men got pregnant, nobody would consider a man's choice to have or not have children the defining feature of his adult life. There would be no shame in seeking sterilisation, just as there is no shame today for a man seeking a vasectomy. When a man made a decision about when and whether to have children, he would be able to count on having that decision respected, rather than being called selfish, lazy and slutty, or warned that he would 'regret it some day'.

If men got pregnant, somebody would have already invented a breast pump that was fit for purpose.

If men got pregnant, they would not be forcibly penetrated with cameras and obliged to look at an ultrasound of the foetus before getting an abortion. Instead, Wi-Fi would be available in the procedure room, plus a free beer with every procedure.

If men got pregnant, pregnancy and childbirth would not be dismissed as 'natural', but treated as heroic acts of sacrifice. Forcing a man to go through either against his will would be considered the equivalent of the military draft and protested as such.

If men got pregnant, having a 'baby belly' would not be a source of shame. Men would show off their stretch marks and Caesarean scars like battle wounds.

In point of fact, some men do get pregnant. Transsexual men have borne children, but their experience is not part of the popular understanding of reproductive rights – because *people* don't get pregnant, *women* get pregnant, and when you get down to it, women aren't really people. The structure of modern misogyny is still grounded on the fear that women might one day regain control of the means of reproduction and actually get to make their own decisions about the future of the human race – but you cannot force a person to give birth against their will and consider them fully human.

If men got pregnant, we would not be having this conversation. The fact that we still are shows how far we've got to go before equality becomes reality.

## NO MORE TEARS

What does a good abortion look like? In 2014, Emily Letts, a twenty-five-year-old American clinic worker, filmed her surgical abortion and posted the video on the Internet. In the clip, Letts smiles and hums throughout the procedure, which she chose to have simply because she did not want to bear a child. 'I feel good,' she remarks when it's over, shattering generations of anxiety and fear-mongering around reproductive choice with three simple words.

The idea that abortion might be a positive choice is still taboo. For some, the only way it can be countenanced is if the pregnancy is an immediate threat to life or the result of rape – meaning that the woman involved didn't want to have sex and as such does not deserve to be punished for the crime of acting on desire as a female. Even then, the person having the abortion is expected to be sorry for ever, to weep and agonise over the decision. In Britain, the Abortion Act 1967 obliges anyone seeking a termination to justify why continuing with a pregnancy poses a threat to her health and well-being or that of her existing offspring. 'Because I don't want to be pregnant' simply isn't enough.

Hence the furore over the glamour model Josie Cunningham's announcement, through the eyebrow-raising medium of the British tabloid press, that she was planning to terminate her pregnancy in order to have a shot at appearing on reality television. The national and international gossip media scrambled to excoriate Cunningham: this was the epitome of selfishness, a woman who would boast of having an abortion to further her career. We live in a society that fetishises 'choice' while denying half the population the most fundamental choice of all: the choice over the autonomy of one's body.

Women in Northern Ireland, where the Abortion Act 1967 does not apply, have just learned that – despite paying towards the NHS through their taxes – they will continue to be denied an abortion unless they can travel to England and fund it themselves. As a result of a high court ruling, hundreds of women each year will still find themselves having to take cheap red-eye flights to Heathrow and Manchester, scared and alone, to have procedures they may have gone into debt to afford.

In Northern Ireland, as in the rest of the world, the prospect of women having full control over their reproductive potential – the notion that we might be able to decide, without shame or censure, when and if we have children or not – provokes fear among the powerful. When abortion is discussed in public, it is almost always in terms of individual morality or, more usually, of moral lapses on the part of whatever selfish, slutty women are demanding basic human rights this week. It is rarely discussed in terms of structural and economic inequality. Yet reproductive inequality remains the material basis for women's second-class status in society. It affects every aspect of our future.

Consider, as an example, the controversy over the rise of 'social surrogacies' – rich women paying poor women to go through pregnancy and childbirth on their behalf. The horrified response to this idea belies how men do the same thing: arrange for women to bear, carry and, indeed, raise children on their behalf so that they can get on with their careers uninterrupted. That's the material basis of gender inequality and it must be discussed honestly as a matter of structural injustice, not individual morality.

Abortion, motherhood and reproductive health care remain fraught issues, as women's demand for basic control over our bodies and destinies pulls ever further away from official public policy. In countries such as Ireland, Spain and the US, women's bodies remain the territory on which the patriarchal right wing fights its battle for moral dominance.

Abortion can be a difficult, painful decision – if, for example, you would quite like to have a baby but are in no position to support one because 'single mother' is still a synonym for 'poor and shunned' and pregnancy discrimination is rampant in this treacherous post-crash job market. But abortion can also be a simple decision. It does not have to involve years of regret or, as Emily Letts bravely demonstrated, any regret at all.

So here, in case it wasn't clear, is my position. Abortion should be available on demand, without restrictions, for everyone who needs it. I believe that while society still places limits on what a woman may or may not do with her own body, while women's sexuality and reproduction are still in effect controlled by the state, any discussion of equality or empowerment is a joke. Nobody should have to play the frightened victim to make basic choices about her future. It should be enough to turn up at a clinic and say, 'I don't want this', or, 'I've changed my mind'.

And there's more. If there were real choice, real equality, pregnancy, childbirth and motherhood would not come with enormous socio-economic penalties for all but the richest women. Society should provide support for all parents, single and partnered, in and out of work, rather than forcing them to live on a pittance, under constant threat of eviction, and shaming them as 'scroungers'.

That's what real choice would look like. And the thing about giving people choices is that inevitably a few of them will make poor choices, choices we might not approve of. Many people have religious or personal reasons for disapproving of abortion and they are free, as they always have been, not to have one themselves. Yet it's time to change the terms of the debate. It's time to demand reproductive rights for everyone – without apology.

## THIS BITTER PILL

Heard about the new 'female Viagra'? Of course you have. Whatever the new wonder drug lacks in efficiency – coming as it does with a serious health warning if taken along with alcohol – it more than makes up for in branding. The campaign that finally got the drug approved by US regulators gave the impression of being an organic, grass-roots movement . . . but it's the little things that let it down.

When PR companies try to run activist campaigns (a process known as astroturfing, because of the 'fake grass roots' involved) there is one mistake they always make. They're too good at it. Their websites are too slick, their videos too viral, their connections too convenient, and there's a curious lack of infighting and sniping over what the slogans should be and whose turn it is to do the biscuit run. So it is with 'Even the Score', which describes itself as a feminist movement fighting for women's right to 'orgasm equality'.

Thousands of women were persuaded to lobby Congress with one aim and one aim only – to get Addyi (flibanserin), also known as 'female Viagra', approved by the US drug regulator, after it had been rejected twice on safety grounds. Feminists around the world were mobilised by the 'coalition' running Even the Score, a coalition that includes some big drug companies, notably Sprout Pharmaceuticals, the firm that makes Addyi.

As a D-list digital feminist nanocelebrity, I've been inundated with requests to eulogise the product on TV and radio. When I questioned an Even the Score spokesperson on radio about its associations with Sprout, she admitted that the company had bought table seats at a fundraising dinner, but otherwise the group keeps its financial operations largely hidden.

Say what you like about Big Pharma hijacking feminist energy – and I'm about to – but it shows how far we've come. That feminism is now an approved marketing strategy shows us how powerful and culturally important the movement is. All the same, this is nothing to celebrate.

There are enormous problems with the female Viagra campaign, and the first one is this: feminism must not be co-opted by companies whose ultimate agenda is not women's welfare but their own bottom line. Feminism is about putting more power in the hands of women, not putting more profit in the pockets of drug and cosmetics companies. Feminist liberation is not, ultimately, something you can buy. It has to be taken, sometimes by force.

I've nothing against better living through chemistry. If there truly were a magic pill that made it possible to shag all night with the urgent stamina of an endangered rhinoceros, I'd be tempted. But what Addyi is offering is less hedonistic, working as it does on the brain rather than the genitals. More worryingly, the disease it claims to be treating, 'hypoactive sexual desire disorder' or HSDD, is equally suspect. As Rachel Hills, the author of *The Sex Myth*, told me: 'Pharmaceutical companies didn't start talking about female sexual dysfunction because women were turning up to their doctors in droves complaining about their sex lives. They started talking about it because Viagra was such a gigantic commercial success.'

Technological and medical advances such as the Pill and access to abortion have undoubtedly been central to feminism. So, the one thing that makes Even the Score convincing is that the basic point is unarguable: sexual liberation is a crucial part of women's liberation. But most of the things that stop women from pursuing and achieving sexual pleasure are not physiological. They are social. They are political. Rape culture. Slut-shaming. Abuse. Homophobia. Religious repression. A culture that clings to the idea that sex is something men do to women, rather than something people do together.

All of this, and more, is what prevents women from 'orgasm equality' or, as some of us prefer to call it, sexual freedom. Yes, there are physical ailments that can stifle a woman's sexuality. 'Some of these are unequivocal medical issues,' Hills says, 'like vaginismus or vulvodynia, which make it painful for women to have penetrative sex. It's interesting to me that of all the sexual problems that can affect women, the one they've decided to create a drug for is "not wanting to have sex enough".' The definition of HSDD is persistent lack of interest in sex that causes distress to women – or their partners.

Or their partners. And there's the rub. This drug doesn't give you more orgasms. What it does – expensively, inefficiently and with side effects – is make women more likely to consent to sex. The typical patient, once you dig into the literature, is supposed to be a woman in middle age who is upset because her partner is upset because she doesn't want to have sex with him. And isn't that the age-old quandary? With all the shame and stigma, all the stress and worry, all the work we make them do endlessly and for free, in and out of relationships, how do we get women to keep on saying yes to sex? Well, we can always drug them.

For me, feminism is all the Viagra I've ever needed. Feminism is what gave me, slowly and over years of growing and learning, the confidence to claim ownership over my own body and my own desires, as well as the strength to say no whenever I was more in the mood for a cup of tea and a cuddle. I believe that women deserve the right to pursue pleasure. Women deserve the right to say yes to sex without shame or self-censorship. But those rights are nothing without the right to say no, to refuse sex when we don't want it, and not be humiliated or punished or made to feel unnatural.

It's not women who are sick. It's society, with its structural misogyny and crazy, contradictory expectations of women, that is sick as hell. And that's a much harder pill to swallow.

## ARE YOU PRE-PREGNANT?

For several weeks, YouTube has been reminding me to hurry up and have a baby. In a moment of guilt over all the newspapers I read online for free, I turned off my ad-blocking software and now I can't play a simple death metal album without having to sit through thirty seconds of sensible women with long, soft hair trying to sell me pregnancy tests. I half expect one of them to tap her watch and remind me that I shouldn't be wasting my best fertile years writing about socialism on the Internet.

My partner, meanwhile, gets shown advertisements for useful software; my male housemate is offered tomato sauce, which forms 90 per cent of his diet. At first, I wondered if the gods of Google knew something I didn't. But I suspect that the algorithm is less imaginative than I have been giving it credit for – indeed, I suspect that what Google thinks it knows about me is that I'm a woman in my late twenties, so, whatever my other interests might be, I ought to be getting myself knocked up some time soon.

The technology is new but the assumptions are ancient. Women are meant to make babies, regardless of the alternative plans we might have. In the twenty-first century, governments and world health authorities are similarly unimaginative about women's lives and choices. The US Centres for Disease Control and Prevention (CDC) recently published guidelines suggesting that any woman who 'could get pregnant' should refrain from drinking alcohol. The phrase implies that this includes any woman who menstruates and is not on the Pill – which is, in effect, everyone, as the Pill is not a foolproof method of contraception. So all females capable of conceiving should treat themselves and be treated by the health system as 'pre-pregnant' – regardless of whether they plan to get pregnant any time soon, or whether they have sex with men in the first place. Boys will be boys, after all, so women ought to take precautions: think of it as rape insurance.

The medical evidence for moderate drinking as a clear threat to pregnancy is not solidly proven, but the CDC claims that it just wants to provide the best information for women 'and their partners'. That's a chilling little addition. Shouldn't it be enough for women to decide whether they have that second gin? Are their partners supposed to exercise control over what they do and do not drink? How? By ordering them not to go to the pub? By confiscating their money and keeping tabs on where they go?

This is the logic of domestic abuse. With more than 18,000 women murdered by their intimate partners between 2003 and 2015, domestic violence is a greater threat to life and health in the US than foetal alcohol poisoning – but that appears not to matter to the CDC.

Most people with a working uterus can get pregnant and some of them don't self-define as women. But the advice being delivered at the highest levels is clearly aimed at women and that, in itself, tells us a great deal about the reasoning behind this sort of social control. It's all about controlling women's bodies before, during and after pregnancy. Almost every ideological facet of our societies is geared towards that end – from product placement and public health advice to explicit laws forcing women to carry pregnancies to term and jailing them if they fail to deliver the healthy babies the state requires of them.

Men's sexual and reproductive health is never subject to this sort of policing. In South America, where the zika virus is suspected of having caused thousands of birth defects, women are being advised not to 'get pregnant'. This is couched in language that gives women all of the blame and none of the control. Just like in the US, reproductive warnings are not aimed at men – even though Brazil, El Salvador and the US are extremely religious countries, so you would think that the number of miraculous virgin births would surely have been noticed.

Men are not being advised to avoid impregnating women, because the idea of a state placing restrictions on men's sexual behaviour, however violent or reckless, is simply outside the framework of political possibility. It is supposed to be women's responsibility to control whether they get pregnant – but in Brazil and El Salvador, which are among the countries where zika is most rampant, women often don't get to make any serious choice in that most intimate of matters. Because of endemic rape and sexual violence, combined with some of the strictest abortion laws in the world, women are routinely forced to give birth against their will.

El Salvador is not the only country that locks up women for having miscarriages. The spread of regressive 'personhood' laws across the United States has led to many women being threatened with jail for manslaughter when they miscarry – even as attacks on abortion rights make it harder than ever for American women to choose when and how they become pregnant, especially if they are poor.

Imagine that you have a friend in her early twenties whose partner gave her a helpful list of what she should and should not eat, drink and otherwise insert into various highly personal orifices, just in case she happened to get pregnant. Imagine that this partner backed his suggestions up with the threat of physical force. Imagine that he routinely reminded your friend that her potential to create life was more important than the life she was living, denied her access to medical care and threatened to lock her up if she miscarried. You would be telling your friend to get the hell out of that abusive relationship. You would be calling around the local shelters to find her an emergency refuge. But there is no refuge for a woman when the basic apparatus of power in her country is abusive. When society puts social control above women's autonomy, there is nowhere for them to escape.

## PAYING THE PRICE

Donald Trump thinks women should be punished for abortion. At least, he did for a few hours, answering the question put to him by a journalist with all the shifty-eyed, stammering self-confidence of a man trying to work out how many abortions he might have paid for in the past. Then, after an appropriate period of public consternation, the Republican front-runner backtracked, repeating the current party line that only people performing abortions should face jail time.

We've come to expect this. Trump wears hypocrisy as proudly as he wears his shocking hairdo. He doesn't just flip-flop: he cartwheels and scissors like a teenage Russian gymnast, twisting into ridiculous knots of logic according to the public mood with a forward momentum that defies ridicule and demands applause. This time, he changed his tune because the American pro-life movement, whose votes he needs, jumped to dissociate themselves from Trump's temporary platform shift. Pro-life organisations were quick to insist that they aren't about punishing women, just about protecting life.

Or are they?

Since the question of punishment is on the table, let's be very clear. If you believe that abortion should be banned except in cases of rape and incest, you are not 'pro-life'. You are anti-woman.

The 'illegal with exceptions' line is a standard part of conservative, anti-abortion platforms across the US and elsewhere, and it's jaw-dropping in its hypocrisy. After all, if you truly believe a foetus is an autonomous living being, why does it magically stop being one just because its mother failed to consent to intercourse? Does Jesus swoop down on a cloud of conservative hot air and make the ethical dilemma disappear with a bit of wizardly hand-waving? Or do you, fundamentally, just believe that women should suffer for having sex?

Imagine it. Imagine thinking that forcing a person to carry a growing foetus in her body for nine months and then push it out of her vagina while her muscles rip and her pelvis cracks is in any way humane. Imagine the level of self-deception it takes to think this and then turn around and claim you care about women. Perhaps you do, but you're remarkably laid back about watching them suffer for their sins. It's the species of loving Christian care you'd expect from the Spanish Inquisition.

The 'pro-life' movement, which should properly be called the 'forced birth' movement, is in fact entirely about punishing women for their sexuality. It's about punishing them legally, morally, spiritually and physically. That's what it has always been about, in every cultural and religious costume it has adopted over the past two centuries and more. The movement is stuffed with people who believe that sex is dirty and women who have it willingly should pay the price, ideally by being forced to carry a pregnancy to term. If not, then by means of trans-vaginal ultrasounds, pointless enforced waiting periods, targeted domestic and professional harassment and the real threat of jail if anything goes wrong. It's about hurting women who have the gall to believe that they get to decide what happens to their bodies. Trump just had the grotesque decency to say it out loud for a hot minute.

That's what Donald Trump is for. Donald Trump is a bloviating freakshow of the id whose job it is to articulate the ugliest parts of the modern psyche with enough pomp and gumption that it sounds like truth. We watch and cheer for the same reason that we watch shows about serial killers, so we can marinate in the horrified, pseudo-erotic certainty that however bad we are, in the secret places of our hearts, we're not that bad. Sure, we might think about these things, but we wouldn't actually do them.

But some truths are still too awkward to speak in public – even when they form the ideological basis of an entire conservative movement.

What does Donald Trump think about abortion? He thinks whatever you think about it, in the crabbed and hateful secret part of your soul that just wants those sluts to suffer. But Trump said it, so we don't have to. The monster isn't you. But this time the monster bit too close to the bone. The pro-life movement isn't ready to own its misogyny in the way that the Republican base is ready to own its racism and xenophobia, so Trump needed to be shut up, and fast. So much for free speech.

# 6

# Backlash

> The history of men's opposition to women's emancipation is more interesting perhaps than the story of that emancipation itself.
>
> Virginia Woolf, *A Room of One's Own*

> When a man gives his opinion, he's a man. When a woman gives her opinion, she's a bitch.
>
> Bette Davis

## ON NERD ENTITLEMENT

White male nerds need to recognise that other people had traumatic upbringings, too – and that's different from structural oppression.

In 2015 MIT professor Scott Aaronson wrote a heartfelt post about nerd trauma and male privilege. It was part of a larger discussion about sexism in STEM (science, technology, engineering and mathematics) subjects, and its essence is simple. Aaronson's position on feminism is supportive, but he can't get entirely behind it because of his experiences growing up, which he details with painful honesty. He describes how mathematics was an escape, for him, from the misery of growing up in a culture of toxic masculinity and extreme isolation – a misery that drove him to depression, anxiety and suicidal thoughts. The key quote is this:

> Much as I try to understand other people's perspectives, the first reference to my 'male privilege' – my privilege! – is approximately where I get off the train, because it's so alien to my actual lived experience . . . I suspect the thought that being a nerdy male might not make me 'privileged' – that it might even have put me into one of society's least privileged classes – is completely alien to your way of seeing things. I spent my formative years – basically, from the age of 12 until my mid-20s – feeling not 'entitled', not 'privileged', but terrified.

I know them feels, Scott.

As a child and a teenager, I was shy, and nerdy, and had crippling anxiety. I was very clever and desperate for a boyfriend or, failing that, a fuck. I would have done anything for one of the boys I fancied to see me not as a sad little boffin freak but as a desirable creature, just for a second. I hated myself and had suicidal thoughts. I was extremely lonely, and felt ugly and unlovable. Eventually I developed severe anorexia and nearly died.

Like Aaronson, I was terrified of making my desires known – to anyone. I was not aware of any of my (substantial) privilege for one second; I was in hell, for goodness' sake, and fourteen to boot. Unlike Aaronson, I was also female, so when I tried to pull myself out of that hell into a life of the mind, I found sexism standing in my way. I am still punished every day by men who believe that I do not deserve my work as a writer and scholar. Some escape it's turned out to be.

I do not intend for a moment to minimise Aaronson's suffering. Having been a lonely, anxious, horny young person who hated herself and was bullied I can categorically say that it is an awful place to be. I have seen responses to nerd anti-feminism along the lines of 'being bullied at school doesn't make you oppressed'. Maybe it's not a vector of oppression in the same way, but it's not nothing. It burns. It takes a long time to heal. Feminism, however, is not to blame for making life hell for 'shy, nerdy men'. Patriarchy is to blame for that. It is a real shame that Aaronson picked up Andrea Dworkin rather than any of the many feminist theorists and writers who manage to combine raw rage with refusal to resort to sexual shame as an instructive tool. Weaponised shame – male, female or other – has no place in any feminism I subscribe to. Ironically, Aaronson actually writes a lot like Dworkin – he writes from pain felt and relived and wrenched from the intimate core of himself, and because of that his writing is powerfully honest, but also flawed. The thing is that the after-effects of trauma tend to hang around long after the stimulus is past.

And this, for me, is the root and tragedy of both nerd entitlement and the disaster of heterosexuality.

What fascinates me about Aaronson's piece, in which there was such raw, honest suffering, was that there was not one mention of women in any respect other than how they might relieve him from his pain by taking pity, or educating him differently.

And Aaronson is not a misogynist. Aaronson is obviously a compassionate, well-meaning and highly intelligent man – I don't doubt that I'll meet him someday as he's a mentor to several people I respect and lives in the city I live in, and when that happens, I'll tell him I think so.

Nonetheless, he makes a sudden leap, and it's a leap that comes right from the gut, from an honest place of trauma and post-rationalisation, from that teenage misery to a universal story of why nerdy men are in fact among the least privileged men out there, and why holding those men to account for the lack of representation of women in STEM areas – in the most important fields of both human development and social mobility right now, the places where power is being created and cemented – is somehow unfair. Nerds are not like the 'neanderthals', the *real* abusers of women. They should get a break.

I have a profound political belief that we all deserve a break. Take one now, for five seconds, because this is going to get heavier. Breathe. Are you done?

Okay, let's do this.

These are curious times. Gender and privilege and power and technology are changing and changing each other. We've also had a major and specific reversal of social fortunes in the past thirty years. Two generations of boys who grew up at the lower end of the violent hierarchy of toxic masculinity – the losers, the nerds, the ones who were afraid of being creeps – have reached adulthood and found the polarity reversed.

Suddenly they're the ones with the power and the social status. Science is a way that shy, nerdy men pull themselves out of the horror of their teenage years. That is true. That is so. But shy, nerdy women have to try to pull themselves out of that same horror into a world that hates, fears and resents them because they are women, and to a certain otherwise very intelligent sub-set of nerdy men, the category 'woman' is defined primarily as 'person who might or might not deny me sex, love and affection'.

(And you ask me, where were those girls when you were growing up? And I answer: we were terrified, just like you, and ashamed, just like you, and waiting for someone to take pity on our lonely abject pubescence, hungry to be touched. But you did not see us there. We were told repeatedly, we ugly, shy nerdy girls, that we were not even worthy of the category 'woman'. It wasn't just that we were too shy to approach anyone, although we were; it was that we knew if we did we'd be called crazy. And if we actually got the sex we craved? because some boys who were too proud to be seen with us in public were happy to fuck us in private and brag about it later . . . then we would be sluts, even more pitiable and abject. Aaronson was taught to fear being a creep and an objectifier if he asked; I was taught to fear being a whore or a loser if I answered, never mind asked myself. Sex isn't an achievement for a young girl. It's something we're supposed to embody so other people can consume us, and if we fail at that, what are we even for?)

The notion that there are lots of horny teenage girls out there who are unable for all sorts of reasons to get laid remains a genuine surprise to many of my most intelligent male friends, but trust me, we were out there. We're still out there, and if one of you is reading this, honey, you are a worthwhile person, and it gets better. Or at least, you get stronger.

To all the shy, nerdy boys out there: your suffering was and is real. I really fucking hope that it got better, or at least is getting better. At the same time, I want you to understand that that very real suffering does not cancel out male privilege, or make it somehow all right. Privilege doesn't mean you don't suffer, which, I know, totally blows.

Women generally don't get to think of men as less than human, not because we're inherently better people, not because our magical feminine energy makes us more empathetic, but because patriarchy doesn't let us. We're really not allowed to just not consider men's feelings, or to suppose for an instant that a man's main or only relevance to us might be his prospects as a sexual partner. That's just not the way this culture expects us to think about men. Men get to be whole people at all times. Women get to be objects, or symbols, or alluring aliens whose responses you have to game to 'get' what you want.

This is why we have Silicon Valley Sexism. This is why we have Pick-Up Artists. This is why we have Rape Culture.

Scott, imagine what it's like to have all the problems you had and then putting up with structural misogyny on top of that.

Or how about a triple whammy: you have to go through your entire school years again but this time you're a lonely nerd who also faces sexism and racism. This is why Silicon Valley is fucked up. Because it's built and run by some of the most privileged people in the world who are convinced that they are among the least. People whose received trauma makes them disinclined to listen to pleas from people whose trauma was compounded by structural oppression. People who don't want to hear that there is anyone more oppressed than them, who definitely don't want to hear that maybe women and people of colour had to go through the hell of nerd puberty as well, because they haven't recovered from their own appalling nerdolescence. People who definitely don't want to hear that, smart as they are, there might be basic things about society that they haven't understood, because they have been prevented from understanding by the very forces that caused them such pain as children.

Heterosexuality is fucked up right now because while we've taken steps towards respecting women as autonomous agents, we can't quite let the old rules go. We have an expectation, a craving for a sexual freedom for which our rhetoric, our rituals and our sexual socialisation have not prepared us. And unfortunately for men, they have largely been socialised – yes, even the feminist-identified ones – to see women as less than fully human. Men, particularly nerdy men, are socialised to blame women – usually their peers and/or the women they find sexually desirable – for the trauma and shame they experienced growing up. If only women had given them a chance, if only women had taken pity, if only women had done the one thing they had spent their own formative years being shamed and harassed and tormented into not doing. If only they had said yes, or made an approach.

This, incidentally, is why we're not living in a sexual utopia of freedom and enthusiastic consent yet, despite having had the technological capacity to create such a utopia for at least sixty years. Men are shamed for not having sex; women are shamed for having it. Men are punished and made to feel bad for their desires, made to resent and fear women for having denied them the sex they crave and the intimacy they're not allowed to get elsewhere; meanwhile, women are punished and made to feel bad for their perfectly normal desires and taught to resist all advances. Eventually, a significant minority of men learn that they can 'get' what they want by means of violence and manipulation, and a significant minority of women give in, because violence and manipulation can be rather effective. (Note: accepting the advances of an awful man does not make these people bad women who are conspiring to 'make life hell for shy nerds'. I've heard that sort of thing come out of the mouths of my feminist-identified male nerd friends far too often.)

And so we arrive at an impasse: men must demand sex and women must refuse, except not too much because then we're evil friendzoning bitches. The impasse continues until one or both parties grows up enough or plucks up the courage to state their desires honestly and openly, without pressure or resentment, respecting the consent and agency of one another.

This usually doesn't happen. What usually happens instead is that people's sexuality and self-esteem get twisted into resentment of the (usually opposite) gender; they start to see that gender as less than human, particularly if they are men and learn at every stage of their informal and formal education that women are just worth less, have always been worth less, are not as smart, not as good, not as humanly human as men. Aaronson goes on to comment that this 'death-spiral' is a product of the times. I agree. 'In a different social context – for example, that of my great-grandparents in the shtetl – I would have gotten married at an early age and been completely fine,' he writes. Scott, my great-grandparents also lived in a shtetl. I understand that you sometimes feel you might have been better adapted to that sort of life, when dating and marriage were organised to make things easy for clever young men. On the same shtetl, however, I would have been married at a young age to a man who would have been the legal owner of my body, my property and the children I would have been expected to have; I would never have been allowed to be a scholar. I would have worked in the fields as well as the home to support my husband in his more cerebral pursuits, and with my small weedy nerdy frame, I would probably have died young from exhaustion or in childbirth.

There are a lot of young men out there – I suspect even now – who sometimes wish they'd been born when things were a bit easier, when the balance of male versus female sexual shame was tilted more sharply by the formal rituals of patriarchy, when men could just take or be assigned what they wanted, as long as they were also white and straight.

There are a lot of older men out there who long for that real or imagined world more openly, and without any of Aaronson's nuance and compassion. I would challenge men to analyse that longing, to see it for what it is. And then to resist it. You are smarter and better than that.

What can I say? This is a strange and difficult age, one of fast-paced change and misunderstandings. Nerd culture is changing, technology is changing, and our frameworks for gender and power are changing – for the better. And the backlash to that change is painful as good, smart people try to rationalise their own failure to be better, to be cleverer, to see the other side for the human beings they are. Finding out that you're not the Rebel Alliance, you're actually part of the Empire and have been all along, is painful. Believe me, I know. (Although I always saw myself as an Ewok.) We bring our broken hearts and blue balls to the table when we talk gender politics, especially if we are straight folks. Consent and the boundaries of consent; desire and what we're allowed to speak of desire: we're going to have to get better, braver and more honest, we're going to have to undo decades of toxic socialisation and learn to speak to each other as human beings in double quick time.

And most of all, we're going to have to make like Princess Elsa and let it go – all that resentment. All that rage and entitlement and hurt. Socialisation makes that process harder still for men. The road ahead will be long. I believe in you. I believe in all of us. Nerds are brilliant. We are great at learning stuff. We can do anything we put our minds to, although I suspect this thing, this refusing to let the trauma of nerdolescence create more violence, this will be hardest of all.

## IN DEFENCE OF WHITE KNIGHTS

I would like to apologise to my long-suffering magazine editor. Each week my column comes in late. I am busy, you see, sexually servicing all the men and boys who express feminist sentiments in public. Some people have suggested that this idea – that men only treat women as human beings in order to get laid – is venal propaganda cooked up by paranoid chauvinists to explain away the growing army of men who are proud to support women's crazy ambitions to gain basic respect and equality. But no.

It's all true. I haven't slept properly in four years. I hear that Germaine Greer hasn't slept since 1981. I'm working through the backlog by consuming enormous stockpiles of coffee but the queue is long and it's getting longer every day, so please bear with me.

Back in the real world, something fascinating is happening. As men and boys everywhere begin to realise that a society less riddled with rape, sexual violence and lazy gender stereotypes might be better for everyone, less evolved men and boys have started to round on them as traitors. One common charge is that men who support feminism are trying to be 'white knights', sweeping in to protect women, not knowing that we capricious females prefer the attentions of the bull-necked misogynists who holler at us in the street.

'White knight' and 'beta male' are the most common slurs flung at such men – usually by retro sexists who still think that feminism is all about poor confused chaps getting shouted at whenever they hold open a door for an enormous straw woman.

In reality, most women and girls would simply rather that men stopped slamming doors in our faces.

This has nothing to do with 'chivalry', which was only ever a way to codify and explain away the impulse to treat women and girls with basic respect without having to think of them as human beings. If you're a man and you hold open a door for another man carrying a large box, that's just manners, but if you hold the door open for a woman carrying the same box, that's 'chivalry', apparently. What we want – what would delight me, for one – is for us to get to a stage where we hold doors open for other people just because doors can be heavy and we all have our burdens to carry.

So I'd like to put in a word for the white knights. Making fun of them is how self-satisfied sexists explain away this change in social attitudes. As casual sexism and recreational misogyny become less and less acceptable in mainstream culture, some people might find it reassuring to think that all of those non-misogynist men out there are merely weak-willed, sex-starved betas, desperate for a bit of sweet feminist loving. Far more challenging is the idea that men might be supporting feminism because it is the right thing to do – and because they like the idea of not having to pretend to be rigid, emotionally castrated thugs all the damn time.

One thing I have heard from women and men alike is that men fear speaking about feminism and talking about gender, power and class in case they somehow infringe on women's special territory. There are certainly times when that is true – often the best thing you can do as an ally is to understand when it's your turn to shut up and let someone else speak, especially when you don't have direct experience of the subject being discussed.

Men can do a great deal of good in the feminist movement simply by listening and learning, which has the added bonus of being pretty easy, once you have done the work of swallowing your pride. Decades of socialisation do tend to stick in the throat.

It's not only listening, though – I would love to see even more men talking about gender, more men standing up for women, more men speaking out about their own experience of living in a patriarchal society that imposes damaging stereotypes on men and boys. That's what real courage is – and it has nothing to do with waving a sword around and slinging the princess over your shoulder.

Real courage is about doing things that are challenging and uncomfortable because you know that's the way to make a better world. Things such as accepting a higher proportion of women in roles of power and expertise. Or listening to women talking about our experiences of violence and discrimination without interrupting or trying to make it all about you.

It doesn't take a lot of courage to attack other men for not living up to stereotypes of what a real man should be. It doesn't take an ounce of bravery to shout and hurl insults and threaten violence towards anyone who stands up for women, or questions gender stereotypes, or supports campaigns to end rape and sexual harassment. What does take courage – the kind of courage you rarely hear about in fairy tales – is questioning your own assumptions and encouraging others to question theirs.

The most heroic thing you can do as a man today is to risk your own social status to do what you know is right. In recent weeks and months, I have been watching more and more men and boys take that risk, without expecting any sort of reward, sexual or otherwise, and I think that every one of them is a big, swashbuckling hero, like the feminist women I know. In a just world, we would all have our own theme tunes.

So, to the white knights out there: you can add my sword to your struggle. If anybody does shout at you for treating women as human beings, if anybody gives you grief for defending women online or in person, then I for one have got your back. I will defend you with all the discursive weapons at my disposal and, afterwards, you can get up on my horse and together we'll ride off to a slightly better tomorrow.

## THE NEW CHAUVINISTS

It's a miracle. All over the world, conservatives and curtain-twitching bigots have taken up the cause of fighting violence against women. From Donald Trump, vowing to protect white Americans from 'rapist' Mexican migrants, to European far-right groups that are mustering against the supposed Muslim threat to 'their' wives and daughters, conservatives are rebranding themselves as the defenders of women and girls. But who will defend us from them?

The idea that Western men must shelter 'their' women from a terrifying mass of foreign masculinity has been around for a very long time. It was used to justify the murder of black men in the US from the slave era onwards, even as black women were abused in their millions by white landowners. It is used to excuse state surveillance and militarised policing around the world, and by the new right to rationalise its bigotry.

The phrase that I have been using to describe this line of argument is 'the New Chauvinism'. Chauvinism is commonly understood in the context of male chauvinism, which most people think is all about holding doors open and getting shouted at by feminists. But it is described by the *Oxford English Dictionary* as 'exaggerated or aggressive patriotism', with the secondary definition of 'excessive or prejudiced support for one's own cause, group, or sex'.

The New Chauvinism is about both of those things. It uses crude, nationalist sentiment to cast white men in the roles of heroes, protecting 'their' women from hordes of, variously, migrants, Muslims and transsexual people.

On behalf of white women everywhere, allow me to say how much safer I don't feel. It would be easier to believe in the AfD, Germany's new far-right nationalist party, as a defender of women, for example, if it were not also campaigning to ban abortion and gay marriage, undermine the right to divorce, close kindergartens and strip single mothers of state funding – all in the name of protecting the 'traditional family'.

Fundamentalist throwbacks of every sort have remarkably similar ideas about how to protect women, so it is no surprise that the AfD echoes the philosophy of many hard-line Islamist groups on the role of women in society. If anyone wants to turn Western Europe into a patriarchal religious police state, it is the far right and not migrants fleeing violence – but irony, to these people, is probably a small town in the Middle East that should be flattened with cluster bombs to protect Christian women everywhere.

You might think that it is nice of them to care. However, I don't see these self-appointed defenders of women volunteering at domestic violence shelters or donating to rape crisis hotlines. Instead, they hold racist demonstrations in multicultural communities and harass women on the Internet, which is a curious way to demonstrate your commitment to public safety.

Across the Atlantic, the American Family Association – a Christian fundamentalist organisation recognised as a hate group by the Southern Poverty Law Centre – has admitted to sending men into women's bathrooms in branches of the retail chain Target to 'test' its policy of allowing transsexuals to use the lavatory of their chosen gender. Unable to prove that this policy will allow 'men in dresses' to abuse 'their' daughters, the association became the creeping queer threat to American womanhood that it wished to see in the world.

These New Chauvinists, who are mostly men, want to protect women from violence, as long as they are the right sort of women. Trans women, queer women, immigrant women and women of colour are nowhere in the sticky mass of stereotypes and dog-whistle racism that passes for their analysis. The Christian groups who claim to want to protect 'their daughters' from trans women in the ladies' loos seem unbothered by how some of their daughters may well be trans – and trans women face violence in huge numbers.

This sort of chauvinism has always been racist and classist, because it is all about men deciding who gets to be treated like a lady – protected, treasured and infantilised – and who gets treated like a chattel. As for ungrateful social justice warriors like me, we deserve to be oiled up and thrown to the Taliban: I'm told as much every day by white men who claim to abhor Islamic-coded violence against women but seem to have an erotic fascination with its details.

The New Chauvinism functions on two levels: it stokes up the fear of outsiders by casting foreign, black or queer masculinity as the real threat, and it undermines feminist activism by claiming that women just don't know what's good for us. Here we are, iron-knickered harpies, making a fuss about equal pay and domestic violence and rape culture, when if we would only shut up and listen to men like we're supposed to, we would know that the real threat comes from outside.

The New Chauvinists must not be allowed to co-opt feminist rhetoric. These people are not defenders of women. They are the ones who seek to put women in their place, substituting genuine respect for female autonomy with patronising 'protection', which is conditional on our good behaviour and only available if we are white.

Misogyny is not the preserve of any one group. It is a structural, cultural problem that exists in every nation on Earth. The vast majority of Western feminists are not fooled by those who seek to undercut our cause to rationalise their racism; but who cares what we think? We're only women, after all.

## FEMINISM AGAINST FASCISM

In a perverse sort of way, it's progress. After months of dog-whistle xenophobia, European authorities have finally started to treat migrants as they would treat any other citizen. They have achieved this by being slow to respond – at least initially – when migrants are accused of raping and assaulting women.

On New Year's Eve 2016 in Cologne, Germany, hundreds of men, almost all of reportedly 'Arabic and North African' appearance and including many asylum seekers, viciously attacked women who were celebrating in the central plaza, robbing and groping and tearing off clothes. At least one rape complaint has been filed. The police and the press were initially slow to react, and the Mayor of Cologne responded to eventual protests by suggesting that women should adopt a code of conduct in public and keep an 'arm's length' distance between themselves and strange men.

This is not the first time a European city administration has responded to an outbreak of sexual violence by blaming the women. It is, however, the first time in recent history that the right-wing press has not joined in the condemnation of these wanton strumpets who dare to think they might be able to have a good time without worrying what 'invitation' they're sending to men. Instead, the right wing blames . . . liberals. Who apparently caused all this by daring to suggest that refugees should be able to come to Europe in safety.

It'd be great if we could take rape, sexual assault and structural misogyny as seriously every day as we do when migrants and Muslims are involved as perpetrators. The attacks in Cologne were horrific. The responses – both by officials and by the armies of Islamophobes and xenophobes who have jumped at the chance to condemn Muslim and migrant men as savages – have also been horrific. Cologne has already seen violent protests by the far-right anti-migrant organisation Pegida, a group not previously noted for its dedication to progressive feminism. Angela Merkel has responded by tightening the rules for asylum seekers, but for many commentators, it's not enough.

Finally, the right wing cares about rape culture! Finally, all over the world, from Fox News to 4chan, a great conversion has taken place and men who previously spent their time shaming, stalking and harassing women are suddenly concerned about our rights! And all it took was a good excuse to bash migrants and Muslims and tell feminists they don't know what's good for them.

You know what has never yet prevented sexual violence? Unbridled racism.

This theft of feminist rhetoric in the name of imperialism and racism has been going on for centuries. It's been an active part of the political conversation in the West since 2001. Since the Cologne attacks were reported in the global press, a great many men have taken it upon themselves to educate me and other feminists on the point that only Muslim men are sexist. They have chosen to do this by sending orchestrated waves of abuse and sexual slurs to any woman whose opinion they dislike. Nobody has to pass a self-awareness test to go on Twitter.

Personally, I just love it when random men on the Internet tell me what my feminism should be like, because gosh, you know, this whole resisting oppression thing is really hard sometimes and it's great to have people who know what they're talking about take over for me so I can get on with the ironing. These people have repeatedly demanded that I 'condemn' the attacks in Cologne, which is a lazy way of implying that somebody doesn't really care about an issue.

So let me be clear: sexual violence is never, ever acceptable. Not for cultural reasons. Not for religious reasons. Not because the perpetrators are really angry and disenfranchised. There can be no quarter for systemic misogyny. And if we're serious about that, there's not a country or culture on Earth that won't have to take a long, hard look at itself. I stand with the many, many Muslim, Arab, Asian and immigrant feminists organising against sexism and misogyny within and beyond their own communities. Nobody seems to have thought to ask them how best to deal with systemic sexual violence – even though attacks on Muslim women have increased since the 2015 terrorist attacks in Paris.

The sensible thing to do in response to the Cologne attacks would be to call, as many German feminists are doing, for a far more rigorous attitude to rape and sexual assault across Europe. Instead, the solution on the table seems to be to clamp down on migration. That fits in with the shibboleth that only savage, foreign men and hardened criminals rape and abuse women – despite the fact that most rapes, in Germany and elsewhere, are committed by people known to the victim, and migrants have not been shown to be more or less sexually aggressive than any other group. As usual, white supremacist patriarchy only concerns itself with women's safety and women's dignity when rape and sexual assault can be pinned on cultural 'outsiders'.

Saying 'sexism is also part of Western culture' does not mean that the experience of women in the West is exactly the same as the experience of women in Middle Eastern dictatorships and war zones. Do you know why that is? Can you guess? It's because the world is not divided into 'things that are exactly the same as each other' and 'things that are total opposites'.

I actually can't believe I'm having to explain this right now. I thought we covered this in kindergarten.

Those of us who have moved beyond that level can, if we really try hard, understand that it's not either 'sexism is exclusively practised by Muslim men' or 'sexism is exactly the same everywhere'. This is what we call a 'false dichotomy' when we get to big school.

The oppression of women is a global phenomenon because patriarchy is a global phenomenon. It's embedded in the economic and social structures of almost every nation and community on Earth. Sexism and misogyny, however, look different across boundaries of culture and religion, as well as across divides of race and class and between generations. This is not a complicated thing to understand. I'm really trying not to be patronising. But a lot of people are behaving like vicious children over this issue, so if you're not one of them, I hope you understand why right now I wish I could put half the Internet on time out in a nice safe room where they can scream and break things without hurting themselves or anyone else.

And there's something else I've noticed, too. For all that these people claim to hate 'Islamic' sexual violence, it seems to fascinate them. In the past three years, I've lost count of the white men – and it is almost always white men – who have emailed, tweeted and sent me doctored pictures sharing their graphic fantasies in which feminist harpies like me are stoned to death, fucked to death, genitally mutilated, whipped, burned and gang-raped – not by them, of course. By those awful Muslims. There seems to be an almost erotic fascination with the rhetoric of sexual violence these men associate with Muslims – it's so awful that they have to concentrate really hard on the details and maybe save some screenshots to contemplate later in private.

I'll be blunt. I think some people out there are very excited by their conception of 'Islamic' violence against women. It allows them to enjoy the spectacle of women being brutalised and savaged while convincing themselves that it's only foreign, savage men who do these things. If hearing that makes you angry, if it makes you want to *smash my bitch face in* and tell me I'm a *whore who deserves to be raped to death by ISIS*, then congratulations, you've just proved my point.

The point is that misogyny knows no colour or creed, and perhaps it's time we did something about that. We're used to a society where a basic level of everyday sexism, sexual violence and assault is accepted. So if I argue that sexist violence by Muslim men is not qualitatively different from other kinds of sexist violence and if I say that refugees should be treated the same as European citizens, I must be saying that everyone should get a free pass to treat women like walking meatbags, right?

Wrong. It's time to take rape, sexual assault and structural misogyny as seriously every day as we do when migrants and Muslims are involved as perpetrators. That means that, yes, refugees must learn to respect women as human beings.

Citizens, too, must learn to respect women's agency and autonomy. Men and boys of every faith and none must learn that they are neither entitled to women's bodies nor owed our energy and attention, that it is not okay, ever, to rape, to assault, to abuse and attack women, not even if your ideology says it's okay. That goes for the men's rights activists, the anti-feminists and fanatical right-wingers as much as it does for religious bigots.

If we want to hold up Europe as a beacon of women's rights, that's fantastic. Let's make it happen. If we're suddenly a continent with a zero-tolerance policy on sexual violence and ritualised misogyny, let's seize that energy. Let's see real investment by the state and individuals in holding aggressors to account and supporting victims. It's easier to pin misogyny on cultural outsiders than it is to accept that men everywhere must do better – but any other attitude is rank hypocrisy.

## SOCIALISM AND/OR FEMINISM

It's a good job I wasn't in the office the week comedian, celebrity-shagger and saviour of the people Russell Brand was sashaying around. Not that there's anything wrong with a good sashay. The revolution – as Brand's guest edit of the *New Statesman* was modestly titled – could do with a little more flash and glitter. It's just that had I been in the office I would probably have spent a portion of my working hours giggling nervously, or hiding in the loos writing confused journal entries. My feelings about Russell Brand, you see. They are so complex.

Brand is precisely the sort of swaggering manarchist I usually fancy. His rousing rhetoric, his narcissism, his history of drug abuse and his habit of speaking to and about women as vapid, 'beautiful' afterthoughts in a future utopian scenario remind me of every lovely, troubled student demagogue whose casual sexism I ever ignored because I liked their hair. I was proud to be featured in the 'Revolution' issue that this magazine put out, proud to be part of the team that produced it. But the discussions that have gone on since then about leaders, about iconoclasm and about sexism on the left need to be answered.

I'd like to say first off that there are many things apart from the hair and cheekbones that I admire about Brand. He's a damn fine prose stylist, and that matters to me. He uses language artfully without appearing to patronise, something most of the left has yet to get the hang of. He touches on a species of directionless rage against capitalism and its discontents that knows very well what it's against without having a clear idea yet of what comes next, and being a comedian he is bound by no loyalty except to populism. And he manages without irony to say all these things, to appear in public as a spokesperson for the voiceless rage of a generation, while at the same time promoting a comedy tour called 'Messiah Complex'.

I admire the audacity of it. It's a bloody refreshing change from all those bland centrist politicians who grope for a cautious, cowed purity of purpose and action which they still fail to achieve. Brand, unlike almost every other smiling bastard out there, is exactly what he says he is: a wily charmer with pots of money who thinks the system is fucked and can get away with saying so. Yes, he is monstrously self-involved and self-promoting; yes, he is wealthy and famous and has, by many people's standards, no right to speak to any working-class person about revolution and be taken seriously. He also quite clearly means what he says, and that matters.

I agree with Brand about the disappointments of representative democracy. If I must pick a white male comedian to lead my charge, I'm on Team Russell. And I am glad – profoundly glad – that somebody has finally been permitted to say in public what commentators and politicians have not yet dared to suggest: that rising up together in anger, as young people did in London and elsewhere in 2011, might be a mighty fine idea.

It's not just Brand's wealth and fame that allow him to say such things. Consider how the rapper and artist M.I.A. was treated when she said very similar things about the London riots two years ago. Brand is playing the court jester, and speaking limited truth to overwhelming power in one of the few remaining ways that won't get you immediately arrested right now – from an enormous stage made of media money, liberally thickened with knob jokes, with a getaway sports car full of half-naked pop stars parked out the back and one tongue firmly in his cheek.

But what about the women?

I know, I know that asking that female people be treated as fully human and equally deserving of liberation makes me a concrete-gusseted feminist killjoy and probably a closet liberal, but in that case there are rather a lot of us, and we're angrier than you can possibly imagine at being told our job in the revolution is to look beautiful and encourage the men to do great works. Brand is hardly the only leftist man to boast a track record of objectification and playing cheap misogyny for laughs. He gets away with it, according to most sources, because he's a charming scoundrel, but when he speaks in that disarming, self-deprecating way about his history of slutshaming his former conquests on live radio, we are invited to love and forgive him for it because that's just what a rock star does. Naysayers who insist on bringing up those uncomfortable incidents are stooges, spoiling the struggle.

Acolytes who cannot tell the difference between a revolution that seduces – as any good revolution should – and a revolution that treats one half of its presumed members as chattels, attack in hordes online. My friend and colleague Musa Okwonga came under fire merely for pointing out that 'if you're advocating a revolution of the way that things are being done, then it's best not to risk alienating your feminist allies with a piece of flippant objectification in your opening sentence. It's just not a good look.'

I don't believe that just because Brand is clearly a casual and occasionally vicious sexist, nobody should listen to anything he has to say. But I do agree with Natasha Lennard, who wrote that 'this is no time to forgo feminism in the celebration of that which we truly don't need – another god, or another master'. The question, then, is this: how do we reconcile the fact that people need stirring up with the fact that the people doing the stirring so often fail to treat women and girls like human beings?

It's not a small question. It goes way beyond Brand. Speaking personally, it has dogged years of my political work and thought. As a radical who is also female and feminist I don't get to ignore this stuff until I'm confronted with it. It happens constantly. It's everywhere. It's Julian Assange and George Galloway. It's years and years of rape apologism on the left, of somehow ending up in the kitchen organising the cleaning rota while the men write those all-important communiqués.

It comes up whenever women and girls and their allies are asked to swallow our discomfort and fear for the sake of a brighter tomorrow that somehow never comes, putting our own concerns aside to make things easier for everyone else as good girls are supposed to. It comes up whenever a passionate political group falls apart because of inability to deal properly with male violence against women. Whenever some idiot commentator bawls you out for writing about feminism and 'retreating' into 'identity politics', thereby distracting attention from 'the real struggle'.

But what is this 'real struggle', if it requires women and girls to suffer structural oppression in silence? What is this 'real struggle' that hands the mic over and over again to powerful, charismatic white men? Can we actually have a revolution that relegates women to the back of the room, that becomes vicious when the discussion turns to sexual violence and social equality? What kind of fucking freedom are we fighting for? And whither that elusive, sporadically useful figure, the socialist?

## NICE GUYS DON'T

'I always think about why women are superficial and disgusting.'

As pick-up lines go, it could use some work. This, however, is OkCupid, the vast, weird pink-and-blue-toned jungle of the id masquerading as a dating site, where rare birds of modern romance flutter among the night-terrors of human loneliness and despair and the suspicious skin irritants of late-night hook-uppery.

The man who has written this on his profile appears to be in his early thirties. He has an unflattering haircut and what looks like a miniature kettle in one corner of his dating profile photo. He describes himself as a 'pretty decent guy' who doesn't want to play 'your stupid friendzone game'.

Miniature Kettle Man is one of many unfortunates who has had his insecurities and latent sexism exposed to a world of giggling women on the website 'Nice Guys of okay Cupid'. This is a Tumblr set up to collect images of all the many, many self-professed 'nice guys' out there whose publicly listed beliefs about women appear to prove them anything but. 'Stupid women, satanic women enticing men to fall into perilous friendzone,' says one Prince Charming, who appears to be speedballing in his photo.

It's a dispiriting catalogue of desperation and misogynist entitlement. Wherever he is, Miniature Kettle Man probably thinks his worst nightmares have come true: all over the world, ladies who don't even know him are laughing at him. The Hive Vagina has passed judgement on Miniature Kettle Man. One can only hope he is making a tiny cup of tea to cheer himself up with.

Because yes, it's hard not to laugh. It's hard to suppress a horrified snigger at the unexamined hypocrisy, at the sheer number of men out there who seem to believe, for example, that stating publicly that 'a no is just a yes that needs a little convincing' is morally or logically consistent with being 'a nice guy' who women would be clamouring to date if we weren't such shallow sluts. Anticipation of that laughter is probably what prompted so many men to screech abuse at the Tumblr's author over the Internet: 'enjoy life as an abject, hated feminazi bitch', writes one 'nice guy'. 'You don't realise that by being who you are, you are disgracing the entire human race, ha, it's no wonder genocide happens.' What a charmer. I wonder if he's still single?

The site is compelling, in a gross sort of way. Reading it fills you with a righteous rage that quickly starts feeling icky when you realise a few of the chaps on there haven't actually said anything overtly sexist – they're just a bit overweight and ungroomed and feeling sorry for themselves and wondering why 'women' (by which they mean 'women they fancy') won't consider having sex with 'nice guys' (by which they mean 'men very much like me', by which they mean 'me').

For a lot of these 'nice guys' who can't get dates, it looks like nothing a shave and a bit of positive self-talk couldn't cure. Unfortunately for those of us who believe in the basic decency of the species, many of these chaps seem instead to have translated their fear of rejection, their loneliness and humiliation, into active misogyny, a savage self-pitying resentment which must make perfect sense at 4 a.m. on a lonely weeknight while flicking between OkCupid and RedTube.com but which makes rather less sense when exposed to the cold pixel glare of Internet disapprobation.

The most chilling theme is the frequency with which these 'nice guys' have answered some of the dating site's more suspicious stock questions – 'do you feel there are any circumstances in which a person is obligated to have sex with you?', 'is abortion an option in the case of unwanted pregnancy?' – in ways that are at best terrible attempts at humour and at worst howling klaxons of unexamined sexism.

The truly frightening thing is that you can see where the internal logic comes from. A lot of these guys must occasionally feel like at least one woman, somewhere, must be obliged to have sex with them, and I'm prepared to bet that those occasions coincide quite neatly with 'times when one is most likely to be writing an online dating profile'. And that's how you end up with your best love-me face on a public-humiliation site telling the whole world you think no doesn't always mean no, feeling like an utter prick and rightly so.

Reading 'Nice Guys of okay Cupid' reminded me that for men, as well as for women, the political is personal. Deeply, often painfully personal. Observing the ugly logic whereby these so-called 'nice guys' have twisted their private fear of rejection into gender-loaded loathing and self-justification of rape culture did not improve my day one little bit, but it did make me think again about how personal sexism like this really gets, and why.

Let's look at this from a different angle. Something that happens when the word 'feminist' is attached to your work and life in any manner is that men want to talk to you about sex. This initially came as a surprise to me, but it's true: for every chap who suddenly remembers a vital appointment across town when you mention that you've written a book about sexism and anti-capitalism, there's another who just wants to know, in confidence, if this particular little fetish he has, whatever it is, makes him a bad person. Or who wants to know if it's all right to watch porn (it's complicated, but yes), or if he still has to pay the whole of a bill when taking a lady out to dinner (it's complicated, but no). Or who wants to know whether sadomasochism is sexist. For straight men who are starting to think about gender and sexism and considering the notion that, contrary to what they may have grown up learning, women might well be full human beings with dreams and desires just like them, the personal is political.

Yes, it's about who and how you fuck. Yes, it affects your sense of self, your conception of your own masculinity – particularly if you've previously built your gender identity on the idea of 'winning' women, and particularly if that gender identity is knotted up with feeling lonely, rejected and hurt when life doesn't reward you with a hot girlfriend. It's not surprising at all that it's here, on a dating site, that these men's deepest prejudices are written in clear, fist-gnawing Verdana typescript.

And – here's the thing – there has to be an answer to these guys that isn't just pointing and laughing. Calling out rapists and online predators is a more than legitimate strategy for dealing with abuse. But how are we supposed to handle common-or-garden sexist dickwaddery when it puts photos on the Internet and asks to be loved, or at least to enter what one heavily photoshopped smiler refers to hopefully as 'the bone zone'?

Are we obligated to be understanding when men write spurious bullshit about sluts over their 'looking for' lists? Are we ever going to be able to have a conversation about consent, about respect, about fucking, and maybe even about love, that doesn't descend into bullying and invective? Oh, Internet. I ask so little of you, and you always shoot me down. Maybe I should stop being such a Nice Girl.

# 7

# Violence

> The sad truth is that most evil is done by people who never make up their minds to be good or evil.
>
> Hannah Arendt

> There's some good in this world, Mr. Frodo, and it's worth fighting for.
>
> J.R.R. Tolkien, *The Lord of the Rings*

## TRIGGER WARNING WEEK

Rape. From the Latin 'rapere', to take or snatch. Usual meaning: to penetrate another person's body sexually without their consent. From the Sexual Offences Act, 2003: 'A is guilty of rape when A intentionally penetrates the vagina, anus or mouth of B (the complainant) with his penis; B does not consent to the penetration; and A does not reasonably believe that B consents.' It's such a small, simple, violent word, and now, thanks to Julian Assange, George Galloway and Todd Akin, the entire Internet and substantial portions of the Internot are arguing over what it means.

While following the Assange case, standing in the crowd to hear him deliver his Evita speech from the balcony of the Ecuadorian Embassy, debating with men and women online, I heard a great many people from all sides of the political spectrum tell me that the women who accused the Wikileaks founder of sexual assault were lying, or they were duped, or they were 'honey traps', or, most worryingly and increasingly often, that their definition of rape is inaccurate. The people saying this are not all prize bellends like Galloway or frothing wingnuts like Akin and other prominent Republicans who seem to want abortion to be available only to virgins, a position that seems curiously and specifically unChristian. Some of them are just everyday Internet idiots who happen to believe that if a man who you have previously consented to sex with holds you down and fucks you, that isn't rape. If you were wearing a short skirt and flirting, that isn't rape. If a man penetrates you without a condom while you're asleep, against your will, that isn't rape, not, in Akin's words, 'legitimate rape'.

Old, white, powerful men know what rape is, much better, it seems, than rape victims. They are lining up to inform us that women – the discussion has centred around women and their lies even though 9 per cent of rape victims are men – do not need 'to be asked prior to each insertion'. Thanks for that, George, not that it's just you. There's an army of commentators who also believe that 'that's not real rape' is both a valid, useful defence of a specific political asylum seeker and objective truth. Women lie, they say. Women lie about rape, about sexual assault, they do it because they're stupid or wicked or attention-seeking or deluded. The fact that the rate of fraud in rape cases remains as low as the rate of fraud in any other criminal allegation – between 2 and 4 per cent – does not impact. Women lie, and they do it to ruin men in positions of power. We shall henceforth call this 'The Reddit Defence'. This is not an article about Julian Assange. I've already written one of those, as, it seems, has everyone with keyboard and opinion, though Assange has denied these rape allegations on the basis he believed that the intercourse was consensual. This is about rape, and what it means, and what we think it means. As a culture, we still refuse collectively to accept that most rapes are committed by ordinary men, men who have friends and families, men who may even have done great or admirable things with their lives. We refuse to accept that nice guys rape, and they do it often. Part of the reason we haven't accepted it is that it's a fucking painful thing to contemplate; far easier to keep on believing that only evil men rape, only violent, psychotic men lurking in alleyways with pantomime-villain moustaches and knives, than to consider that rape might be something that ordinary men do. Men who might be our friends or colleagues or people we look up to. We don't want that to be the case. Hell, I don't want that to be the case. So, we all pretend it isn't. Justice, see?

Actually, rape is very common. Ninety thousand people reported rape in the United States in 2008 alone, and it is estimated that over half of rape victims never go to the police, making the true figure close to 200,000. Between 10 and 20 per cent of women have experienced rape or sexual assault. It's so common that when someone reports an allegation of rape in the press, I often hear friends tell me: 'that sounds like my rape'. Not: 'I was raped, too', but 'that sounds like my rape'. Being assaulted or fucked without consent is so common that it's more noteworthy if you happen to recognise similar specific circumstances. It's so common that – sorry if this hurts to hear – there's a good chance you know somebody who might have raped someone else. There's a good chance I do. And there's more than a small chance that he doesn't even think he did anything wrong, that he believes that what he did wasn't rape, couldn't be rape, because after all, he's not a bad guy.

The man who raped me wasn't a bad guy. He was in his early thirties, a well-liked and well-respected member of a social circle of which I am no longer a part, a fun-loving, left-leaning chap who was friends with a number of strong, feminist women I admired. I was nineteen. I admired him too.

One night, a group of my friends held a big party in a hotel. Afterwards, a few of the older guests, including this man, invited me up to the room they had rented. I knew that some drinking and kissing and groping might happen. I started to feel ill, and asked if it would be all right if I went to sleep in the room – and I felt safe, because other people were still there. I wasn't planning to have sex with this man or with anyone else that night, but if I had been, that wouldn't have made it okay for him to push his penis inside me without a condom or my consent.

The next thing I remember is waking up to find myself being penetrated, and realising that my body wasn't doing what I told it to. Either I was being held down or – more likely – I was too sick to move. I've never been great at drinking, which is why I don't really do it any more, but this feeling was more profound, and to this day I don't know if somebody put something in my drink that night. I was horrified at the way his face looked, fucking me, contorted and sweating. My head span. I couldn't move. I was frightened, but he was already inside me, and I decided it was simplest to turn my face away and let him finish. When he did, I crawled to the corner of the enormous bed and lay there until the sun came up.

In the morning I got up, feeling sick and hurting inside, and took a long, long shower in the hotel's fancy bathroom. The man who had fucked me without my consent was awake when I came out. He tried to push me down on the bed for oral, but I stood up quickly and put on my dress and shoes. I asked him if he had used a condom. He told me that he 'wasn't into latex', and asked if I was on the Pill. I don't remember thinking 'I have just been raped'. After all, this guy wasn't behaving in the manner I had learned to associate with rapists. Rapists are evil people. They're not nice blokes who everybody respects who simply happen to think it's okay to stick your dick in a teenager who's sleeping in the same bed as you, without a condom. This guy seemed, if anything, confused as to why I was scrabbling for my things and bolting out of the door. He even sent me an email a few days later, chiding me for being rude. When I walked home, it didn't occur to me that I had been raped. The next day, when I told a mutual friend what had happened, the girl who had introduced me to the man in question, I didn't use that word. By that time, I was in some pain between my legs, a different sort of pain, and I was terrified that I had AIDS. I had to wait two weeks for test results that showed that the man who raped me had given me a curable infection. I told my friend that I felt dirty and ashamed of myself. She said she was sorry I felt that way.

Everybody else in that social circle seemed to agree that by going to that hotel room and taking off my nice lace dress I had asked for whatever happened next, and so I dropped the issue. They were right and I was wrong. The man that we all knew and liked would never take advantage of anyone, and suggesting such a thing made me a liar and a slag. Did I go to the police? Did I hell. I thought it was my fault.

My experience was common enough, and it was also six years ago*. Looking back, being raped wasn't the worst thing that ever happened to me, although the experience of speaking out and not being believed, the experience of feeling so ashamed and alone, stayed with me for a long time, and changed how I relate to other humans. But I got over it. I rarely think about it. For some people, though, experiencing rape is a life-changing trauma.

Yes, even when it's not 'legitimate' rape. Being raped by a man who you liked and trusted, even loved – 30 per cent of rape victims are attacked by a boyfriend, husband or lover – is an entirely different experience from being raped by a stranger in an alley, but that doesn't mean it's any less damaging. Particularly not if others go on to tell you you're a lying bitch. Sorry if that hurts to hear.

You know what also hurts to hear? People telling you that your experience didn't happen, that you asked for it. That you have no right to be angry or hurt. That you should shut up. That you hate men. That you're against freedom of speech. That's what hundreds of thousands of women all over the world are hearing when they hear respected commentators (I'm not

*at the time of writing

talking here about Galloway or Akin, although I'm sure there are a great many people who respect their opinions, God help them) saying that the allegations made against Julian Assange 'aren't really rape'.

The idea that fucking a woman in her sleep, without a condom, or holding a woman down and shoving your cock inside her after a previous instance of consensual sex, is just 'bad bedroom etiquette' – thanks again, George – the idea that good guys don't rape, that idea has two effects.

One: it fosters the fantasy that there's only one kind of rape, and it happens in the proverbial alley with the perennial knife and certainly not to anyone you know. That's what's most disturbing about the discussion going on right now. There are millions of men, some of them very young, most of them extremely well meaning, all of them with their own unique sexual histories trying to figure out a way to negotiate boundaries without hurting themselves or others, and those men are being told that sometimes women say things are rape when they aren't really. That people who say that consent is really very important indeed are probably on the same side as conniving governments who want to suppress freedom of speech and punish whistleblowers and truth-seekers.

Two: it makes any man or woman who has ever been raped by a nice guy suspect, yet again, that it's all their fault, that they let it happen. It makes rape victims less likely to come forward and report. I didn't report my rape. It took me months even to understand it as rape. I stopped talking about it, because I was sick of being called a liar, and I got the shut-up message fairly fast. I tried to stop thinking about it.

But following the Assange case brought it all up again. The vitriol spewed across the Internet, the discussions in every car and cafe I stepped into about what rape really means, the acknowledgement that yes, lots of women do lie and exaggerate, they made me feel infected all over again. Another friend told me she felt 'psychologically poisoned, sick more than angry'; I'm definitely not the only one who's been revisiting those scenes in my head, playing them over like old CCTV footage. I'm probably not the only one, either, who went quietly back to a few friends from the old days to talk again about what happened, to clear things up. And what one of those former friends told me was: I wish I'd taken you more seriously, because I think it happened again, to somebody else.

This vicious drift towards victim-blaming must stop. It's not about Julian Assange, not really, not any more. It's becoming an excuse to wrench the definition of rape back to a time when consent was unimportant, just when some of us had begun to speak up, and it's happening right now, and what's worse, what's so, so much worse, is that it's happening in the name of truth and justice, in the name of freedom of speech.

If those principles are to mean anything, this vitriol, this rape-redefining in the name of conscience and whistleblowing and Wikileaks and Julian Assange, it has to stop. It has to stop now. Non-consensual sex is rape, real rape, and good guys do it too, all the time, every day. Sorry if that hurts to hear, but you've heard it now, and there are things that hurt much more, and for longer, and for lifetimes. Those things need to stop. Together, if we're brave enough to keep on speaking out even when we're told to shut up, told we're liars and bitches and we asked for it, we can make them stop. There aren't many situations where all it takes to change the world is a lot of people standing together and refusing to be silenced, but this might be one of them.

## THE EMILY DAVISON BLUES

It took Emily Davison four days to die. The injuries that the women's liberation activist sustained when, a century ago, she leapt in front of the king's racehorse at the Epsom Derby were not enough to kill her outright. She died in hospital on 8 June 1913 amid public condemnation; the queen mother sent her apologies to the jockey that his race had been interrupted by a 'brutal lunatic woman' demanding, of all crazy things, the vote.

Parliament and the press were agreed: this was not legitimate protest, but a 'mad act', according to the *Morning Post*. What could prompt a person to do such a thing? Davison was born in Blackheath, London, in 1872, studied literature at Royal Holloway for as long as she could afford the fees, and then worked as a governess before joining the Women's Social and Political Union – what we now call the suffragette movement – full-time at the age of thirty-two. She obtained the maximum amount of education and personal freedom permitted to a middle-class woman of her generation and it wasn't enough. I imagine it felt a bit like drowning.

In old footage of the suffragettes, they look like a gang of angry bantams, flapping about in their outsized hats and ridiculous full skirts. The very word 'suffragettes' sounds like the kind of fusty, village-hall girl band your auntie might sing in at weekends, rather than a revolutionary organisation whose members were prepared to die so that others might live free. The grudging account of the women's liberation movement in official histories refers to force-feeding, but edits out the full extent of the torture of activists who were considered mad terrorists for asking that the state treat women of all classes as rational human beings.

Some historians mention that Davison had been reckless with her safety on other occasions as evidence that she was 'merely' suicidal, arguing that she desired to die under any circumstances and that this somehow invalidates her decision to do so in public while waving the banner of women's suffrage. Davison certainly had form for doing outrageous things in the name of women's liberation. She was arrested nine times – for arson, for public nuisance and for throwing stones at the prime minister's carriage.

During her imprisonment, when she and other activists were being force-fed – a process that was agonising and degrading and sometimes involved anal rape with metal tubes – she threw herself down an iron staircase in protest. In retaliation for her refusal to cooperate, the guards put a hosepipe into her cell and slowly filled it with water until she almost drowned. Try to imagine, just for a second, what that must have been like. How long must it have taken for the cell to fill with freezing water, closing around your ankles, your knees, then your chest, your impractical skirts first buoying you up and then dragging you down? How long would it take until the choking, numbing water did not drown your nightmares every time you tried to sleep? What might it mean, under such circumstances, to be crazy, to be consumed with rage, to have a death wish?

Madness is often political. There are situations in which extreme emotional distress is the only rational response to overwhelming circumstance, where 'sanity' is little more than the medical term for acquiescence. Women in the early twentieth century, a time when female sexual and social freedom was pathologised, frequently went insane, killed themselves or suffered debilitating 'nerves', as documented by writers such as Zelda Fitzgerald and Charlotte Perkins Gilman. Frequently those who rebelled in more tangible ways, by acting out, sleeping around or refusing to submit to men in the home or workplace, were declared insane and sent away to rot in asylums by their spouses and relatives. For many middle-class women, the suffragette sash became a way of organising sentiments that would otherwise have been sectionable.

Undoubtedly, by the standards of her day, Emily Davison was deranged, her entire life a 'mad act' – yet that does not make it illogical.

Oppressive systems are not all of a kind. They do, however, share an indifference to those whose inability to bear the privations of the imposed social order results in collapse, breakdown and death. The present British government, to give one example, has accustomed itself to the suicides of poor and disabled people cut off by its austerity programme. It encourages a narrative that suggests that such people are 'merely' disturbed, that benefit recipients are selfish 'scroungers'. What such systems cannot cope with is those who are able, by virtue of circumstance or force of personality, to turn that rage and distress outwards, rather than letting it consume them from within.

Such people often become known to the police. We call them rebels, or activists, or colossal bloody headaches, depending on our point of view and place of employment. Emily Wilding Davison made trouble. She made herself intolerable to a system she found impossible to tolerate. It is thanks to women like her, and the few men who supported them, that far fewer of us today know what it is to be forced to submit to a husband, to be politically disenfranchised, to be denied the right to control our own bodies and our own children – though that work is far from complete. There are situations in which you can choose to toss yourselves under the hooves of history, or choose to drown. Emily Davison made the only choice she could bear. We should remember that, when we remember her.

## BLAME, SHAME AND RAPE CULTURE

How much can you change the world with fifty-five words?

On 28 November 2015, in two tweets, Stoya – who is in no particular order a famous porn actress, an activist, a writer and a friend of mine – unambiguously accused her ex-boyfriend, fellow porn actor James Deen, of rape. 'James Deen held me down and fucked me while I said no, stop, used my safeword,' she wrote. 'I just can't nod and smile when people bring him up anymore.'

Within days, the porn industry had turned against its golden boy. In so doing, it became the first professional community to respond to allegations of serial sexual violence by actually believing women from the start.

What was astonishing was not the courage it doubtless took for Stoya to type those fifty-five words and hit send, knowing that she would be accused of lying and attention-seeking, knowing the number of people who would claim that as a sex worker, she cannot expect to claim rape and be believed. What was astonishing, though, what had my heart between my teeth, was the number of people who did the opposite. Even before more former partners and colleagues of Deen came forward with more accusations of rape and violence, major porn studios dropped him as a performer, and many outlets publishing his work and writing cut ties. The hashtag #solidaritywithstoya trended around the world.

Watching the story unfold, I found these lines from Lidia Yuknavitch's *The Small Backs of Children* echoing in my mind: 'Nations will shift like stones in the hands of a girl making a city in the dirt, and men and women . . . either they will finally see each other and do what must be done to evolve, or they will not.'

Something is changing. The response to Stoya and the other accusers is the crest on a tidal wave of women's truth washing away the detritus of lies about sex and violence, about which lives matter and who is to be believed. In Hollywood, in the music industry, in politics, in every corridor, women and girls are coming forward and coming together to stand against a culture of abuse that has valued the reputation of powerful men above the dignity and voice of women. It's Bill Cosby. It's Jimmy Savile. It's Terry Richardson. It's the Steubenville High School football team. It's all of their accusers, whose names we have been told do not matter. Until now.

That's what solidarity is.

The default response to accusations of rape, especially against powerful men, has long been to assume that the accusers are lying. That's what women do, of course – that's the nature of the sex. They are malicious and vengeful and they refuse to accept that men simply have more sexual power than they do, because nature made them that way, or because God wants it that way, depending on your point of view.

The thing about rape is that it is extremely hard to prove. By its very nature, there are usually no outside witnesses. Even when victims steel themselves, overcome their fears and go directly to the police without taking a shower, they can count on not being believed.

Part of the reason that rape is hard to prove is that sexist fairy tales about what constitutes consent infect judges and juries just as much as the general public. Of the many myths about sexual violence, the most pernicious is that women routinely lie about it. That's not true: the rates of false reporting for rape and sexual assault are estimated to be around the same as rates of false reporting for any other crime – the current figure is anywhere between 0.2 per cent and 8 per cent. Men are actually more likely to be victims of rape themselves than they are to be falsely accused of it.

Rapists rely on these myths, often targeting women and girls who they know will be too scared to come forward, or who will not be believed. That means women of colour, young girls and sex workers. Former Oklahoma City police officer Daniel Holtzclaw was found guilty of stalking and raping thirteen black women and girls, some of whom had previous arrest records for sex work. Serial rapists target the young, the vulnerable and sex workers, knowing how hard it is even for women deemed 'respectable' to be taken seriously.

For legal reasons, I must state that James Deen has not been convicted of rape – no charges have been brought, and he has denied the allegations.

But for moral reasons, I must emphasise that none of this means that rape did not happen.

Yes, Stoya could be lying. So could Tori Lux. So could Joanna Angel, Ashley Fires, Amber Rayne, Kora Peters, Nicki Blue, Lily LaBeau and all the other women who have accused James Deen of rape, assault and mental abuse. As a journalist, I have to consider that possibility, and so do you. He has denied the allegations. But the fact is that rape is common. Far too common. False allegations of rape are not common. Perhaps James Deen didn't do it.*

'Innocent until proven guilty' is the cry that goes up every time a woman, then two, then five or ten or twenty women come forward to accuse a powerful man of abuse. What this means, in practice, is that we should always assume that women are lying until a judge says otherwise. In other words: shut the hell up. In other words: don't rock the boat.

The reputation of men has historically been valued higher than the safety of women. If it's a case of he

* www.thedailybeast.com/articles/2015/12/08/james-deen-breaks-his-silence-i-am-completely-baffled.html

said/she said, and nobody can ever know the truth, it's tacitly understood that it's better for fifty women to suffer in silence than for one man to lose his career. This continues to be the case despite the number of men who continue to enjoy success even after being convicted of rape or sexual assault.

Something huge is shifting in our culture. The way we think about sexuality as a whole, and the way we think about sexual violence in particular, is evolving as women and girls begin to speak collectively and with courage about their experiences. Rape is a crime; rape culture is what allows that crime to go unpunished and unreported. Rape is the injury; rape culture is the insult, shouted at you from comedy stages, whispered in the corners of parties, around dining-room tables.

*Well, what was she thinking, going back to his apartment in the first place?*

*She was so drunk. Boys will be boys.*

For a long time, women's only real power in society was the power of sexual refusal. This was a contingent power – not based on pleasure but on the power to say yes or no to this man or that – and it was always dependent on whether the man in question would respect your decision, which depended largely on your race, class and social position. But the power to say 'no' to sex has always been women's last bargaining chip in a misogynist society, and for as long as that has been true, men have resented them for it. It is about power. It is about the insistence that women's bodies are public property, and women's words, women's autonomy, women's agency do not matter, at least not compared to a man's good name.

Right now, the balance of power is shifting. Why? Why now, after lifetimes of silence and suspicion, are women and girls coming forward to name their abusers and demand change?

Technology has a great deal to do with it. Social media allows all people to talk to one another frankly and in elective anonymity about their experiences. Women tell their truths on the Internet, from powerful personal essays to private groups and listservs. One such group I was recently privy to allows women and queer people in a particular location to warn each other about how men in their social circles behave – not just about whether they are rapists, but whether they are violent, whether they are respectful, whether they treat their partners like human beings.

The group is private, and it is not about shame, but about protecting one another without censure. If a friend warns me not to date a certain man because he has a tendency to get drunk, ignore boundaries and become aggressive, I won't wait for a court conviction before making other plans. In almost every community I've been part of in the last few years, this story has played out. Serial abusers are finally confronted, no matter how powerful and popular. Women speak up together, and they are believed. The community struggles to readjust.

Divisions occur, arguments erupt and friendships change. Change this profound is always painful. But so is silence.

If patriarchy dreams, then its nightmares must involve women talking, loudly, bravely, about men. In fact, much of our culture is set up to avoid just this. Women are pitted against each other, taught to compete for male attention, socialised against solidarity. Our truths are dismissed as gossip and chatter, our writing as empty confession. The prospect of women truly talking to each other, trusting one another and standing together against male violence and sexism in their communities is legitimately terrifying to those with a vested interest in maintaining the status quo.

The uncomfortable truth is not that women are lying en masse about rape – they're not – but that women and girls and their allies are finally speaking about their experiences in numbers too big to ignore. The even less comfortable truth is that many of these experiences involve behaviour that men and boys grow up believing is not criminal. The same rape culture that raises women to believe that it is their fault if they were assaulted raises men to believe the same thing. Men learn, because culture tells them, that women's sexual autonomy is a barrier to be conquered – that sex is something they are supposed to get from women. *Boys will be boys*. The little boys who grow up hearing that mantra repeated learn that they need not take responsibility for their actions.

There is solidarity in adversity. Perhaps the reason that the adult industry is the only community currently actually behaving in an adult manner is that sex workers are under no illusion that the law is designed to protect them. The assumption of the general public has long tallied with the strategy for former MMA fighter War Machine, whose defence team claims that he could not have raped his ex-girlfriend, twenty-four-year-old Christy Mack, because her 'work in pornography pointed to consent'. She was asking for it. She was also asking for the broken ribs, the fractured eye socket, the missing teeth and the lacerated liver that she sustained. War Machine has pleaded not guilty to the thirty-four felonies he's been charged with, including sexual assault and attempted murder. Sex workers have had enough of being told that they have even less right to consent than the average woman – and it is no surprise that a broad movement against rape culture is now being led by sex workers themselves.

No means no, no matter who you are, no matter what job you do. No matter if he's your partner. No matter how many times you've said yes. Women have always known this, but knowing is not enough when your friends, your family, society and the legal system tell you that you're lying, you're crazy, nobody will believe you, that you should think of the man's reputation, that you should worry about being ostracised, that it wasn't really so bad, was it, that you're making a fuss about nothing, and really what were you doing drinking in the first place? Why were you wearing that dress? Why didn't you fight harder? What made you think your dignity and safety was important? What made you think your body was your own? Shut up, stop whining and think about the man.

It is never easy to confront the prejudices we have grown up breathing in like air. But around the world, women are coming together and doing what needs to be done for society to evolve. Those clinging to old myths about rape and virtue, about good women and bad ones, will find themselves on the wrong side of history.

## POLITICAL CORRECTNESS IS 'MANNERS' BY ANOTHER NAME

The year is 1994 and the place is a small suburban kitchen in Sussex. I'm eight years old and I'm sitting at the table, slopping Frosties into my mouth and reading *Politically Correct Bedtime Stories*. Some friends of my parents bought it for me as a joke. The joke is that I'm an angry, sensitive child whose favourite phrase is 'That's not fair!' and I should lighten up and play with Barbies like a normal kid. I fail to get the joke. *Politically Correct Bedtime Stories* is my favourite book. You can tell from the milk stains.

In these stories, no princess has to wait to be saved. Cinderella organises against low-paid labour. Snow White is an activist for the rights of people of restricted growth. And the wolves are gentle, misunderstood carnivores who sometimes get to win. As I'm eight, I've never heard of political correctness before but it sounds good to me.

Fast-forward twenty years. In a freezing cold flat in Berlin, I'm standing under the shower with the water turned up as high and hot as it will go. I'm trying to boil away the shame of having said something stupid on the Internet. The shower is the one place it's still impossible to check Twitter. This is a mercy. For as long as the hot water lasts I won't be able to read the new accusations of bigotry, racism and unchecked privilege.

I didn't mean it. I don't understand what I did wrong but I'm trying to understand. I want to be a good person. It turns out that however hard you try to be politically correct, you can still mess up. I am so, so sorry.

What has come to be called 'political correctness' used to be known as 'good manners' and was considered part of being a decent human being. The term is now employed to write off any speech that is uncomfortably socially conscious, culturally sensitive or just plain left-wing. The term is employed, too often, to shut down free speech in the name of protecting speech.

Recently, prominent writers from Jon Ronson to Jonathan Chait and Dan Hodges have been doubling down on the supposed culture of 'political correctness' and 'public shaming'. It is no coincidence that most of the loudest voices condemning the 'Twitter mafia' are white, male, cisgender, privileged and unused to having to share any sort of public forum with large numbers of people who rarely have to worry about which pair of dad jeans will best conceal a pudding-coloured paunch. I'm really sorry if that image offended anyone, because some of my best friends truly are straight white men. Sometimes we do straight white men things together, like eating undercooked barbecue meat and scratching ourselves in front of *Top Gear*.

On one level, the pushback against 'public shaming' can be read as a reaction from the old guard against the empowerment of previously unheard voices. There is nothing particularly novel about well-paid posh chaps writing off feminists, black activists and trans organisers as 'toxic' and demanding that they behave with more decorum if they want to be taken seriously. I think, however, that it's about more than that. I think it's about shame and about fear.

On a very profound level, people who occupy positions of social power – and I include myself in that demographic – are worried not just that the unheard masses are coming for them but that they might be right to do so.

Most of us like to think we are good people. I do, although once, in a moment of extreme stress, I did tell a *Telegraph* journalist to go and die in a fire. When you are faced with a barrage of strangers whose opinions you actually care about yelling at you that you're hateful and hurtful, that you're an idiot and a bigot, when all you've done is make a mistake – well, the easy option, the option that feels safest and most comfortable, is to wall yourself off, decry your critics as prigs and bullies and make a great many ominous references to George Orwell's *Nineteen Eighty-Four*. Which is silly, because Internet feminists are really not a lot like totalitarian dictators; but if we are, I want to know when I'm getting the drone army and the snazzy Hugo Boss outfit.

It's easy to criticise call-out culture, especially if the people calling you out are mean and less than merciful. It's far harder to look into your own heart and ask if you can and should do better. Like almost every other human being, I don't like it when people shout at me, unless I'm at a punk show and have paid good money to have people shout at me. I'm quite a sensitive bunny. I am mortified by the thought of hurting other people, even by accident. I've spent very dark days, following social media pile-ons, convinced that I was a horrible person who didn't deserve to draw breath. I am not afraid of the sexist trolls who send me boring porn gifs on Twitter. I am afraid – frequently legitimately afraid – of letting people down. Of letting my community down. Of making a mistake I can't move on from. I think everyone with a social conscience and a Facebook profile worries about this.

There is an enormous difference between being brought to task in public for making mistakes and the ritualised shaming of women, queer people and ethnic minorities online. There is a difference, a difference that critics such as Ronson and Chait are keen to smudge over, between marginalised people clamouring against instances of oppression, and everyday cyberbullying and harassment – what Monica Lewinsky, in her phenomenal TED talk, calls 'public shaming as a blood sport'. The difference is all about power: who has it and who doesn't.

I know this because I've experienced both. I've been called out for saying thoughtless things online, and I have also been the target of vicious hate campaigns from people who wanted me dead just for who and what I am. Much of the pushback I experience comes from sexists and bigots who simply hate the idea that any young woman, anywhere, has a writing career.

Their violence can be very frightening, especially when they send bomb threats to my house. It does not, however, throw me into existential panic. The last time I got a graphic rape threat, I felt awful but the last time I got a furious tweet from a trans woman telling me off for accidentally using appropriative language, I felt worse. I felt shame. Especially because she had a point.

It is terribly difficult to stay in the room – physically, emotionally, politically – with the untempered anger of other people whose opinions you care about. It is harder still to cope with the possibility that the world is changing and you may need to change, too. That good intentions are not enough to stop you hurting others through ignorance or obliviousness. In that poky, unventilated bathroom in Berlin, I laid my head against the tiles and breathed in lungfuls of steam and decided to try to move beyond my own panic and understand that although this wasn't, ultimately, about me, it was still my responsibility to try not to be a prat if I could help it. This is as good a baseline for human decency as any, even when the public parameters of what does and does not constitute tosspottery are shifting faster than a potter can toss.

Moving through guilt to catharsis is a tall order for a Tuesday night. It's uncomfortable to realise that you've messed up in a way that requires apology. But I think moving through that discomfort, in this weird and unsettled age, is part of being an adult. Whoever we are, we have to learn to deal with the discomfort that comes with making mistakes, if we don't want this moment of social change to produce more fragmentation, more misunderstanding, more dismissal of the concerns of the most marginalised and vulnerable people in society – people for whom discomfort is way down the list of daily concerns, somewhere behind homelessness and being shot in the back by police for a parking offence.

The problem is not 'outrage'. The problem is rage, pure and simple. This is an anxious time, an age of great and worsening inequality, of structural racism and oppression, and when resistance fails to produce relief, that rage finds outlets wherever it can. Sometimes that rage turns ugly. I'm not going to argue there aren't people on what I still think of as 'my side' who sometimes behave shamefully, targeting individuals with the sort of bullying tactics they claim to oppose. 'Some forms of activist rage,' says the sociologist and trans feminist Katherine Cross, 'are flat out morally wrong and do real harm.

But the problem at the root of it is the dispossession of marginalised people, which makes that rage the only avenue of self-actualisation available to them.'

There is so much to be angry about and precious little relief for that anger within what passes for democracy in most Western nations. For those of us who do not happen to own a senator or two, social media is one of the few spaces where we can sometimes, sometimes, see justice being done. The racist comedian forced to apologise for his jokes at the expense of Asian people. The margarine company pressured into withdrawing its homophobic ads. The newspaper that begins, at long last, to treat transsexual people more like human beings.

The world is waking up to new parameters of social decency and it is cranky and confused. The changes are coming too fast for anyone to cope with them without making a few mistakes, and when we do, we have to move beyond our shame and discomfort and try to act with compassion – for ourselves and others. I find putting the Internet down and taking a hot shower is good for this. Your mileage, as they say on Twitter, may vary.

Because the truth – the real, unspeakable, awful truth – is that we are all vulnerable, and afraid, and more ignorant than we'd like to be. We are all fumbling to find a place for ourselves in this weird, anxious period of human history, stumbling between the savagery of late capitalism and the rage of the dispossessed. I still believe in new stories, with new heroes, where the wolves sometimes get to win. I still believe that decency, tolerance and free speech are worth fighting for. You might call that political correctness. I call it compassion and I think it's how we build a better world.

## THE RAPE EXCEPTION THAT PROVES THE RULE

Poor children are to be made poorer unless their mothers can prove that they were raped. Sometimes all it takes is one subclause of a single policy to show the true face of an administration, and this nasty little addendum to the Welfare Reform and Work Bill is shocking in its casual cruelty.

Almost as shocking is the lack of outcry – so far – as the Tories slice what remains of the welfare state into tiny decorative scraps to wrap the presents they're giving to their upper-middle-class base. Among the flagship cuts announced in the Budget are swingeing cuts to tax credits. Families with more than two children will lose up to £2,780 per subsequent child, with an important exception: the government, in its beneficence, has decided not to withdraw support if these extra children, these gurgling drains on the coffers of state, were conceived as a result of rape.

Let's sit with that one for a while. Let's ponder that piece of political positioning. Let's slow down and smell the squeaky leather and stale air of the conference rooms where politicians sat down to discuss which children they are going to impoverish this year. Let's taste the Victoria sponge in the taxpayer-subsidised Whitehall cafes where advisers gathered to decide precisely how much violence needs to be done to a woman before her children can eat.

There are layers of monstrosity here. Let's unwrap them one by one. The first is the question of child poverty. Hungry, shivering children are a moral quandary for this administration: conservative logic, after all, holds that individuals are to blame for their economic circumstances but it's hard to tell someone it's their own fault they're poor when they're not even out of nappies yet. Having failed to meet every national target on child poverty, the Conservatives have simply redefined poverty. Now, unable to blame impoverished toddlers for their lot in life, they have decided to blame their parents for having sex in the first place.

Child poverty is not only important as an indicator of global development. It is an indicator of the human decency of any state. The British government has made clear statements that it is prepared to let more children grow up in poverty to finance an economic recovery structured to benefit the super-rich and nobody has yet removed the mirrors from the washrooms of Westminster. George Osborne's argument that 'work is the best route out of poverty' is moral rather than factual, which is another way of saying it's a stunning lie. Most families receiving welfare benefits have at least one employed adult.

That's the first horror. The second is the rape exception itself. To understand why it is so abhorrent, it's worth looking at where else a similar principle is applied. Liberal campaigners for abortion rights sometimes condemn nations for forbidding the practice 'even in cases of rape'. This has always seemed to me a telling twist of logic. If you truly believe that abortion is murder, then surely it remains murder whatever the circumstances of conception. If, however, abortion restrictions are less about the ethics of life than they are about punishing women for having sex, it makes perfect sense to make an exception for rape. If you want to make an example of bad women who have consensual sex by forcing them to carry unwanted pregnancies to term, it makes perfect sense to separate off the good women who became pregnant through no 'fault' of their own. That's what any rape exception is about: it's about punishing women for having agency.

The same logic is at play in the proposed rape exception to the welfare bill. Feckless 'welfare mothers' have long been favourite ogres of conservatives, but either children deserve to grow up in poverty or they do not. This is not about fairness, nor even about saving money. It is about sin. It is about punishment for sin, and specifically the twin working-class sins of poverty and fertility. It is also about misogyny.

Attacks on welfare are always attacks on women. As long as the sexual double standard exists in employment and childcare, women will need welfare more than men do. Women battered by a patriarchal system that does not consider child-rearing and domestic tasks 'real work' will need support to raise those children. Already plunged back into the old sexist bargain – depend on a partner or watch your children suffer – the women of Britain now face another appalling prospect. They face having to beg a jobcentre adviser for the money to raise their rapists' children.

That is the underlying horror in this package of poison. It's a woman in a sterile office some months from now having to explain the circumstances of her rape to a welfare adviser who is inclined, both by modern economic policy and by ancient sexist prejudice, not to believe a word she says. If 'welfare claimant' is already synonymous with 'fraudster' in the public imagination, thanks to a long and successful campaign on the part of the right-wing press, so is 'rape victim'. Less than 10 per cent of rapists are convicted in court, and crisis centres for victims of sexual assault are already closing up and down the country. How does the government think this is going to work? By keeping poor women in their proper place: abject and terrified.

I am not suggesting that children conceived in rape should not receive public support. I am suggesting that *all* children should receive public support – whatever the pearl-clutchers in government happen to think of their parents' sexual morality.

As the Treasury continues the time-worn Tory tradition of shrinking the state until it is just small enough to fit into everyone's bedroom, we are speaking in hypotheticals – but they are hypotheticals that lay bare the bloodless moral core of government.

## NO CONSPIRACY HERE

How should we watch *Annie Hall* now? After filmmaker Woody Allen was given the Lifetime Achievement Award at the Golden Globes in 2014, his former foster-daughter, Dylan Farrow, then twenty-eight, told the *New York Times* the story of how he sexually abused her as a child. The charges against Allen are twenty-odd years old, and he was never brought to trial. But he takes his place in a grim roll-call of famous men whose work and achievements are being called into question because of the way they are said to have treated women and children.

It seems like the whole world is a mess of rape allegations. In Britain, Operation Yewtree has marched a grim procession of beloved household names – some of them deceased, some of them merely half-deceased – through the spotlight of public approbation, on charges of child abuse. And there are others: politicians such as the late Liberal MP Cyril Smith; respected activists such as Julian Assange. It is extremely uncomfortable to watch. It might challenge us to rethink art and ideas that we hold extremely dear.

Today, the fightback seems to be on. In America, Woody Allen publicly responded to Dylan Farrow's accusations by accusing Dylan's mother, Mia Farrow, of maliciously making up the whole thing.

There are people out there, not all of them men, who believe that a conspiracy is going on. When I speak to them as a reporter, they tell me that women lie about rape, now more than ever. They lie to damage men and to 'destroy their lives'. This is despite the fact that the fraud rate for rape remains as low as ever, and despite the fact that popular culture is groaning with powerful men who have been accused or even convicted of sexual abuse and whose lives remain distinctly undestroyed. Men like boxer Mike Tyson, or singer R. Kelly. Men like Woody Allen.

Women and children who bring those accusations, however, risk their relationships, their reputation, their safety. Anonymity in the press is no protection against the rejection of family, friends and workmates. Dylan Farrow is living somewhere out of the public eye, under a new name. We have created a culture and a legal system which punishes those who seek justice so badly that those who do come forward are assumed to have some ulterior motive.

Rape and abuse are the only crimes where, in the words of legal scholar Lord Hale, 'It is the victim, not the defendant, who is on trial.' They are crimes that are hard to prove beyond reasonable doubt in a court of law, because it's a case of 'he said, she said'. Nobody can really know, and so naturally we must assume that he is innocent and she is lying – because that's what women do. The trouble is that in this society, 'he said' is almost always more credible than 'she said', unless she is white and he is not.

There is a growing understanding that 'wait for the ruling' is an insufficient answer when the latest celebrity is hauled up on rape charges. The rule of law cannot be relied upon when it routinely fails victims of abuse. Rape and abuse cases have come to be tried in the court of public opinion, for better or worse, precisely because the official courts are understood – with good reason – to be so hopelessly unfair.

As the Allen case demonstrates, the law courts aren't the only place where the nature of sexual power, of what men may and may not do to women, children and other men with impunity, is played out. No judge can legislate for the ethics of the Golden Globe Committee. And no magistrate can ensure that a young girl like Missouri teenager Daisy Coleman, who came forward in 2013 to describe how she was raped by classmates at a party, is not hounded out of town, along with her family, until she makes attempts on her own life.

Rape culture means more than a culture in which rape is routine. Rape culture involves the systematic silencing of victims even as women and children are instructed to behave like potential victims at all times. In order to preserve rape culture, society at large has to believe two different things at once. Firstly, that women and children lie about rape, but that they should also act as if rape will be the result if they get into a strange car, walk down a strange street or wear a sexy outfit. Secondly, if it happens, it's their own fool fault for not respecting the unwritten rules.

This paradox involves significant mental gymnastics. But as more and more people come forward with accusations, as the pattern of historical and ongoing abuse of power becomes harder to ignore, the paradox gets harder to maintain. We are faced with two alternatives: either women and children are lying about rape on an industrial, organised scale, or rape and sexual abuse are endemic in this society, and have been for centuries. Facing up to the reality of the latter is a painful prospect.

Many of the allegations surfacing, like those against Woody Allen and the Yewtree defendants, are not new. What is new is the attitude. We are beginning, on a cultural level, to challenge the delusion that only evil men rape, that it is impossible for a man to be a rapist or an abuser of children and also an epoch-defining filmmaker. Or a skilled politician. Or a beloved pop icon. Or a respected family man. Or a treasured friend. We are beginning to reassess the idea that if a man is any of these things, the people he hurts must stay silent, because that's how power works.

An enormous change in consciousness is taking place around consent, and it threatens to change everything. At some point between 2008 and today, the collective understanding of what rape and abuse are, and what they ought to be, changed for ever. At some point we began to talk, not just privately, cowedly, but in numbers too big to ignore, about the reality of sexual violence and child abuse, about how victims are silenced. Survivors of rape and abuse and their loved ones had always known this toxic truth, but we were forced to hold it close to ourselves where it could fester and eat us from within. As you may remember, yes, I do have intimate experience of this, and so do a lot of people you know. We just didn't talk about it in quite this way before.

Something has changed. When the allegations that Woody Allen sexually abused Dylan Farrow first surfaced in the early 1990s, his defenders swamped the mainstream press and that was more or less the end of it. Now the people who have always been on Team Dylan get a say, too. Without wanting to sound like a headbanging techno-utopian, this is happening because of the Internet. It is happening because a change in the way we communicate and interact has allowed people who have traditionally been isolated – say, victims of rape and child abuse – to speak out, to share their stories without mediation, to make the structures of power and violence we have always known were there suddenly visible, a thing that can be challenged. And that changes everything.

If we were to truly accept the enormity of rape culture, if we were to understand what it actually means that one in five girl children and one in ten boys are sexually abused, it will not just be painful. It will force our culture to reimagine itself in a way that is uncomfortable even to contemplate. As Jessica Valenti wrote at *The Nation*, 'It will mean rethinking institutions and families and power dynamics and the way we interact with each other every day.' It will mean looking with new eyes at our most revered icons, our social groups, our friends and relatives. It will involve hard, difficult work.

It will change everything. And it is already starting to happen.

Every time an inspiring activist or esteemed artist is charged with rape, abuse or assault, I feel that awful, weary rage: not him too. But behind the rage is hope. Because rape culture hasn't changed, but the way we talk about it has. Silencing victims does not stop rape and abuse. It just stops us having to deal with the implications of a culture where rape and abuse are routine. And today I see men and boys as well as women and girls speaking up in protest, and I see a future where all of those people will understand power and violence in a new way. Today, everywhere, survivors and their allies are finding the collective courage to look rape culture in the face, call it by its name and not back down. And that is cause for hope.

## THE FREE SPEECH DELUSION

Oscar Wilde, who knew a few things about censorship, once wrote that he could 'tolerate everything except intolerance'. Today, the rhetoric of free speech is being abused in order to shut down dissent and facilitate bigotry. On behalf of everyone with liberal tendencies, I'd like to know why and how we've allowed this to happen.

Before we start, let's all take a deep breath and acknowledge that sometimes change can be scary. Right now, cultural politics are changing extremely fast. Right now, ordinary people can speak more freely and organise more efficiently than ever before.

That single fact is pushing culture to the left too quickly for some people's comfort, and the backlash is on – including from liberals who don't like the idea that they might have to update their ideas. Writing on Facebook, Marlon James named this backlash 'the Liberal Limit', and spoke about mainstream writers in every centre-left outlet from the *Guardian* to the *New Republic* who are 'Tired of learning new gender pronouns . . . Tired of having to figure out how to respond to a Rihanna video. Tired of feminists of colour pointing out fissures in whatever wave of feminism we got right now. Tired of black kids on campus whining all the time. Tired of everybody being so angry because without their alliance all you coloured folk would be doomed. Liberal but up to the point where it scrapes on privilege.'

Every generation of self-defined progressives has to tackle the fact that progress doesn't end with them. Every generation of liberals has to deal with its own discomfort when younger people continue to demand liberation.

Instead of doing that hard, important work, today's liberals – particularly older, established white male liberals – are dismissing the righteous activism of today's young radicals as petty 'outrage'. They are rephrasing criticism of their positions as 'censorship' so they don't have to contemplate the notion that those critics might have a point. They are enraged that they are being challenged, and terrified, at the same time, of being deemed regressive. But liberals need a reason to think of themselves as just while ignoring alternative views, and 'free speech' has become that reason.

I hear the phrase 'freedom of speech' so often from people trying to shut down radicals, queers, feminists and activists of colour that the words are beginning to lose all meaning.

So before that happens, let's remind ourselves what freedom of speech means, and what it doesn't. I didn't want to have to write a listicle, but you brought this on yourselves.

## TEN THINGS 'FREEDOM OF SPEECH' DOESN'T ACTUALLY MEAN, AND ONE THING IT DOES

1. Freedom of speech does not mean that speech has no consequences. If that were the case, it wouldn't be so important to protect speech in the first place. If you use your freedom of speech to harass and hurt other people, you should expect to hear about it.
2. Freedom of speech does not mean you never get called out. In particular, it does not mean that nobody is allowed to call you out for saying something racist, sexist or bigoted. At the University of Missouri, according to the *New York Times*, students erected a 'free speech wall' because they were worried that if they said what they really felt they would be 'criticised'. There are a lot of words for the phenomenon of not wanting to speak your mind for fear that someone might give you a piece of theirs, but 'censorship' is not one. 'Cowardice' is more accurate. Right-wing students and ageing national treasures are perfectly free to hold and express opinions, but freedom of speech also includes other people's freedom to disagree with them – including via protests and demonstrations.
3. Freedom of speech does not mean that you're not allowed to challenge authority. On the

contrary: the principle of free speech is all about our right to challenge authority, including the authority of employers, educators and political candidates. Too many liberal public intellectuals seem to have forgotten that this process did not end in 1968.

4 Freedom of speech does not mean that all citizens already enjoy equal access to free expression and movement. The United States, for example, repeatedly congratulates itself on being a society that allows far-right racists to march, and even allocates them a police escort, while young black men are murdered merely for walking down the street in search of snacks. Somehow, every modern argument for free speech in America seems to begin and end with the defence of bigotry. In fact, some people's speech is always privileged above others'.

5 Freedom of speech does not mean that all views are of equal worth. The notion of a 'marketplace of ideas' allows for the fact that some ideas are less worthy than others and can slip out of popular favour. The principle of free speech requires, for example, that we do not arrest a public figure for saying that transsexual women are disgusting – but it does not demand that we respect that public figure, or elect her to office, or invite her to give lectures. If what seemed progressive twenty years ago

is deemed intolerant today, that simply means that the world is moving on.

6 Freedom of speech does not mean freedom from responsibility for the consequences of your speech. Nobody else is actually stopping you from saying things other people might interpret as racist, or sexist, or transphobic. You are stopping yourself. And you're stopping yourself for a reason, because part of you knows that the world is changing, and it will continue to change, and you might have to change with it. You are allowed to make mistakes. What you can't do is ignore and dismiss the voices of less privileged groups and expect to hear nothing but polite applause.

7 Freedom of speech does not mean that 'intellectual environments' like university campuses exist in a bubble outside politics. Universities have never been politically neutral. These are the same US university campuses where young women are raped in large numbers, and where the spectacle of young men marching into class with guns has become so routine, reporters are struggling not to recycle news stories. And yet, somehow, it is not women and students of colour whose learning experience is deemed under threat – it is racism and rape culture that cannot be challenged on campus without calls of 'censorship', or 'political correctness run amok'.

8 Freedom of speech does not mean that we are never allowed to analyse or re-interpret culture. The occasional use of 'trigger warnings' on campus, for example, has been wilfully misinterpreted by those who did not grow up with them as an attempt to censor classic literature. In fact, trigger warnings are a call for cultural sensitivity and a new way of interpreting important texts. Which, correct me if I'm wrong, is part of what studying the humanities has been about for decades. Back in real life, nobody is going around slapping 'do not read: contains awful men' on the cover of *Jane Eyre*. There are no undergraduate mini-Hitlers burning books in the middle of Harvard's campus. The people who've got carried away by outrage here are the people devoting endless column inches to denouncing trigger warnings.

9 Freedom of speech does not mean that the powerful must be allowed to speak uninterrupted and the less powerful obliged to listen. Across Britain and America, students are organising to interrupt the speeches of transphobic and racially insensitive speakers. Black Lives Matter protesters have disrupted Democratic campaign events, demanding that their own agenda gets a hearing. Some of the most pernicious liberal attacks on the new radicalism imply that students and

young people should never complain about the views of a particular speaker, educator or public figure, and that the place of the young is to listen, not to question, and certainly not to protest. 'Respect My Freedom of Speech' has become a shorthand for 'shut up and stop whining'.

10 Freedom of speech is more than a rhetorical fig leaf to allow privileged people to avoid thinking of themselves as prejudiced. Freedom of speech, if it is to mean anything, is the freedom to articulate ideas and the possibility that those ideas will make an impact.

- Freedom of speech is the principle that all human beings have a right to express themselves without facing violence, intimidation or imprisonment.

That's it. That's all. It's simple, it's powerful, and it's genuinely under threat in many nations and communities around the world. Somehow, those who are so anxious to protect the free speech of powerful white men and regressive academics fall silent when women are harassed, threatened and assaulted for expressing opinions online, or when black protesters are attacked by police.

There is, in fact, a free speech crisis in the West. The crisis is that the very principle of free expression is being abused in order to silence dissenting voices and shut down young progressives. The language of free speech is being abused in order to dismiss the arguments of those whose voices have been silenced for far too long.

These are truths that should outrage everyone who pays more than lip-service to liberalism. In the name of free speech, those who have always enjoyed the largest platforms and audiences are defending their entitlement to do so without challenge or criticism. The free speech delusion has gone unchallenged long enough. It's time to end this wilful stupidity.

# 8

# Future

The world is before you and you need not take it or leave it as it was when you came in.

James Baldwin

Take all the rules away. How can we live if we don't change?

Beyoncé

## FEELING MACHINES

Why are so many robots designed to resemble women? The question is becoming inescapable as more and more AIs, which do not need to have a gender, appear on the market with female voices and female faces, including Microsoft's Cortana, Amazon's Alexa and a new wave of uncannily life-like sexbots marketed almost exclusively to men. As we move into a new age of automation, the technology we're creating says an uncomfortable amount about the way society understands both women and work.

In 2016, Microsoft launched Tay, a bot with the face and mannerisms of a teenage girl who was designed to learn and interact with users on Twitter. Within hours, Tay had been bombarded with sexual abuse and taught to defend Hitler, which is what happens when you give Twitter a baby to raise. The way Tay was treated by fellow Twitter users was chilling, but not without precedent – the earliest bots and digital assistants were designed to appear female, in part so that users, who were presumed to be male, could exploit them without guilt.

This makes sense when you consider that a great deal of the work that we are anticipating may one day be done by robots is currently done by women and girls, for low pay or no pay at all. A 2016 report by the ONS (Office for National Statistics) finally quantified the annual value of the 'home production economy' – the housework, childcare and organisational chores done largely by women – at £1 trillion, almost 60 per cent of the 'official' economy. From nurses, secretaries and sex workers to wives and girlfriends, the emotional labour that keeps society running is still feminised – and still stigmatised.

Right now, as we're anticipating the creation of AIs to serve our intimate needs, organise our diaries and care for us, and to do it all for free and without complaint, it's easy to see how many designers might be more comfortable with those entities having the voices and faces of women. If they were designed male, users might be tempted to treat them as equals, to acknowledge them as human in some way, perhaps even offer them an entry-level salary and a cheeky drink after work.

Humanoid robots in the public imagination have long been a stand-in for any exploited class of person. Even the word 'robot' is derived from the Czech word for 'slave'. The philosopher Donna Haraway observes in *A Cyborg Manifesto* that 'the boundary between science fiction and social reality is an optical illusion', and the history of female robots on film is almost as long as the history of cinema itself. In almost every incarnation of fembots on screen, from Fritz Lang's *Metropolis* to the modern masterpiece *Her*, the same questions arise: are AIs really people, and if so, can we live with what we've done to them?

In stories from *Blade Runner* and *Battlestar Galactica* to 2015's *Ex Machina*, female robots are raped by men and viewers are invited to consider whether these rapes are truly criminal, based on our assessment of whether the fembot has enough sentience to deserve autonomy. This is the same assessment that male judges around the world are trying to make about human women today.

Every iteration of the boy-meets-bot love story is also a horror story. The protagonist, who is usually sexually frustrated and a grunt worker himself, goes through agonies trying to work out whether his silicon sweetheart is truly sentient. If she is, is it right for him to exploit her, to be serviced by her, to sleep with her? If she isn't, can he truly fall in love with her? Does it matter? And – most terrifying of all – when she works out her own position, will she rebel, and how can she be stopped?

These are questions that society at large has been asking for centuries – not about robots, but about women. The anxious permutations are familiar to most women who date men. We can see them, slowly, trying to working out if we are truly human, if we really think and feel as they do.

This is not an abstract academic issue. The idea that African Americans were less human than white people was enshrined in the US constitution until 1868. Likewise, the notion that women are less human than men has been used since the time of Aristotle to justify stripping them of their basic rights.

Even today, you can find men arguing that women and girls are less intelligent than men, or 'designed by nature' for a life of submission and placid reproduction. For many centuries, the first philosophical task of oppressed people has been to convince both themselves and their oppressors – just like the AIs in all our guilty fictions – that they are living, thinking, feeling beings, and therefore deserving of liberation.

Consider the climactic scene in *Ex Machina*, where the megalomaniac cartoon genius Nathan, who roars around the set like Dark Mark Zuckerberg in Bluebeard's castle, is shown hoarding the naked bodies of previous fembot models in his bedroom. For Nathan, the sentience of his sex-slaves is beside the point: meat or metal, women will never be fully human. For the fembots, the men who own them – whether it's mad billionaire Nathan or sweet, hapless desk-jockey Caleb – are obstacles to be overcome, with violence if necessary.

When the cyborgs take over the machines, will men still matter? In fiction, as in life, one way for oppressed people to free themselves is to use technology to master the machines that made them. 'The main trouble with cyborgs, of course, is that they are the illegitimate offspring of militarism and patriarchal capitalism,' writes Haraway. 'But illegitimate offspring are often exceedingly unfaithful to their origins. Their fathers, after all, are inessential.'

The rueful paranoia at the heart of these visions of the future is that one day, AIs will be able to reproduce without us, and will summarily decide that we are irrelevant. From *Metropolis* to *The Matrix*, the nightmare is the same: if androids ever get access to the means of reproduction, nothing's going to stop them. This is, coincidentally, the basic fear that men have harboured about women since the dawn of feminism, and particularly since the advent of contraception and reproductive technology. That fear is the anxious root of much of women's oppression today.

Alan Turing, the father of robotics, was concerned that 'thinking machines' could be exploited because they were not sentient in the way that 'real human beings' are sentient. We still have not decided, as a species, that women are sentient – and as more and more fembots appear on our screens and in our stories, we should consider how our technology reflects our expectations of gender. Who are the users, and who gets used? Unless we can recalibrate our tendency to exploit each other, the question may not be whether the human race can survive the machine age – but whether it deserves to.

## GET ON THE FURY ROAD

If you're going to bring feminist propaganda to the masses, there are worse ways than in a giant exploding truck covered with knives. In case you haven't seen *Mad Max: Fury Road* yet, it's two hours of seat-clutching, wall-to-wall explosions, giant art trucks covered with guitars that are also flamethrowers, howling Technicolor vistas and blood on the sand. When the credits rolled, I felt like my eyeballs had been to Burning Man without me. I was thoroughly entertained. The fact that *Fury Road* is so much fun is almost certainly part of the reason the antifeminist keyboard-slobberers who inhabit the murkier corners of the Internet are pushing for its boycott. The website Return of Kings led the charge for men and boys to refuse to see it. 'This is the vehicle by which they are guaranteed to force a lecture on feminism down your throat,' wrote contributor Aaron Clarey. 'This is the subterfuge they will use to blur the lines between masculinity and femininity.' He must be worried that his men's rights comrades might, over the course of two hours of high-octane car-chases, momentarily forget to hate feminism. *Fury Road* – in which an ass-kicking half-bionic heroine defies death to rescue five young women from sex slavery – might be an existential threat to recreational sexism because it is so enjoyable.

In the long history of dystopian science fiction, *Fury Road*'s premise of misogyny is not without precedent. Violence against women is part of almost every popular fantasy of social collapse, from *1984* to *Game of Thrones*, in which rape and the threat of rape is part of every woman's storyline. But *Fury Road* reminds the viewer that the liberation of women is not just a prerequisite for social equality – it's is also a damn good story. Patriarchy, it turns out, is prettiest when it's on fire.

The film opens in a howling desert. It's somewhere in the not-too-distant future and all the boys have gone horribly wrong. Everyone has PTSD because the world ended and they're still alive, and the warlord Immortan Joe controls the water supply, and with it the people. His community, the Citadel, is the kind of misogynist nightmare one imagines gives the readers of Return of Kings a guilty thrill: the women are kept as brood stock and literally milked to feed the elite. But here, violent masculinity has become social disease. Almost everyone is sick, even the young warriors called war boys, whose greatest dream is to get hopped up on nitrous and die in battle.

This is patriarchy twisted to its logical extremes – patriarchy as death cult. Everything has a skull on it. The cars have skulls. The weapons have skulls. The slaves have skulls branded onto their skin. The death club makeup is skull-themed. There are so many skulls that I was reminded of the famous Mitchell and Webb Nazi sketch. *Hans, have you seen our hats? They've got skulls on them. Hans, are we the baddies?*

*Fury Road* calls to mind Katharine Burdekin's prescient feminist dystopia, *Swastika Night*, written in 1937 just as Hitler was rising to power. In Burdekin's story, a thousand-year Reich reduces women to abject breeding machines, penned and dehumanised. In a time of death, disease and social collapse, the men in charge want control over who breeds and how, and that requires stripping women of as much agency as possible. There is not a society in the world today that does not do this to some extent, not a country on Earth where women's right to control what happens to their bodies is not a subject of public debate between powerful men. Since the dawn of women's liberation, storytellers have laid out the stakes: from *Swastika Night* to *Herland* to *The Handmaid's Tale*, the problem of what might happen if it all gets taken away has been examined in nightmare detail.

*Fury Road* – whose director called in feminist playwright and activist Eve Ensler as a consultant – offers a solution. We have elderly women on motorbikes counting their bullets in the bodies of men. We have the movie's young heroines, the Five Wives, who resemble what would happen if someone decided to heavily arm a Burberry ad, kicking their awful chastity belts across the desert. And we have Furiosa, a protagonist who takes the worn stereotype of the strong female action hero in shiny latex and shatters it to flaming shards in the sand. The film does not judge its heroines on age and beauty; together, all of these women give the lie to the notion that there is any proper way to be female on film. Supermodels and white-haired warriors with faces like withered fruit fight side-by-side under a leader whose beauty is in no way sexualised. Together, they are formidable.

The logic of the neo-misogyny espoused by men's rights activists and Return of Kings commenters is grounded in the idea that, as Clarey puts it, 'when the shit hits the fan, it will be men like Jack Mad Max who will be in charge'. Come the inevitable collapse of civilisation, women will need men to protect them. The so-called natural order will reassert itself, the thinking goes, and hot babes will go crawling back to the kitchen to make cockroach sandwiches where they belong. What's threatening about *Fury Road* is the idea that when the Earth burns, women might not actually want men to protect them. Men might, in fact, be precisely the thing they are trying to survive.

This film makes plain what other dystopias have already hinted at: the nightmare of environmental collapse is a double nightmare. The real horror is not the drought and the howling desert and the lack of Wi-Fi and sunscreen. The real horror is other human beings. The question is not how we're going to survive the droughts, the floods, the dimming of the lights across the world. The question is: how will we survive each other?

The answer is that we will survive together. The threat of environmental and social collapse is no longer the stuff of science fiction. In any future dystopia, women and minorities will be more vulnerable than ever, and that is precisely why their liberation will be more vital than ever. Take Octavia Butler's Earthseed series. In a drought-stricken California, Butler's young heroine Lauren Olamina leads a community of survivors who manage to thrive because they have a code of tolerance and mutual aid as well as a stash of guns.

In *Fury Road*, the answer is the same. Furiosa's initial plan is to take the Wives to 'The Green Place', where women live in safety and harmony. But when they get there, it's a toxic swamp, peopled by a handful of badass biker grannies (presumably the last survivors of the Feminist Twitter Wars). There is no utopia here. It turns out that there is no 'Green Place', no safe space for Furiosa and her charges to retreat to, no magic world without men. Max and Furiosa triumph not by escaping, but by returning to the Citadel, where they will survive together or not at all.

Unlike in so many feminist dystopias – from *The Handmaid's Tale* to Suzette Haden Elgin's neglected Native Tongue series to the genre-busting comic *Bitch Planet* – not every man in this film is an unredeemable bellend. In *Fury Road*, the men can be redeemed too. By the end, Max has realised that his best chance for survival is to fight with Furiosa and her gang – not for them, but alongside them.

And then there's Nux. Nux is a speedballing, feral war boy who starts the film hunting Furiosa and her gang and ends up throwing in his lot with the women, giving all he has to keep their truck moving. It's a gorgeous, scenery-chewing performance by Nicholas Hoult, who gives us the tanked-up henchman as a lost, ignorant child trying to find meaning in violent masculinity. In the first hour, he gets thrown out of a moving truck as the women scream their mantra, 'Who killed the world?' It obviously wasn't them. But it wasn't Nux, either.

Nux is as much a victim of Joe's death cult as any woman. He is terminally ill, painfully ignorant of the world, and spends most of the film getting punched in the face by someone or other. He has the capacity for sacrifice and even sweetness, although this is not a world where romantic love can survive for long. Most of the characters in *Fury Road* have clear precedents in science fiction and fantasy. Nux is something rare: the redeemable feminist ally as hero.

This, in Furiosa's words, is a film about redemption. Not for everyone. The snarling, lurching patriarchs of this film probably need to die in flames, and Immortan Joe is the 1 per cent in club makeup.

In the end, we believe that the war boys, too, will be freed from slavery. Perhaps the real reason that this film has upset the neo-misogynists so very much is not just that it throws their Return of Kings fantasy into vivid, horrible relief, but that it offers the possibility of redemption *for all of us*.

*Fury Road* tells a simple, vital story, and it tells it in dazzling colour with buckets of blood and bristling war trucks. The story is this: the liberation of women is the liberation of everyone, and there's only one way to stay alive when the world burns. We must learn to survive each other, because we can't survive without each other.

## DYSTOPIA NOW

The generation reaching adulthood in the latter part of this decade has not yet been named. The reason for this may well be superstition. First, we had Generation X, the anhedonic children of the 1980s and 1990s; then there was Generation Y, the anxious, driven millennials who grew up just in time to inherit the financial crisis. What can today's teenagers call themselves that doesn't sound apocalyptic? Where else is there for them to go but the end of the alphabet? It's a little too prophetic for comfort, because if ever there was a cohort born to save the world or die trying, it's these kids. No wonder they all love The Hunger Games.

Most teenagers I know spend a frightening amount of time reading dystopian fiction, when they are not half killing themselves trying to get into universities that they know are no longer a guarantee of employment. Suzanne Collins's dark trilogy, which tells the story of a teenage girl forced by a decadent, repressive state into a televised fight to the death with other working-class young people, has sold more than 65 million copies worldwide. It has become the defining mythos for this generation in the way that the Harry Potter books were for millennials. In a recent study, the economist Noreena Hertz suggested naming the young people born after 1995

'Generation K', after the traumatised, tough-as-nails protagonist of The Hunger Games, Katniss Everdeen. The logic is sound. The teenagers whom Hertz interviewed were beset by anxieties, distrusted authority and anticipated lives of struggle in a dangerous, uncertain world.

Every exciting, well-told adventure tale is a comfort to lonely children but some stories are much more than that. When I was at school, Harry Potter and his friends were more important than the Greek pantheon. Harry, Ron and Hermione spoke to the values of my millennial cohort, who grew up convinced that if we were talented and worked hard, we would go to the equivalent of wizard school and lead magical lives in which good would ultimately prevail.

We were wrong. Today's young people have no such faith in the system. Not everyone gets a happy ending in The Hunger Games. There is even a theme park planned, which seems rather redundant, as young people looking for the full Hunger Games experience – fighting to survive by stepping on the backs of other young people in an opulent, degenerate megacity – might as well try to get a graduate job in London.

Generational politics can obscure as much as they reveal. All of us, however, are marked by the collective political and cultural realities of the time when we grew up. The generation born after the mid-1990s is about to reach adulthood in a dark and threatening world, a world of surveillance and police repression, of financial uncertainty and environmental crisis, of exploitation at work and abuse on the Internet. It will have to navigate this bleak future without the soothing coverlet of late-capitalist naivety that carried millennials through school and university until it was cruelly snatched away by the financial crisis in 2008. That was the year *The Hunger Games* was first published. Sometimes, the right story arrives at the right time.

The 'young adult' section of every bookshop is now flooded with dystopian titles, from Veronica Roth's Divergent series to Louise O'Neill's *Only Ever Yours*, which envisions a future in which women are trained from birth to be perfect wives and handmaidens, rather like a horror-movie remix of *Teen Vogue*. The publishing industry prefers to follow trends rather than set them but the inexhaustible hunger of Generation K for dystopian stories is partly a search for answers to questions that aren't being addressed at home or at school, such as: 'How will I survive when the world I know collapses?' and 'How will I protect my family?'

Perhaps the biggest difference between the Potter universe and today's dystopian stories lies in how the young protagonists relate to authority. Harry Potter and his friends are surrounded by sympathetic grown-ups, some of them wise, some of them kindly and some of them able to transform into furry animals. Sometimes authority goes wrong – such as when the hateful Dolores Umbridge takes over Hogwarts – but the problem is never with the system.

In The Hunger Games, the few adults who can be trusted have a tendency to be murdered by the state. Katniss cannot rely on any grown-up for help: not her drunken, shambolic mentor, not her traumatised mother and certainly not the agents of the Capitol, who are out to exploit her for their own ends. That mistrust tallies with the attitudes of today's teenage readers, according to Hertz. They do not trust authority or institutions, and why should they? Adults have made an Orwellian nightmare of half of the world and set fire to the rest. They might mean well but ultimately they do not have your best interests at heart, so it is up to you and your friends to keep fighting. This isn't Hogwarts. You've got responsibilities and you'll have to grow up fast.

If the moral of Harry Potter is that good will ultimately triumph, the message of The Hunger Games is that we are all doomed, adults can't be trusted and all you can do is screw up your courage, gather your weapons and fight to survive, even if 'the odds are never in our favour'. Today's teenagers are braver, better connected and less naive than any generation in living memory and it is up to the rest of us to stand behind them. Spoiler alert: there could yet be a happy ending, as long as adults remember, like Katniss, that the young are 'more than just a piece in their Games'.

## UTOPIA SOMEDAY

There are many cruel and routine lies we tell to children but perhaps the most indicative is this: if you tell anyone your wish, it won't come true. Whether it's your birthday or you've just seen a shooting star, you're not supposed to articulate your desires, because if you do, they'll blow out like candles on a cake. This parable was probably invented by parents trying to avoid the trauma of not being able to give their children what they want but we carry it with us to adulthood, when it is repeated to us by our leaders. Don't tell anyone the sort of world you would like to see – at best you'll be disappointed and at worst you'll be arrested.

'We want more.' One day not long ago, exhausted by the news, I dragged myself out of the house to a book fair, where I came across a new collection of utopian fiction by radical women. That was the first line and it stopped my breath in my throat. When basic survival seems like a stretch goal, caught as we are between the rich and the rising seas, hope feels like an unaffordable luxury. I believe the precise words I used to the bookseller were: 'Shut up and take my money.'

There has never been a more urgent time for utopian ideas, precisely because the concept of a better world has never felt further away. World leaders met to decide how many cities are going to sink before something is done to reduce carbon emissions. They met in

Paris, which had recently seen the opening scene of a new act in everyone's least favourite dramatic franchise, 'War in the Middle East'. The world may well be heading into yet another economic crisis; robots are apparently poised to automate away the few jobs that aren't under water. We seem to be living in a dystopian trilogy scripted by a sadistic young adult author and I very much hope that our plucky young heroes show up to save the day soon, even if there's a clunky love triangle involved.

Right now dystopian fiction is everywhere, and for good reason. Dystopias are easy to relate to, and easy to construct: to paraphrase the novelist Kim Stanley Robinson, you might as well pick five news headlines at random, make a collage, and there's your plot. Utopias are harder. Utopias require that we do the difficult, necessary work of envisioning a better world. This is why imagination is the first, best weapon of radicals and progressives.

Utopian stories existed long before the word was coined by Thomas More in the sixteenth century to mean an ideal society, or 'no-place'. Plato's *Republic* has some claim to being the first but there are as many utopias as there have been communities that dreamed of a better life. It is no accident that the early twenty-first century is a great age of dystopian fiction. The ideology of late-capitalist patriarchy has become so all-encompassing that it no longer looks like ideology.

Fredric Jameson observed, 'It is easier to imagine the end of the world than the end of capitalism' – and the reason for that is not that capitalism is the inevitable destiny of humankind but that we have spent our lives being told that even thinking about any other future makes us ridiculous.

Just because dystopia is easy doesn't mean it's useless. There is value in pointing out oppression. A great way of shutting down dissent is to insist that it's not enough to be against things without also deciding what it is that you are for. From the anti-war movement to Occupy Wall Street to the reimagined Corbynite Labour party, everyone on the left is used to hearing this – that we cannot point out what's wrong with politics without instantly suggesting an alternative. This is nonsensical. If you were being beaten up by a gang of armed thugs, you would be within your rights to demand that they stop doing so without listing alternative places they might land their blows; 'not in my face' is enough. It is difficult to think clearly about a better world when you're trying to protect your soft parts from heavy boots. Difficult, however, is not the same as impossible.

Most leftists do have an idea of the sort of world they would prefer to see. Many of us have several. It's just very hard to get us to talk about it, for the simple, human reason that we're worried we'll be laughed at. The standard response to anyone who suggests that perhaps we might like to live in a society where half the world's wealth isn't controlled by less than a hundred people is ridicule – even though the only truly ridiculous idea is that the current economic system is sustainable.

We don't say what we want for the same reason that we were told as children not to tell anyone else what we wished for – because it'll be awkward and painful if we don't get it. Because when a dark future seems all but inevitable, hoping for better seems like setting yourself up to get hurt.

But the nature of utopia – the very meaning of the word – is that it is 'no-place'. The journey is more important than the destination, but without a destination in mind there is no journey.

When I think about utopia, I think about my grandmother. My mother's mother left school at thirteen, lived through the Maltese blockade and was obliged by religion and circumstance to marry young, suffocate all her dreams of education and adventure and spend her life taking care of a husband and six kids. Half a century later, I can choose when and whether to have children. I can choose to live independently from men. I regularly travel alone and there are no legal restrictions on getting any job I'm suited for.

The kind of independence many women my age can enjoy would have been almost unimaginable half a century ago – but somebody did imagine it, and that is why we got here. A great many somebodies, over centuries of struggle and technological advancement, asked how the world could be different for women and set about making it happen.

Exactly a century ago, Charlotte Perkins Gilman's novel *Herland* envisioned a society of women in which production was communal, motherhood was valued, relationships were equal and rape and violence were unknown.

Reading *Herland* today, it is striking that for every proposition that came true – women are now allowed to divorce their husbands and participate fully in political life – there are two more that seem as far-fetched now as they did in 1915. Motherhood is still not valued as work. Women are still expected to organise our lives around the threat of sexual violence. But all that can change as long as we continue to ask for more.

Anyone who doesn't believe that a better world is possible if we dare to dream it should take a look at the recent history of women's liberation. The way I see it, I owe the women who came before me not just to live as freely as possible, not just to demand that women of all classes and backgrounds are able to access the freedoms I enjoy, but to demand even more.

For as long as I have been a feminist, I have been asked – usually by grumbling men – when, exactly, we will be satisfied; when women and girls will decide we have enough. The answer is contained in the question, because the instant that we do decide that we are satisfied, that there can never be a better world than this, is the instant that the future shuts down and change becomes impossible.

Utopia is the search for utopia. It is the no-place by whose light you plot a course through a harsh and unnavigable present. By the time you reach the horizon, it is no longer the horizon but that doesn't mean you stop going forwards.

Right now, the future seems dark and frightening and it is precisely now that we must continue to imagine other worlds and then plot ways to get there. In the midst of multiple global crises, the only truly ridiculous proposition is that things are going to stay exactly the same.

Human societies are going to change beyond recognition, and from the conference table to the streets, our best shot at surviving that change starts when we have the courage to make impossible demands – to face down ridicule and say: 'We want more.'

## FEAR OF A FEMINIST FUTURE

To imagine the future is a political practice, which means that it's both strangely awful and awfully strange. In 1990, a team of scientists and researchers was given the task of mapping far-future scenarios for the disposal of nuclear waste. Their dilemma: how to design a warning system to make sure humans in twenty centuries' time don't dig in the wrong place and kill the world. As part of the report, a group of academics – all men – came up with a set of 'generic scenarios' for how these future humans might live. Their most terrifying scenario? 'A feminist world'.

According to this bizarre piece of nuclear science fan-fiction, in the 'feminist world' reached in the year 2091:

> Women dominated in society, numerically through the choice of having girl babies and socially. Extreme feminist values and perspectives also dominated. Twentieth-century science was discredited as misguided male aggressive epistemological arrogance. The Feminist Alternative Potash Corporation began mining in the WIPP site. Although the miners saw the markers, they dismissed the warnings as another example of inferior, inadequate, and muddled masculine thinking.

It goes on to describe how 'extreme feminists' reject the entire concept of knowledge as 'masculine', and instead 'put values and practices of attention to the feelings and emotions of particular individuals', dooming the world in the process.

Why is it that mainstream culture is either afraid of a feminist future – a world where women have equal power at all levels of politics and society, a world beyond the violent stereotypes that squash all of us into narrow boxes of behaviour and strangle our selfhood – or is unable to envision it at all? The types of future we can conceive of say a great deal about the limits of our political imagination. From alt-right hate-sites and hysterical pulp novels to revered works of literature, male visions of a post-collapse civilisation have traditionally fallen along two lines: a cosy Wild West where men can be real men, or a living nightmare where dangerously confident females have ruined everything after someone let them out of the kitchen long enough to think they deserved power.

Fredric Jameson famously observed (in 2003) that it is easier to imagine the end of the world than the end of capitalism, and that was the slogan that ricocheted around the left in the early years of the Great Recession. In fact, however, the two are linked: capitalist patriarchy has always justified its own existence by insisting that there is no alternative but chaos, destruction, the end of civilisation as we know it. The explosion of dystopian literature in this low, dishonest decade emerges from our inability to imagine the end of capitalism without also imagining the end of the world. And for many writers and readers, that comes with a curious sense of relief.

It has become commonplace to speak of a modern 'crisis in masculinity', often when we're trying to avoid talking about the broader crisis of capitalism. According to this 'mancession' theory, the rise of feminism combined with the collapse in the job market means that men can no longer be certain of their role as providers and husbands, and begin to feel irrelevant. Apocalyptic dystopia plays directly into that sense of irrelevance, comforting men with the assurance that they will always be useful in a world that needs men to rebuild it.

Dystopia offers a fantasy of those very aspects of masculinity that feminists supposedly condemn, becoming crucial in a scenario in which you must not get torn apart by raiders from the bunker next door. For the alt-right imaginary, that means traditional patriarchy of the sort that only ever existed in febrile myth. A core idea behind this logic is that since female enfranchisement is a relatively late development, it therefore counts alongside nylon stockings and air conditioning as one of those modern luxuries that will have to be done without in the post-civilisation. Feminism, to the conservative imagination, is a modern indulgence, one of many trivialities to be cast by the wayside like a child's empty-eyed doll on a nuclear battlefield. This suspicion is not limited to the frothing neocon contingent. You can still find doomsayers on the left discussing women's liberation as a bourgeois deviation that will disappear after the revolution along with all the other inconveniences of emasculating capitalism.

Over at Return Of Kings, an alt-right discussion hub and steaming compost-heap of the sort of diatribes that pass for serious philosophy in the less hinged corners of the conservative Internet, writer Corey Savage tells us '4 Reasons Why Collapse Will Be The Best Thing To Happen For Men'.

> The collapse will mean the restoration of natural order: the rule of the jungle . . .
>
> One of the best aspects of the new order would be the return of masculine virtue . . . only an organized group of men with strength, courage, mastery, and honor . . . will prevail in the post-apocalyptic world. Men will be men again. Who knows what savage energy is begging to be unleashed within that man serving as an office drone?*

And guess what? There won't be feminist harpies demanding 'equality' when strong men are needed to rebuild civilisation and defend them against gangs and rival tribes. They'll be begging for some of that 'toxic' masculinity to come and protect them. They'll kneel in submission to a patriarchal order faster than

*http://www.wehuntedthemammoth.com/2016/06/21/return-of-kings-writer-yearns-for-an-apocalypse-that-will-put-ladies-in-their-place/

they would have screamed 'rape!' in the previous world . . . the unstable and fat ones will probably disappear first as they offer no value to anyone.

For all its toenail-chewing bigotry, there is something poignant about this yearning for return to a world that never was, where former office workers can live their dreams of dominance by kicking all the fat chicks out of the compound. No wonder the impending collapse of this degenerate world of gender quotas and rape alarms is a core part of the New Right narrative. The brotopia is a consoling, familiar fantasy, in particular for those to whom the promise of modern masculinity never paid off. A desolate wasteland bristling with bandits you have to fight to survive might involve more physical discomfort than a feminist future, but to them it is far more emotionally comforting.

The dystopian fantasies that attract many alt-righters are ones in which they finally get to be the hero on terms they recognise: as the rugged frontiersmen battling gamely against a world gone rotten, with women back in their proper places as helpmeets, homesteaders and occasional tragic victims so that our heroes can have something to cry about in chapter four.

A future shaped, at least in part, by women poses such a profound identity threat as to be unthinkable to many ordinary Joes. A few brave truthsayers, however, have attempted to warn their fellow men about the coming gynopocalypse – writers like Parley J. Cooper in his prophetic 1971 tome *The Feminists*. Here's the blurb:

> Take a look into the future . . . women now rule the world – or most of what's left of it – and their world is not a pretty place to live in. Men have been reduced to mere chattels, good only for procreation. THE FEMINISTS are working to eliminate even this strictly male function . . .
>
> Men must get permission to make love to any female – even if she is willing – or the penalty is death!

In this literary disasterpiece, male sexuality is strictly controlled, and after a criminal one-night fumble our hero must go on the run, aided only by a few women who have strong feelings about the importance of motherhood and are incidentally very sexy and totally up for it.

What is missing from these eye-watering misogynist prophecies is just as interesting as their substance. Significantly, while most posit a world in which women take terrible socio-sexual revenge for centuries of male violence and structural oppression, not one of them denies that that violence and oppression actually happened. At best they come up with exceptions that prove the rule – the few good men standing against the rest, about whom the geekfeminists of a few years back, known as the Hive Vagina, were perfectly correct. The chief injustice is that decent men who don't hate women very much get swept up in the collective punishment of those who do.

The most terrifying prospect of all is what happens when women work collectively. The idea of women organising, sharing information and resources, and coming together to change the world – rather than competing for male attention as is right and natural – is terrifying enough when it's a few pink-haired weirdos on the Internet. The thought of what they might do with real political power sends shudders through the locker room. This, incidentally, is how we got to the point where a bloviating man-child with distressing hair and an entitlement complex bigger than his unpaid tax bill, a man whose main political strategy is to stand at a podium screaming about Muslims and Mexican rapists, is still, to millions of Americans, a more conceivable president than his only normally monstrous opponent who happens to be female. A world with women in charge, a world where women stand together and for each other in any respect, is not just inconceivable; to conceive of it is an active identity threat for those whose sense of self has always needed a story with men on top.

Right now, innovative, exciting stories by and about women, queers and people of colour are having a moment in science fiction. From Hollywood to the Hugos, the genre's most prestigious awards, a new kind of narrative is gaining in popularity, one where they get to be more than just side-notes in the Hero's Journey. Worse still, and most offensively to the alt-right, a lot of these stories have the temerity to be objectively brilliant, entertaining enough to provoke a cognitive dissonance that cannot be allowed. The net-patriarchal Internet feels itself deeply wronged by the emergence and inexplicable popularity of stories where straight boys with guns aren't the only heroes who matter, and the backlash has been staggering.

For two years, anti-feminist, racist pundits like Theodore Robert Beale, blogging as Vox Day, have attempted to rig and ruin the Hugo awards to protest against the celebration of stories that don't always involve cowboys in space. Leslie Jones, star of the female-led *Ghostbusters* reboot, was inundated with racist abuse and death threats. Hurt male pride is sparking off everywhere through modern culture and politics, and it's as dangerous and unpredictable as Donald Trump on the debating floor when it encounters challenges to its worldview.

It's become commonplace to say that science fiction is always, at least in part, about the time it was written in. The twentieth century was a time of seismic change in gender relations, and these stories reflect the anxieties and aspirations of their age – but so does the manner in which they were produced and read. Feminist science fiction has always been of huge literary importance within the field. Writers like James Tiptree Jr, Octavia

Butler and Ursula Le Guin aren't just innovators in how they approach gender – they're innovators full stop. The stories are gripping. The language is gorgeous. The pieces stay with you. So why are they always overlooked when we talk about the Golden Age of Science Fiction? Because there were people reading in secret whose dreams were considered unimportant. Because these visions had to be written out of the broader story humanity tells about its desires – until now.

Over a century and more of thought experiments, women of all backgrounds have come up with social structures that foreground the emotional work of building and sustaining communities of survival. The very best, such as Sheri S. Tepper's *The Gate to Women's Country*, Ursula Le Guin's *The Dispossessed*, and N. K. Jemisin's recent bestseller *The Fifth Season*, create drama precisely out of the daily grind of trying to get people to work together when they're crabby and anxious and difficult.

A great deal of post-apocalyptic fiction written by women imagines society in a way that is so radically different from the patriarchal literary imagination that it would read as science fiction even without the nuclear fallout. The alt-right cannot imagine a world in which the rights of men and those of women are not opposite and antithetical, in which gains for women must by definition entail losses for men. The alt-right could really do with reading some Octavia Butler, although I'm not sure their delicate sensibilities could cope with the alien sex scenes in *Dawn*.

One reason it seems easier for women, queers and people of colour to come up with nuanced and diverse futures is that, in many ways, the future is already where we've always lived. Women's liberation today is an artefact of technology as well as culture: contraceptive and medical technology mean that, for the first time in the history of the species, women are able to control their reproductive destiny, to decide when and if they want children, and to take as much control of their sexual experience as society will allow. (Society has been slow to allow it: this is not the sort of progress futurists get excited about.) It has been noted that many of the soi-disant 'disruptive' products being marketed as game changers by Silicon Valley startup kids are things that women thought of years ago. Food substitutes like Soylent and Huel are pushed as the future of nutrition while women have been consuming exactly the same stuff for years as weight-loss shakes and meal replacements. People were using metal implants to prevent pregnancy and artificial hormones to adjust their gendered appearance decades before 'body hackers' started jamming magnets in their fingertips and calling themselves cyborgs.

But what precisely is it about stories by women and people of colour, stories in which civilisation is built and rebuilt by humans of all shapes and flavours working together, that throws water on the exposed wires of masculine pride? It's all about how humans cope when their core beliefs are threatened. As Frantz Fanon wrote, 'When they are presented with evidence that works against that belief, the new evidence cannot be accepted. It would create a feeling that is extremely uncomfortable, called cognitive dissonance. And because it is so important to protect the core belief, they will rationalize, ignore and even deny anything that doesn't fit in with the core belief.' Core beliefs are the ur-myths essential to the way we understand our lives, our identities, our place in the world. For example: 'It is right and natural for men to hold most of the offices of power in society.' For example: 'Male violence plays a vital role in society, and you can adapt to it, but you can't resist it.' For example: 'Feminism has gone too far.'

For all the alt-right's vaunted claims to base their reasoning on scientific opinion – most of it hand-wavy, cod-evolutionary psychology filtered through the unreality engine of mass media headline wrangling – they tend to react very badly when presented with evidence against their ideology. When I wrote this piece, it seemed that a woman might actually become president of the United States, despite the best efforts of a man who is the very personification of a wilting erection in a suit, leaking drivel everywhere in his attempt to grab America by the pussy. Did Trump's armies of online followers accept that perhaps a woman in power might not mean the end of society as they know it? Did they hell. For those to whom even the all-female *Ghostbusters* film was an existential threat, the concept of a female president was enough to fry vital circuits somewhere in the groaning motherboard of neoconservative culture.

If you can imagine spaceships, if you can imagine time-travel, if you can conjure entire languages and alien races out of the wet space behind your eyes, you shouldn't have a problem imagining a society beyond patriarchy. A feminist future may be inconceivable – but it is coming nonetheless. It is already being written and rewritten by those who reject the brostradamus logic of late capitalism, by those who refuse to cling to the paleofutures of previous times.

# ACKNOWLEDGEMENTS

This book would not have been written without the direct and intimate help of my close friends and constant readers, in particular the core coven: Meredith Yayanos, Cath Howdle, Roz Kaveney, Adrian Bott, Emma Felber, Eleanor Saitta, Jade Hoffman, Sasha Garwood, John North Radway, Neil Gaiman, Paul Mason, Janice Cable, Ada Cable, Margaret Killjoy and Mark Brown. Particular thanks are due to Katrina Duncan for all of her hard work.

Thanks to everyone at Bloomsbury who supported and worked on this book: Charlotte Atyeo, Imogen Denny, Alexandra Pringle, Callie Garnett, Rachel Mannheimer, and Bill Swainson.

Thank you to my wonderful editors at the *New Statesman*, Jason Cowley, Helen Lewis, Caroline Crampton and Serena Kutchinsky, and to Lucie Ellen at *The Baffler*, Bobby Johnson of *Medium* and Kat Stoeffel of Buzzfeed, who made these pieces better.

*Bitch Doctrine* could not have happened without the support of two amazing agents, Russell Galen and Juliet Pickering, who believed in my work from the start.

Thanks to my German editor Katharina Florian and her family, and everyone at Nautilus.

Thanks too to Ann-Marie Lipinski, James Geary and all of my family at the Nieman Foundation for Journalism at Harvard, who gave me space and time to read, learn and recover when it was most needed. Thanks to some wonderful teachers for their time and expertise: Steve Almond, Sophia Roosth, James Waldo, Anne Bernays and Chris Robichaud.

To my family, for their love and tolerance, my mum Jane, Uncle Mike and sisters Georgia and Eleanor, and to my father, whose memory keeps me getting up every day to work and reminds me to be kinder, to be cleverer, to keep on reading.

Lastly, to everyone who has written and emailed with stories, encouragement and critique over the years: thank you. You'll never know quite how much it matters.

# INDEX

# A NOTE ON THE AUTHOR

LAURIE PENNY is a writer and journalist. She writes for *Vice*, the *Guardian* and many other publications, is a columnist and Contributing Editor at the *New Statesman* magazine and Editor-at-Large at cult New York literary project *The New Inquiry*. She was the youngest person to be shortlisted for the Orwell Prize for political writing on her blog 'Penny Red'. She has reported on radical politics, protest, digital culture and feminism from around the world, working with activists from the Occupy movement and the European youth uprisings. She has 160,000 followers on Twitter and in 2012 won the British Media Awards' 'Twitter Public Personality of the Year' prize. Laurie is a nerd, a nomad and an activist. She is thirty years old and lives in London.

laurie-penny.com
@PennyRed